The Wellbeing of Children in Care

Because of their previous damaging experiences, many children and young people enter the care system having already developed emotional problems or at a greater risk of developing them. However, in addition to this, research and experience consistently show that being in care is likely to aggravate or worsen developmental problems. Why does public care have these negative effects on children and what is needed to alleviate their problems?

This important book looks at how children in care can best be helped to attain desirable developmental outcomes. Owusu-Bempah introduces his notion of socio-genealogical connectedness to help explain why children in kinship care fare better than children in non-relative foster care. He argues, using recent empirical research as well as a wide range of literature from the adoption field and attachment theory, that knowledge about one's hereditary background is an essential factor in looked-after children's long-term adjustment to placement. As with all children, this knowledge forms the basis of their identity, self-worth and general outlook.

An invaluable contribution to the area, this book offers promising routes to understanding better and working more effectively with virtually all families, irrespective of their cultural, ethnic and religious backgrounds. It will interest researchers and students of attachment theory, adoption and fostering, child development and children's mental health.

Kwame Owusu-Bempah is Emeritus Reader in Psychology at the University of Leicester, UK.

The Wellbeing of Children in Care

A new approach for improving developmental outcomes

Kwame Owusu-Bempah

Routledge
Taylor & Francis Group

LONDON AND NEW YORK

First published 2010
by Routledge
2 Park Square, Milton Park, Abingdon, Oxon, OX14 4RN

Simultaneously published in the USA and Canada
by Routledge
270 Madison Avenue, New York, NY 10016

*Routledge is an imprint of the Taylor & Francis Group, an informa
business*

© 2010 Kwame Owusu-Bempah

Typeset in Sabon by
Pindar NZ, Auckland, New Zealand
Printed and bound in Great Britain by
TJ International Ltd, Padstow, Cornwall

British Library Cataloguing in Publication Data
A catalogue record for this book is available from the British Library

Library of Congress Cataloging-in-Publication Data
Owusu-Bempah, Kwame.
The wellbeing of children in care: a new approach for improving
    developmental outcomes / Kwame Owusu-Bempah.
       p. cm.
    Includes bibliographical references.
    1. Children—Institutional care—Psychological aspects. 2. Foster
home care—Psychological aspects. 3. Adoption—Psychological aspects.
4. Child development. 5. Child welfare. I. Title.
    HV873.O98 2010
    362.73'2—dc22   2009046042

ISBN10: 0–415–47939–8 (hbk)
ISBN10: 0–415–47940–1 (pbk)
ISBN10: 0–203–85172–2 (ebk)

ISBN13: 978–0–415–47939–4 (hbk)
ISBN13: 978–0–415–47940–0 (pbk)
ISBN13: 978–0–203–85172–2 (ebk)

Contents

Preface

Throughout history, fostering has functioned as a childcare mechanism and family support system. It remains a normal and important childcare service in most societies outside the Western world. In these cultures, fostering occurs among kin. Anthropological studies from these cultures indicate no link between fostering and negative psychosocial developmental outcomes. In contrast, in Western societies where fostering is perceived as an anomaly, there exists abundant evidence showing that children growing up in foster care exhibit myriad psychosocial developmental problems, notably mental health and behavioural difficulties. It shows, however, that, within the public care system, children being raised by relatives fare better than their peers growing up in non-relative foster care and those in residential settings.

Whilst theorists and practitioners tend to explain the developmental difficulties facing children in care in terms of attachment concepts, this book offers the innovative theory of *socio-genealogical connectedness* as providing a more helpful approach to understanding these children's difficulties and to designing effective interventions and developing appropriate services to meet their psychosocial developmental needs. This idea proposes that a sense of socio-genealogical connectedness is an essential factor in children's adjustment to separation, and forms the basis of their emotional and mental health. A central argument of the book is that although non-kin foster families seek to meet the children's physical and other needs, they cannot meet their need for a sense of connectedness or continuity. The author presents evidence from the anthropological, clinical and professional literature indicating that kinship care meets this essential need; he argues that, in the best interest of the child, kinship care is superior to other placement options.

Organization of the book

Since antiquity, the institutions of adoption and fostering have always formed an important feature of all human societies. Chapter 1 provides an historical overview of these institutions, how they were perceived and practised, and the functions they served in ancient civilizations, for example, in ancient Greece and Rome. The main objective of this chapter is to enable readers to appreciate not only the importance of fostering, but also how and why it is practised in different modern-day societies across the world. Chapter 2 draws material from the social anthropological field to provide definitions of adoption and fostering, and illustrate how those definitions vary across cultures. It discusses also cultural values and belief systems regarding children and childcare, since these influence a given society's child-rearing patterns and attitudes towards fostering in profound ways. Chapter 2 provides examples from studies in diverse regions: Africa (notably West Africa), Oceania, North America and South America.

While Chapter 2 examines fostering patterns in traditional settings, Chapter 3 looks at fostering in contemporary Western societies. It considers changes in societal attitudes since the industrial revolution and the consequences of those changes for children who require alternative care. It discusses the factors associated with why, in today's Western societies, even the extended family or kin are reluctant or unable to care for their own or even deterred from doing so.

The motives for fostering, as opposed to adoption, are diverse and complex, particularly from a cross-cultural perspective. Whatever the motives for child fostering or the circumstances in which fostering takes place today, it entails considerable costs or challenges for the caregiver. Chapter 4 examines theories of fostering and the reasons why families and individuals are prepared to invest in children who are not their progeny. It examines also the motives for giving up a child to be raised by others.

Chapter 5 discusses the two broad forms of foster care in contemporary Western societies: non-kin (or non-relative) foster care and kinship foster care. It further considers the two emergent types of kinship care: formal (or public) and informal (or private) kinship care. This chapter deals with the question: 'When does kinship care become public care?' It considers also the implications of this dichotomy for children cared for by kin and their caregivers.

Chapters 6 and 7 examine the psychosocial developmental outcomes for children growing up in the care system in general. Chapter 6 discusses traditional theoretical explanations, notably attachment concepts, for the children's vulnerability. It discusses also professional interventions derived from these theories which attempt to help these children to surmount their negative experiences of being in care. The chapter further discusses the limitations of these theories and interventions. It then presents the new theory of socio-genealogical connectedness. This new theory complements existing developmental theories and contributes towards a fuller understanding of these children's difficulties. From theoretical as well as empirical perspectives, Chapter 7 then addresses the crucial question: 'What type of placement best serves the child's interest?' In so doing, it examines the observed disparity in psychosocial developmental outcomes according to type of placement.

Chapter 8, the final chapter, considers the implications of the main arguments of the book for theory and research, policy and professional childcare practice.

Acknowledgements

I must express my special gratitude to Professor Stewart Petersen for his understanding and support for this project. Thanks also go to the University of Leicester for granting me special study leave during the initial stages of the preparation of this book. I am grateful also to Mark Peel for his helpful comments on parts of the manuscript.

1   Fostering and adoption in historical perspective

Fostering and adoption are the two main alternative mechanisms of child-care utilized in all human societies when parents are unable or unwilling to care for their offspring. Thus, both forms of childcare have always been a common feature of every human society. In the Judaeo-Christian scriptures, for example, Joseph (son of Jacob), Moses and Jesus provide archetypical examples of adopted or fostered figures. In antiquity, legendary examples include Oedipus, Alexander the Great (King of Macedonia) and Aristotle. In and around the Victorian era in Western societies, Jean Jacques Rousseau (philosopher) and Charles Dickens may represent well-known adopted persons. In modern times, we have such grandees as Eleanor Roosevelt (First Lady), Winston Churchill, Malcolm X, Nancy Reagan (First Lady), Nelson Mandela, US Presidents Gerald Ford, William (Bill) Clinton and Barack Hussein Obama.

Fostering and adoption in ancient civilizations

This section sketches Goody's (1969) detailed summary of the institution and purpose of adoption in major ancient civilizations, especially Greece and Rome. He contrasts the functions of adoption in these prehistoric societies with the role it played in Eurasian societies which he further contrasts broadly with the role of fostering in sub-Saharan Africa. His analysis of the anthropological literature indicates that fostering and adoption played a major part in the traditional laws of many ancient societies. For example, he argues that in ancient China, Greece, Rome and other civilizations both written laws and conventions afforded the practice a particular status. In these primeval civilizations, as in modern societies, as we will see in subsequent chapters, fostering and adoption served several purposes: political, economic, social, religious and psychological.

Greece

Adoption in ancient Greece, according to Goody, was undertaken principally for the purposes of inheritance. That is, it commonly occurred when a man had no offspring at all or had only a daughter or daughters, and wanted to forestall or prevent a close relative from claiming his daughter as an heiress, with the motive to benefit from his estate. In such a case, he would arrange a husband for her, and then adopt either him or one of his sons (i.e., the man would adopt one of his grandsons). By Goody's account, adopting their grandsons or their agnatic (patrilineal) nephews or (rarely) their nieces to succeed them was a common practice among men of means. In these cases, adoption could be carried out even posthumously by will. Goody's (1969) scrutiny of the literature indicates that adoption in primordial Greece was, thus, mainly of close kin, although sometimes of affine (relatives by marriage). No one who had a biological son would adopt. If having adopted, a man later begot a son, the biological and adopted sons would both inherit his estate, share the property between them.

In ancient Greece, as in modern Western societies, adoption severed the relationship between the adopted person and his kin. In other words, all the rights and status that might have been bestowed upon him by his birth family were revoked and replaced with the rights and status granted him by the adoptive family. However, he was unable to make a will and so could only bequeath his property by direct descendants. This made his position potentially precarious, since an adopted person could be easily disowned. Besides, as in some modern societies, such as Poland (Stelmaszuk, 2006) and the Netherlands (Strijker *et al.*, 2003), a citizen could only adopt a citizen. As far as inheritance was concerned, only citizens could own Greek property. It must be pointed out also that only males could adopt.

In summary, in ancient Greek society, adoption essentially involved ancestor worship; it entailed a continuation of the worship of the family shrine. This, according to the Greeks, could not be properly observed by a foreigner or, presumably, by a woman. In addition, an adopted son had to provide for his adoptive father in his old age, bury and worship him after his death (Goody, 1969). All this means that, in olden Greece, the practice was closely linked with genealogical continuity, continuity not just of property, but, more importantly, of ancestor worship.

Rome

According to Goody, the context in which adoption took place in ancient Rome was somewhat different from that which prevailed in Greece. In Rome, it occurred in 'crisis' situations; its primary function was to avert the extinction of a family; it was undertaken to ensure the continuity of a family, especially a high-ranking family. Such a crisis also created an opportunity for rank or social mobility for a lower-status family or a family of equal or similar status to enhance its standing. Namely, a family with a son to spare could affiliate with a noble family at risk of annihilation by giving him in adoption.

Goody identifies two distinct forms of adoption that existed in Rome: adrogation and adoption. Adrogation of a person always required public approval since that person was, in principle, head of a family, which, along with its cult, would suffer annihilation as a result of its mergence in another family. Adoption, on the other hand, entailed just the transfer of a person from one family to another. A man adrogated automatically took his entire property and all his descendants across with him. In contrast, an adopted man or woman entered their new family by themselves; their children and property (if any) remained with their original paternal family. In either case, however, the separation was fundamental and uncompromising. The adopted person became an alien to his birth parents, siblings and other relatives; and a person adrogated repudiated the gods of his family by the act of *sacrorum detestation* (i.e., detestation of the sacred). By this act, he was obliged to renounce his ancestral gods, to have strong hatred for the gods of his birth family in order to embrace the gods of his new family. In adoption, not only was the separation irrevocable, but also an adopted son (who joined his new family alone) could not, of his own volition, rejoin his biological family under any circumstance, even when they were experiencing difficulties, for example, bereavement. Adoption in modern Western societies, based on the principle of giving the child 'a fresh start', bears some of the hallmarks of the practice in ancient Rome.

The completeness and irrevocability of the act of both forms of adoption, their possible consequences for donors as well as beneficiaries, meant that it was never undertaken without due consideration. The conditions under which the transfer could take place were significant. Regarding adrogation, Cicero is reported to have argued that only a man who had no children could undertake this. '*What, gentlemen,*' he asked, '*is the law relating to adoption? Clearly, that the adoption of children should be permitted to those who are no longer capable of begetting children, and who, when they were in their prime, put their capacity for parenthood to the test*' (in Goody, 1969, p. 60). Because adrogation destroyed a family, it was only permitted in order to save another family, to provide an heir. It provided an individual with a son and heir, and one who could inherit his property, continue his line and perpetuate his worship. Cicero is said to have justified the practice on patriotic grounds, by arguing that the inheritance of property and worship of the dead were ultimately associated in Roman society, that is, it was in the interest of Romans, and it was for this reason that a man wanted to provide himself with a specific descendant to carry out those tasks. Consequently, it was those with most to inherit who were most concerned to provide themselves with a specific heir to carry out these tasks.

Goody claims that the institution of adoption fulfilled other functions in Roman society, typically child welfare functions; for example, it enabled an uncle to adopt an orphaned nephew. In the main, though, it was a mechanism whereby the great and noble families provided themselves with heirs to their property and worship, successors to office or a political following. Goody's (1969) studies show that from Julius Caesar and Augustus onwards, a considerable number of emperors, failing to sire sons or have sons of their own, adopted them instead. Adoption was, therefore, essentially a male-to-male transaction. Even though females could be adopted, they could not adopt or be adrogated. Also, as in Greece, only citizens could be adopted, often the sons of other high-ranking families. For the donor, there was a gain in the shape of alliance between two families, while the beneficiary perpetuated his own line. Hence, adoption in ancient Rome entailed an exchange relationship.

As in ancient Greece, Rome and other ancient societies, the perpetuation of the lineage, the continuation of a man's personal line of descent, was the chief object of adoption in the traditional laws of other olden societies (Goody, 1969). By this act, the adopted son entered into a new inheritance and its concomitant obligations. Under Hindu law, for example, the adopted son maintained only a minimal link with his birth family, since he was debarred from marrying there. In brief, in prehistoric Greece, China, India and Rome, to an extent, as described by Goody, adoption had little to do with the assimilation of strangers (i.e., non-kin). Rather, the adoptive relationship often fell within descent groups; the adopted person was very often the paternal nephew who had no automatic right of inheritance unless he was adopted formally. A formally adopted person inherited from his father (biological uncle), carried on his direct line and worshipped at his ancestral shrine. He acquired his uncle's chattels in return for continuing another man's line of descent.

Adoption and fostering in medieval Western Europe

In today's Western Europe, adoption serves three main purposes: 1) to provide homes for orphans, foundlings and children whose parents are incapable, for whatever reason, of providing them with adequate care; 2) to provide childless couples with social progeny; and 3) to provide an individual or a couple with an heir to their property (Goody, 1969). We may add to these a fourth function, the current fad among celebrities and others to undertake cross-country adoption for the purpose of enhancing their social status or to portray themselves as humanitarian or philanthropists (Owusu-Bempah, 2007). Although these functions are clearly not dissimilar to those fulfilled by adoption in ancient societies, the context in which contemporary Western European adoption and fostering take place has not always been the case. In the contemporary context, it is the welfare or the standard of 'the best interest of the child', giving 'adequate' care to children in need of care, which provides the rationale.

Anglo-Saxon England

Crawford (1999) points out that the Anglo-Saxon family is generally presented as a common ideal, a family characterized by a close, warm and loving relationship between parents and their children. Yet, as researchers (e.g., Crawford, 1999; Parkes, 2001, 2006) point out, fostering out, sending one's child away to be raised by another family, was integral to Anglo-Saxon child-rearing practices. Crawford (1999) stresses, nonetheless, that the extent to which children were brought up by those outside their nuclear family, and the purpose of this, varied widely according to the age and status of the child. He points out also that the term 'fostering' carried a somehow different meaning among the Anglo-Saxons. That is, they used the word 'foster' generically to cover a range of nurturing patterns, from the equivalent of a mother's help or live-in nanny to what we might recognize today as full-scale adoption outside the biological family.

Crawford distinguishes three broad categories of fostering in Anglo-Saxon England. In the first category, and by far the most common type of fostering, a nurse (nanny) was brought into an upper-class or elite household to assume some, if not all, of the childcare responsibilities, the duties of bringing up the child. This very often resulted in the development of attachment and a strong bond or warm and enduring ties of affection between the nanny and the child. The second type of fostering in Anglo-Saxon England is what today is often referred to as 'fostering out'. In this type of childcare arrangement, children were often fostered outside their homes to be raised in another household, often that of a relative. This type of fostering took place either through necessity, such the death of a parent(s) or, as Crawford points out, it might be the equivalent of sending a child to a boarding school. While a foster-mother who was a nanny might be of low status, a child sent to be trained and to acquire good manners in another household would customarily expect to be fostered into a family of equal or higher status than his biological family. We will see in subsequent chapters that fostering children out in order to learn valued skills or to acquire culturally appropriate manners is one of the major motives for fostering children out in many contemporary societies.

In the third category of fostering in Anglo-Saxon England, as in ancient Greece and Rome, for example, there were instances where the child entered another household not simply on a temporary basis or as a visitor; rather he would acquire rights of inheritance from his new family, and might even abandon his biological family permanently. Thus, Crawford argues that secular 'adoption' as a feature of the Anglo-Saxon child-rearing system and oblation (the offering of the child as a gift to God) whereby children were donated to the Church might, today, be interpreted as an act of adoption as opposed to fostering.

Crawford provides examples indicating the commonplaceness of foster-mothers or nannies being recruited by Anglo-Saxon elite households. In fact, he claims that it is beyond dispute that noblemen and their wives delegated the task of looking after their children to others as a matter of course:

[T]he *childfoster* was expressly included in the list of servants indispensable to a man of status in the eighth-century law codes of Ine of Wessex. The nurse was considered an indispensable part of the thane's entourage.
(Crawford, 1999, pp. 123–4)

Crawford uses this and other examples to stress that the children of noble-men needed to be kept within the household even when that household was peripatetic (on the move), but the day-to-day task of looking after and car-ing for the child was assumed not to be the business of either parent of the elite Anglo-Saxon child. In other words, it was seen as a menial task. Thus, nannies and foster families were usually of a lower status than the foster-child. Nonetheless, fostering a royal or noble child seems to have been an attractive prospect; it could be advantageous for the foster family, just as it could be for the child.

> [T]he *Prognostications* advised that the 7th day of the moon was an auspicious one to ask a favour of a lord, and 'if you propose to foster a royal child or a nobleman's, fetch it to your home and household, and so foster it; it will be well for you'.
>
> (Crawford, 1999, p. 126)

The account given by Crawford of fostering in Anglo-Saxon society suggests that children were raised by foster-carers either within the family home or away from it, in another household, at some time during their childhood. It suggests that at some stage, boys in particular were sent away from home to gain an education or training for their adult lives. Crawford is not the only one to equate this form of fostering with the act of sending a child away to boarding school today; others (e.g., Cleaver, 2000) do so too and, so, warn that it does not necessarily mean that noble families gave up all interest in their child.

Crawford claims that the evidence regarding girls being fostered out is vague. Thus, he relies on literary and legal sources to show that it was uncommon for parents to give up their infant daughters from birth to be reared away from the home. From these sources, he cites the examples of King Edwin's daughter Eanflaed, King Edward's daughter Eadberga and King Edgar's daughter Edith, all of whom were given to monasteries from birth. Today, this might seem to represent the clearest form of abandonment of children by their parents, but Crawford warns against such an assumption. He points out that, in fact, the parents seem to have continued to take a warm interest in their growing children. For example, '*Edgar was present when Edith was formally dedicated to the Church, and her mother, as abbess of the convent, was of course always present in the growing girl's life*' (Crawford, 1999, p. 126).

Like contemporary societies, Anglo-Saxon society was concerned about the likelihood of child maltreatment or exploitation, especially orphans and those being raised outside their biological family. To safeguard such children's welfare, according to Crawford, there were laws advocating, for instance, that widows and orphans should be properly looked after. Crawford cites a law of the Kentish King Æthelbert as evidence of the Anglo-Saxons' concern for vulnerable children. This law advocated that, if a father died, his widow should receive half his estate if he had had a living child. Crawford sees this as suggesting that the heir of the man's estate needed protection, and this would best be ensured by providing the child's mother with means of sustenance. He cites also the early seventh-century law of Hlothhere and Eadric which made provision for a man dying, leaving a wife and child: *'it is right that the child should remain with the mother, and one of its father's relatives who is willing to act, shall be given as its guardian to take care of its property, until it is ten years old'* (Crawford, 1999, p. 127). Given the prevalence of fostering in this society, the emphasis on the mother as the right person to care for the child raises one or two questions. For example, might it be that fostering worked effectively for the child only while his/her father, his/her male guardian, was alive to champion his/her cause in case of maltreatment or exploitation? Crawford surmises that an orphan child lacking the status and security provided by a living father was vulnerable, at a disadvantage. In other words, fostering by kin in Anglo-Saxon England served to protect the child's physical safety, rights and interests.

Family, kin and fostering

Notwithstanding Crawford's caveat, it appears that Anglo-Saxon parents nonchalantly put their children in foster care or delegated their care to others. If so, then how do we reconcile that with the picture of ideal Anglo-Saxon families, of parents who showered upon their children tender and loving care? Crawford's guess is that in selecting the foster family, parents were not callous about their choice of foster-parents for their children; nor did they count on the altruism or benevolence of strangers. Rather, like their ancient Greek and Roman counterparts, they would select potential foster caregivers from among their own kin or social networks. Although, as we have already seen, there existed laws designed to protect the child against abuse or exploitation, as it is the case today, one could not always guarantee enforcement of legislation. Kinship, by its very nature, brought with it strong legal, moral and social obligations as well as solidarity, and so provided assurance that the child would be well looked after. Thus, Crawford (1999) suggests, by entrusting kin with one's child or placing the child close to kin, those bonds of obligation and solidarity were reinforced, more so in a society founded upon and maintained by kinship and loyalty.

Crawford cites mortality rates as a rationale for Anglo-Saxon parents' placing their children not just in care, but for preferring kin as foster-parents. They believed that it was in the children's best interest to become members or fictive members of other families. He estimates the average adult life expectancy in Anglo-Saxon society to have been 33 to 35 years. If that was the case at that time, then a large number of children would have experienced the death of one or both parents before they reached maturity or could fend for themselves. *'What could parents do to ensure that their children would be cared for, and that other adults would protect and defend their rights if the worst happened?'*, Crawford asks (p. 130). His answer is that the parents saw fostering out their children as an insurance policy for the children. In other words, the act of taking a child into one's own family automatically brought with it serious moral obligations – the child in one's household is one's child; s/he is part of one's family. Hence, in raising the insurance premium by increasing the number of adults who had 'parental' responsibility for their children, Anglo-Saxon parents, in foresight, were creating an insurance policy in order to guarantee the best possible future for their children.

This insurance policy was further affirmed if the foster family was kin. In short, the exchange of children between families had both tangible and intangible advantages for the parents, in creating or reinforcing bonds between kin groups; and for the child, not only as s/he grew up, but also, as an adult, s/he could call on his/her foster family in times of need. Crawford stresses that such real and potential benefits should not be underestimated. We will see in later chapters that this form of guarantee (or insurance policy) may be one of the conscious or unconscious motives for the preponderance of kinship fostering in many contemporary societies.

Attachment and bond

Those trained in child development, especially in attachment theory and techniques, must not hasten to charge or blame Anglo-Saxon society for instituting and supporting a system of fostering, especially in situations where the biological parents were clearly able and capable of providing the child with optimal care. It is obvious that not all fostered children would have experienced an auspicious environment. Thus, from a developmental perspective, some pertinent questions need to be raised: Does the fact that children were not always placed in a favourable environment necessarily mean that they would routinely have been deprived of a secure base? In short, would they have routinely experienced a lack of love and affection? Would their psychosocial development have been impaired as a consequence?

These questions will be addressed in subsequent chapters. Meanwhile, we must remind ourselves that studies of modern children raised by adults other than their genetic parents have reported mixed findings and have reached conflicting conclusions. What is undisputed, though, is that a child fostered in infancy or from an early age will develop an attachment and as close a bond with his foster-parents as s/he would with his/her genetic parent(s), regardless of whether or not the biological parents live in the same household or in close proximity. In his review of the literature, Crawford cites Winston Churchill as a famous example. Winston Churchill was raised by his nanny, Mrs Everest, with whom he formed a deeply emotional bond. Of his biological mother, he is claimed to have stated: *'She shone for me like the evening star. I loved her dearly – but at a distance. My nurse was my confidante. Mrs Everest it was who looked after me and tended all my wants'* (in Crawford, 1999, p. 130).

For some time now, we have known from psychosocial developmental theory that a child will usually form the closest of attachments with his/her primary carer(s), and that the carer does not have to be the biological mother. Hence, Crawford argues that in cases where a child is lovingly fostered, if the primary bond is not with the biological mother it may be that it is only the parent who loses out emotionally; it is the parent who suffers from emotional deprivation, rather than the child who suffers unduly. It will be clear in later chapters that this does not mean that fostering meets the child's identity needs in all fostering situations. The moral here is simply that we should not hasten to make the easy assumption that all cultural practices carry the same social and emotional implications at all places and times.

Fostering in other regions

The practice of fostering was widespread not just in medieval England. Fostering formed an important aspect of Eurasian social, economic and political landscape. Parkes (2001, 2006) summarizes the act of fostering in the Hindu Kush (the Mountain Kingdom of Pakistan), Celtic Northwest Europe and the Mediterranean. He argues that allegiance fostering, for example, was a characteristic feature of many polities in Eurasia. Distinct from the crisis fostering of orphans by close family or kin, he identifies two related forms of fostering in these early societies: *cliental allegiance fostering*, and *patronal allegiance fostering*. Cliental allegiance fostering refers to the raising of a high-status child by low-status foster-parents, while patronal allegiance fostering is the converse; it describes a situation where a low-status child is brought up by high-status foster-parents. Both forms of fostering were used to reinforce old or to establish new affiliations between rank status grades by delegating infants and children for nursing and raising to social subordinates or vice versa.

Fostering often also created fictive relationships (or 'milk' relationships). According to Parkes (2001), constructing 'milk kinship' (or kinship by milk) through infant fostering was a common social phenomenon throughout the ancient Mediterranean. Milk kinship refers to the fictive kinship relationship between two (or more) children suckled by the same woman but otherwise unrelated. Such relationships became important since they were *de jure* bonds of cliental affiliation. That is, they were recognized by law as well as *de facto* in the administration of justice, rights and obligations in eastern Christendom and Islam (Parkes, 2006).

Allegiance fostering in medieval Ireland

Parkes (2006) deduces from the anthropological literature that references to nursing clothes and breastfeeding indicate that, in medieval Ireland, it is likely that the act of fostering was undertaken within a few days of birth. This seems to suggest that a child would be suckled by its foster-mother before being trained by its foster-father. Parkes believes that fostering usually lasted from infancy until marriage – 14 years for a girl, 17 years for a boy. He believes also that it is likely that separate nursing and educational or training duties were subcontracted to successive foster-parents. He infers from the literature that, given the close-knit local networks of consanguinity or descent relationships and affinity which prevailed in medieval Irish society, foster-parents were likely to have been related along either paternal or maternal descent lines to their foster-children.

As elsewhere in that epoch, fostering in Ireland was a solemn contractual relationship and formed an important bond between families and individuals so related. As Parkes points out, this bond was, on occasions, firmer than the bonds between actual kin, since allies acquired in this way could never become one's rivals for office within one's own lineage. Patronal allegiance was therefore expedient; fostering out one's children served to consolidate dependable supporters in struggles against rivals in a society where a lord's rank and honour depended very much upon the size and resoluteness of his following. Similarly, fostering a lord's child could be an advantageous move; it could provide a ladder for upward social mobility for the foster-parents.

Parkes presents English accounts of Irish fostering in the sixteenth century, confirming its commonplaceness during that era:

> Women, within six days after their delivery, return to their husband's bed, and put out their children to nurse. Great application is made from all parts of the nurses to the children of these Grandees, who are more tender to their foster-children than to their own … nay, though they think it a disgrace to suckle their own children, yet for the sake of nursing these, man and wife will obtain from each other, and in case they do not, they find another nurse at their charge … The foster-fathers take much pains, spend much more money, and bestow more affection and kindness upon these children than their own …
>
> (William Good, 1566, quoted by Parkes, 2006, pp. 368–9)

Parkes believes that this account shows that nursing the infant of a high-status family necessitated infants and children to be cared for by low-status foster-parents. He believes also that this, in turn, resulted in serial chains of fictive kinship among successive social strata, as was the case in western Eurasia as a whole.

There existed other types of fostering in medieval Ireland, apart from allegiance fostering and patronal fostering. These were ecclesiastical fostering and spiritual kinship. Parkes' (2006) research indicates that, modelled on secular fostering, the early development of Celtic monastic school introduced a new framework for adoptive kinship that was tied to literate education, spiritual affiliation and ecclesiastical advancement. He discerns from the evidence that by the ninth century, noble families availed themselves of this new opportunity for their children. Namely, many parents interrupted their children's nursing and training by lay foster-parents at the age of around seven and transferred them to monastic schools in order for them to acquire monastic education.

Fostering in Celtic Wales and Scotland

The institution of fostering formed a significant element of medieval child-rearing not only in Ireland, but also in Wales and Scotland (Aldgate, 1977; Anderson, 2004; Parkes, 2006). However, Anderson (2004) claims that, although there exists a substantial body of linguistic, legal and literary evidence that gives a fairly clear picture of the institution of fostering in early medieval Ireland, the picture regarding the situation in Wales is unclear. She attributes this to the fact that scholarly works, especially those examining the Early Middle Ages, have tended to focus on the linguistic, legal and literary commonalities between Ireland and Wales. Consequently, she claims, scholars have used Irish evidence to fill in the gaps between the two regions with regard to fostering. Having examined the evidence, her conclusion is that there is certainly enough convincing material to suggest that fostering was practised in high medieval Wales. She argues that although it may have developed from an early tradition that was close to the Irish model of fostering, fostering existed in Wales, but it was practised in a distinctive and much more limited way than it was in Ireland and possibly Scotland.

Other researchers, however, claim that cliental fostering was widespread also in Scotland and Wales, as elsewhere in medieval times (Aldgate, 1977; Aldgate and McIntosh, 2006; Parkes, 2006). In other words, contrary to popular belief, kinship care in Britain is not new; it has always been used for various purposes. In Scotland, Aldgate (1977) points out that, in the seventeenth and eighteenth centuries, fostering among clans was the norm and was designed to consolidate and reinforce kinship ties, solidarity and loyalty. Through fostering, sons of chiefs, lords, thanes and other leading clan gentry would foster one anther's children for a minimum of seven of the child's formative years (Aldgate, 1977; Parkes, 2006). This child-rearing arrangement was hierarchical; the foster-parent was always of a lower rank than that of the biological parent.

The literature indicates that the main purpose of fostering among these high-ranking groups in medieval Scottish society was education, for the child to acquire etiquette and skills commensurate with his position in society. Foster-parents were responsible not only for the children's education or training, but also for their welfare. Fostering was, therefore, an economic as well as a socio-political transaction that required a lifetime's commitment. As elsewhere in the Celtic regions, Aldgate and McIntosh (2006) argue that, although cliental fostering in Scotland was practised to a limited extent by the twelfth century, kinship foster care continued among ordinary families. For example, a grandparent, an uncle, an older sibling or even a neighbour would take charge of an orphan. Similarly, families experiencing hardship would transfer their children to their more fortunate kin. Among ordinary families, fostering also involved sending children to another household, usually within close proximity, to learn valued skills or trade. In these situations, the children did not just learn from their masters, they lived with them.

Aldgate and McIntosh point out that in Britain as a whole, informal arrangements for fostering children among kith and kin continued until the introduction of the Poor Laws, when the system of boarding out children with strangers within the Poor Laws became generally accepted. According to these investigators, when the system of boarding out children became more recognized, informal kinship care, and even boarding out children with relatives, fell out of favour, with a corresponding increase in non-relative foster placements. Aldgate (1977) suggests that this was largely motivated by a developing philosophy of giving children 'a fresh start' away from a 'pathogenic' environment, from the influence of their 'lackadaisical' and 'defective' families.

Fostering in medieval France

As in all human societies, past and contemporary, there existed mechanisms in Europe for the care of orphans, foundlings and abandoned children. Although the philosophy underlying these mechanisms and their utilization may have somehow varied between different states, regions or localities, depending on their cultural or religious beliefs and values, they were designed to serve the same end, ensuring the welfare and survival of infants and children who would otherwise not have thrived or who, at least, needed care. As an illustration, this section provides a brief sketch of the situation in pre-industrial France.

In Europe as a whole, there existed no adoption in the technical sense until as recently as the beginning of the twentieth century. In France, for example, there was no legal adoption of young children before 1923. Indeed, until then, adoption of a child, as understood today, was impossible (Fauve-Chamoux, 1996). This is reported to have been the case also in other societies. For example, Goody (1969) has noted that ancient Hindu law forbade the adoption of orphans. So, what was the alternative, what mechanisms were there for the care and protection of children who required alternative or substitute care?

In France, as described by historians of the French child welfare system, until the advent of legal adoption, relatives had duties towards orphaned children and the children, in turn, had to work and serve their substitute parents and to obey them (Culvillier, 1986, in Fauve-Chamoux, 1996). These duties, usually carried out in the form of guardianship or curatorship of children of deceased or absent parents, were most often devolved upon the maternal kin. In other words, a maternal grandfather or uncle would assume responsibility for his daughter's or sister's orphaned children. This was the case in most European societies; orphans and semi-orphans were usually taken in by close relatives (Culvillier, 1986, in Fauve-Chamoux, 1996).

This does not mean that foster-carers or guardians, although kin, were left completely to their own devices regarding the care, wellbeing, protection and the interests of the children in their charge. Other bodies oversaw the duties of the guardians. According to Fauve-Chamoux, customary, local and national agencies were involved in the welfare of the children by creating patterns to control their fate and to establish protection for their survival. Under the watchful eyes of these agencies, kin were duty-bound to provide them with foster care, to secure their sustenance in the broadest sense of the term. Thus, the law did not merely provide them with a guardian; the law was strengthened by the fact that these guardians were subject to the further control of a family council, sometimes with the addition of a judiciary delegate. A family council comprised four relatives from each side of the family. Family councils supervised the orphan's fostering until age 15, when s/he usually began to earn a livelihood. A semi-orphan was controlled by a family council, and the future of an orphan was submitted to a large familial debate, controlled by neighbours and relatives, often in front of public and judicial authorities (Fauve-Chamoux, 1996). One wonders if 'family conference' (or 'family meeting') is a watered-down variant of a family council in medieval France.

Briefly, Fauve-Chamoux points out that, although there was no legal adoption in Europe before the beginning of the last century, following Roman times, the custom of western European societies was to provide for the care and protection of children in need. For example, Christian societies were motivated to find a new family framework for such children. They made careful provision to ensure the protection of orphaned and semi-orphaned children and the correct management and transmission of the assets such children inherited. In other words, they endeavoured to provide the best placement according to conditions and common moral values. Fauve-Chamoux points out further that joining a foster family entailed responsibilities on the part of the child. This, however, did not make the child or the family a stranger:

> Entering a foster family in France implied a respectful behaviour of the child – but this child remained a member of his family of birth, even if at a young age he considered himself as a member of his 'milk-family' ...
> (Fauve-Chamoux, 1996, p. 11)

We will see in later chapters that such is the experience of most children in kinship care globally.

Summary

Examination of the historico-anthropological evidence regarding adoption and fostering may help us understand not just their cultural meanings, functions and outcomes for the child, but also how fostering, for example, has evolved and why it is practised differently in different cultures today. It helps us also to appreciate cultural variations in the concept of kinship and its meaning, for instance. Although there is a surprising scarcity of adoption studies outside Western societies (Goody, 1969; Leon, 2002), as subsequent chapters show, there is more than ample material to highlight how dramatically different kinship, adoption and fostering are structured in other places and at other times. They show that Leon is justified in challenging using blood ties as an essential, if not the sole, criterion in the definition of kinship which has prevailed throughout contemporary Western cultures.

> Even when religious, cultural, and legal norms discouraged adoption ... as occurred in sixteenth- and seventeenth-century France, people persisted in the practice, motivated by a desire to establish the same affective bonds that were formed between biological parents and children.
>
> (Leon, 2002, p. 657)

Using blood ties as *sine qua non* to define kinship holds true only if one defines kinship in its narrowest sense. Kinship by milk is a clear case in point. Similarly, 'adoption' possesses different meanings in different cultures. Consequently, its practice in many societies differs from how it is practised in Western societies. For instance, researchers draw our attention to traditional Hawaiian culture in which adoption was common among tribal chieftains as a means of promoting communal solidarity; a culture in which placing a child for adoption was typically viewed as a generous rather than shameful act (e.g., Griffin, 2006; Leon, 2002).

In his review of anthropological studies from Oceanic cultures, Leon (2002) concludes that, among some of these cultures, it is considered selfish to keep all of one's biological children if one had many and a relative had none. Furthermore, adoption in these cultures is a private transaction between biological and adoptive parents; in most cases the latter are close relatives and almost never strangers. Other studies support Leon's observation. Griffin (2006), for example, points out that the root meaning of Hawaiian adoption (*hanai*) is to feed or nourish. Its associations all relate to parenting non-biological children and it embraces fostering as well as adoption because, in the past, the Hawaiian language did not distinguish between the two. *Hanai* was a verbal covenant: the promise to another family of a child before birth and the giving of that child at birth as a gesture of friendship and esteem. Griffin stresses, however, that the covenant was not always observed since a first child could not be *hanaied*, and no child could be *hanaied* without the consent of biological parents.

In today's Western societies, adoption serves much the same functions as it did in ancient civilizations. Of these functions, as some see it, it is the welfare aspect of children in need of care that is the one most stressed (e.g., Goody, 1969; Leon, 2002). The emphasis on this aspect of the institution has by no means prevailed throughout history or across cultures. As we have seen, the context in which adoption is found in ancient Rome or Greece, Anglo-Saxon

England or Celtic Ireland contrasts markedly with contemporary ideology and convention. As Griffin (2006) argues, adoption served semi-feudal agrarian society in different ways from its functions in modern industrialized society. In other words, since antiquity, adoption has reflected the social reality of the society for which it was designed and in which it existed. This reality is constructed from, or at least influenced by, a given society's ecology – its economic, religious and political ecology – which, in turn, is constructed from or shaped by its history.

It is clear from the foregoing discussion that adoption or fostering in Europe was once a covenant or agreement among extended families and allies, and did not always or necessarily entail severance from birth families. Instead, the primary purpose of the act of adoption was to benefit all parties, birth families and adoptive families alike. In ancient Rome, adoption was a culturally accepted means of providing heirs – perpetuating decent lines, cementing kin ties and reinforcing alliances. In some cases, a boy assumed his adoptive father's name, plus a surname indicating his birth family, and enjoyed the privileges of both his biological and adoptive families (Griffin, 2006). In essence, adoption was a covenant between families of equal or similar status who were members of the same kinship network and, often, political allies; the rationale was economic and political as well as religious.

If successful, as it invariably was in most cases, adoption became a principal means of accruing social and economic capital for the adopted child's birth family; and for the adoptive families, fulfilment of their need for continuity and, consequently, an ancestral niche in society (and perhaps the world beyond). Materially, they derived through adoption *'social and economic benefits on which sovereignty and commonwealth once depended'* (Griffin, 2006, p. 39). That is, adoptive families used the institution to build alliances and foster allegiance upon which their status, power and influence depended. Through those benefits, adoption became a way of promoting social cohesion and kinship or filial integration and solidarity. In short, in the primeval or medieval context, adoption or fostering was a covenant; it was a social contract, verbal or written, explicit or implicit, between families. Indeed, one may wonder if, apart from adrogation in Rome, which was rare in any case, 'adoption' in ancient civilizations and pre-industrial Europe was adoption in the technical sense or, rather, fostering. Whatever the answer may be, that is the context in which the practice is to be found in most contemporary cultures beyond Western borders.

This chapter has confined itself to the institution of fostering and adoption in ancient civilizations and medieval Europe. This by no means implies that the practice did not exist in other civilizations. Such an assumption would be clearly presumptuous. It is rather because of a lack of pertinent material. However, in his attempt to contrast adoption in Eurasia with the situation in sub-Saharan Africa, Goody (1969) highlights the absence of adoption in anthropological accounts of African societies. *'The situation of the Ashanti seems typical; legal analysts and sociological observers agree that adoption as such is not known in Ashanti law'* (Allott, 1966; quoted by Goody, 1969, p. 55). The bourgeoning contemporary evidence of foster care or quasi-adoption in Asante (Ashanti), in fact, in the whole of Ghana and sub-Saharan Africa (and Oceania), indicates clearly that the institution existed in ancient African and other societies. For instance, the ancient obligation that men marry the widow of a deceased brother or uncle meant that many children grew up in the home of an uncle-father. In other words, they were cared for by kin.

The next chapter discusses the practice of fostering in contemporary traditional societies, from a cross-cultural perspective. Also, we will see throughout this book that kinship foster care is the primary alternative child-care arrangement in most cultures outside the Western world.

O'Sullivan (1988) states: *'The physical is a pathway to the metaphysical and the metaphysical does not exclude the physical'* (in Griffin, 2006, p. 50). In the context of this book, this statement may be rephrased thus: 'Fostering is a pathway to adoption and adoption does not exclude fostering.' This book takes the position that the institution and practice of fostering and adoption, whether considered comparatively or not, should be studied not as a phenomenon or entity independent of other social phenomena. Rather, it can only be understood in the context of other social relationships or constructs, in the context of other fictive kinship relationships such as, for example, godparent-hood. This, among other things, calls for a preparedness to approach each culture with respect; it calls for a willingness to seek to understand a given culture on its own terms. To do otherwise, to try to understand any element of another culture from an ethno-historic and/or ethnocentric or, indeed, from any other perspective would be a futile, if not fatuous, endeavour; and that certainly includes that culture's institution of adoption and fostering.

2 Fostering in cross-cultural perspective

In Western societies, it is not only lay members of the public who are prone to viewing alternative child-rearing as aberrant; child welfare professionals – social workers, schoolteachers, family therapists and family lawyers – are also susceptible. In other words, to most people in Western societies, it is axiomatic that children should be raised by their natural or genetic parents, so much so that they find it difficult to believe or even envision that this is not always and everywhere the case. Many are unaware that fostering has a long history in the Western world, as it has in all human societies. Indeed, the placement of children with relatives is among the oldest and commonest traditions in child-rearing throughout the world. As such, as we saw in the preceding chapter, it has not always been perceived as anomalous in Western societies. Fostering was a common institution among the Celts of Britain and Ireland, particularly among high-ranking families who exchanged children to foster political and commercial links. In early modern England, high-ranking families would regularly put their babies out to wet nurses and might not see them at all during what is believed now to be the crucial period of bonding.

Although fostering and adoption have a long history, and continued to be practised everywhere, research indicates that perceptions and definitions of these concepts vary across space and time, historically and culturally. There are societies in which fostering in particular is not just a commonplace practice, but rather an essential and often preferred means of raising children. In short, the practice of sending children away to be raised by relatives, friends or neighbours on a temporary basis or permanently is ubiquitous in the modern world. This chapter draws examples from studies in diverse regions: Africa (notably West Africa), Oceania, North America and South America to demonstrate its commonplaceness and normativeness. In these societies, the interests of children or the fosterer-parents' wishes are not the only motives for circulating children between families and social groups. In many societies, from Latin America to Asia and Africa, the lineage or clan may assume 'ownership' of children, and various strategies are employed to share or to keep children within a lineage (e.g., Alber, 2003, 2004; Bowie, 2004; Castle, 1995; Donner, 1999; Goody, 1982; Kay, 1963; Notermans, 2004; Oni, 1995;

Peers and Brown, 2000; Shomaker, 1989; Stack, 1974; Talle, 2004; Verhoef, 2005). In other instances, adoption and fostering are used to form alliances between groups.

Fostering and adoption: definitions

Shomaker (1989) recognizes that the concept of fostering has not yet been fully defined, so its use in the literature varies. Writers use the term variously to refer to fostering, adoption, child circulation, child transfer, child holding, babysitting, and more. Shomaker argues that the fluidity of the term muddles the literature, and clouds the child's status in many societies. Adoption, in contrast, seems to convey a clear meaning; in its technical sense, there appears to be no confusion about it. Simplistically put, it relates to legal ownership of a child who is not one's offspring. It represents a situation in which full parental rights are transferred from biological parents to 'social' parents, as opposed to fostering in which only a partial transfer occurs. In 'closed adoption' the birth parents are legally and socially erased from the record and the adopted person may not be aware that s/he is not the genetic child of the adoptive parents. This may be seen as almost akin to adrogation in prehistoric Rome.

Although Western conception of adoption is straightforward, its application in other cultural settings is fraught with both conceptual and practical difficulties. In these settings, researchers tend to conflate adoption and fostering. The verb 'to foster' has its roots in the Latin word *nutritura* (the act of suckling). Thus, in English, 'to foster' has several synonyms: to nourish; to nurture; to feed; to educate; to train; to promote; to develop; to cultivate. In the context of child-rearing, these verbs collectively mean promoting and sustaining the growth and development of a child by adults other than his/her biological parents. In fostering, although the foster family exercises the same child-rearing duties (and sometimes responsibilities) as does an adoptive family, the biological parents retain their parental rights. Thus, in contrast to adoption, transfer of a child (and in some cases parental rights) is only partial, tentative or conditional.

There are also cultural variations in the meaning of fostering or adoption. As we will see in this chapter, some societies do not have different words for the two forms of childcare, that is, one for adoption and another for fostering. In some situations there is no easily translatable word (into English) for either of these concepts; in others, the word 'adoption', for instance, does not exist. Allott (1966, in Goody, 1969, p. 55) gives the example of the Asante (or Ashanti) who do not have adoption in their statute. Similarly, Alber (2003, 2004) and Talle (2004) report, respectively, that the Baatombu in Northern Benin and the Maasai in East Africa do not have different terms for biological and social parents, and the term for 'giving birth' is used by both biological parents and foster-parents when speaking about 'their child'. Likewise, a child will use the same designatory term 'mother' for both his/her biological mother and foster-mother(s). In these cultures, many children have multiple 'mothers' because new mothers do not supplant old ones, rather they compliment one another in their parenting tasks; and a child is regarded as fostered only in rare circumstances where s/he is placed outside the kinship network (Verhoef and Morelli, 2007).

In societies where fostering is normal and part of a wider system of relationships, it is often considered to be the preferred means of bringing up children. Children are precious, but may be claimed by others (most often, kin); frequently, foster-parents are perceived to be more suitable than biological parents to raise and educate a child. Children may be claimed (fostered) before or at birth, and it is not thought to harm them in any way to leave their birth families (Alber, 2003; Donner, 1999; Talle, 2004). Alber reports that in Baatombu society, to refuse to give a child to someone who has a culturally validated right to ask for it is considered selfish and morally blameworthy. This does not suggest that parents are indifferent regarding to whom they entrust their children. Biological parents are often very selective in their choice of prospective foster- and adoptive parents; they typically prefer adults who can offer their children better economic prospects than they can themselves.

Nothing contrasts more markedly with the Western ideal regarding child-rearing than these fostering patterns. In Western societies, it is a taken-for-granted assumption that responsibility for a child's physical and emotional wellbeing, the task of promoting and sustaining a child's growth and development, falls solely on his/her birth family. The question is: What is 'family'? To most people in Western societies the term 'family' automatically conjures the nuclear family, an atomized unit of individuals composed of a woman, a man and their biological children and living under the same roof. Even then, some will regard this unit as a family only if the parents are 'properly' married, if they have taken the matrimonial vow. Since the industrial revolution, the 'sacrosanct' nuclear family has been presented as an enduring and universal institution transported and expected everywhere, so that even the thought that some people deliberately choose others to raise their children is abhorrent to many Western families and individuals. However, historical and contemporary studies show that this is far from the reality in most, if not all, societies.

In other societies, characterized by those described below, transfer of children between different caretakers and households is not exclusive; although the fostering may last for years, it does not permanently separate the children from their biological parents. Payne-Price (1981) differentiates fostering from the formal judicial action of adoption, stating that the latter is:

[a] legal process by which a child is taken into a family and raised as a natural offspring; the biological parents give up all their rights to the child ... fostering [is] the raising of a child by people other than his/her natural or adoptive parents ... parents do not give up their rights to the

child and may retrieve him/her. There is no permanent transfer of primary parental rights.

(p. 134)

This and subsequent chapters adopt Payne-Price's definition of fostering.

The African context

Fostering among relatives, friends and neighbours is an established custom in many African societies. As in Oceania (the Pacific regions), the fostering of children within extended kinship networks is a time-honoured cultural practice in many parts of sub-Saharan Africa. The accumulated literature contains descriptions of patterns of fostering in East Africa and Southern Africa (e.g., Page, 1998; Umbima, 1991) and particularly West Africa (Alber, 2003; Castle, 1995; Goody, 1973, 1982; Isiugo-Abanihe, 1985; Lloyd and Blanc, 1996; Notermans, 2004; Nsameng, 1992; Oni, 1995; Oppong, 1973; Talle, 2004; Vandermeersch, 2002; Verhoef, 2005). Briefly, since Goody's research in the region during the 1970s and 1980s, her followers have described West Africa as one of the major centres of kinship fostering. Evidence bears out this description. For example, in a study by Isiugo-Abanihe (1985), 25–40 per cent of parents in Ghana, Liberia and western Nigeria reported that one or more of their children were living in another household; the proportions were even higher in Sierra Leone.

To understand the preponderance of fostering in sub-Saharan Africa, we must understand the African conception of 'family'. In this vast region, family is conceived inclusively, as more than just the nuclear family. Often, the term 'family' encompasses a whole village or community. Hence, it is natural for children to grow up with many relatives – aunts ('mothers') uncles ('fathers'), grandparents, older siblings and even friends or neighbours. We will see in this section that in West Africa as a whole, fostering is a traditional and commonplace childcare practice. In some communities, more than half of all children spend a substantial part of their childhood and adolescence away from their biological parents. In some instances, children are claimed for fostering at birth (Alber, 2003); others remain with their parents until they are weaned. In the main, however, children are cared for by their genetic parents until they are five to eight years old. Some foster-children live in the same village or town as their biological parents do, but others may be sent over long distances, sometimes as far away as another country (Goody, 1982; Verhoef, 2005). Foster-parents are primarily responsible for feeding, clothing, socializing and training their foster-children, although natural parents contribute or are expected to contribute in one way or another to the costs of their formal education and maintenance (Alber, 2003; Goody, 1982; Notermans, 2004; Verhoef, 2005).

Although investigators agree that child fostering is a common phenomenon in sub-Saharan Africa, it needs stressing that it is not practised systematically through this region of the continent (Vandermeersch, 2002). Summarized below are selected studies which, together, give an indication of how deeply embedded and pervasive fostering among kin networks is in Africa; not just in West Africa, but also in many other communities. These are selected for the purposes of illustration, rather than on the basis of their empirical or methodological rigour.

Fostering in Cameroon

> '*A child is only its mother's in the womb.*'
>
> (Interviewee, quoted by Verhoef, 2005, p. 373)

The above statement captures, in its entirety, the value attached to a child in Cameroonian society, the prize children carry with them in African societies generally. Deciphered, it means that a child has many mothers, that a child belongs to the wider family or community. A version of this is the often-quoted African maxim, 'it takes a whole village to raise a child'. As in other African societies, fostering in Cameroon is undertaken not just in response to crisis. Rather, it is a conventional and often preferred childcare arrangement (e.g., Alber, 2003).

Verhoef (2005) argues that whether or not it is acceptable to send children to relatives and others, and under what circumstances fostering is even considered, is inextricably linked to culturally shaped views of family, parenthood and child development. Like others, she claims further that general beliefs about the nature of children and families play a major role in designing, shaping or reshaping the cultural frameworks that mothers, caregivers and community members use to understand and make fostering arrangements. Throughout sub-Saharan Africa, relationships among community and family members are complex and organized hierarchically according to age, gender, designation and number of dependants. Regardless of blood or marriage ties, kin are expected to show appropriate respect for those with higher status. People of one's grandparents' generation are especially revered for their wisdom, if nothing else. Thus, among the Nso of Cameroon, for example, children and young people use terms of address such as *ba* (father) for elder men and *mami* (mother) or *ya* (grandmother) for elder women.

The Nso ideal

Verhoef (Verhoef, 2005; Verhoef and Morelli, 2007) provides the following portrait of fostering among the Nso, an urban community in south-western Cameroon. The governing principle regarding children among this community, as elsewhere in sub-Saharan Africa, is that a child does not belong to the biological parents alone, but rather to kith and kin and the wider community, that one should treat all children as one would treat one's own. This precept requires families to work collectively to raise their collective children so that they may develop bonds with extended family members. To facilitate the multi-bonding process, children circulate among their various 'mothers' with little fuss. Verhoef (2005) reports that the Nso believe that being part of a close network of family relationships is essential for children's success, that the more relatives take active interest in the children's wellbeing, the greater their chances of thriving in a harsh and volatile world. In other words, the extended family represents an insurance policy for the children.

According to this Nso ideal, all children are 'gifts from God' and are meant to be shared. Therefore, when they move between households, they are welcomed with open arms and encouraged to 'feel free' in these households. By Verhoef's (2005) description, children 'fit' into caregivers' households, adapting easily to the routines of caregivers' children. They eat, walk to school and perform household chores with them. Within the household, there should be no distinction between birth children and foster-children, and all children are treated as if they came from the caregiver's own womb – receiving equal love, attention, food, clothes and school materials. Even when children are born out of wedlock, their status within the household is no different from that of other children. As one participant stressed:

> I think it would be abnormal if you have a child and your brothers or sisters neglected the child in your absence. Or keep your child at a distance … That is not part of our culture. Because with us [Nso families], a child is a child no matter what. It is a child and we value all children.
> (in Verhoef, 2005, p. 374)

This Nso ideal, according to Verhoef, involves a kin network in which everyone contributes to one another and their children according to their means. It describes a situation in which relatives, including those abroad, pull their families together by sending food from recent harvests or giving money for school fees, and the more fortunate take in the children of the less fortunate if they can do more for them than can the parents. *'If there is a place where a child can be helped, they should be sent'* (in Verhoef, 2005, p. 374).

The Nso reality

Verhoef (2005) used fostering among this community to test their ideal and, by extension the sub-Saharan African ideal, concerning children. The study involved 20 fostering arrangements. In-depth interviews were conducted with 20 foster-parents and 20 birth parents. The interviews were supplemented with casual conversations and observations during regular visits and participation in family gatherings. Analysis of the interviews with caregivers and birth mothers suggests that the nature of the relationships between the foster-parents and the biological parents was an influential factor in the children's living arrangements. Verhoef categorized these relationships as:

1) joint venture, 2) the ambivalent takeover and 3) the tug-of-war. She then contrasted these with the culturally ideal foster-care arrangements.

Analysis of the interviews revealed varying degrees to which actual fostering arrangements met or deviated from the cultural ideal. While some corresponded to the cultural ideal, others somehow deviated from it. The following are Verhoef's descriptions of the extent to which pairs of mothers (biological mothers and foster-mothers) worked together to raise their children, and the categories into which they fell.

The joint venture: In seven (35%) of the 20 fostering arrangements, involving three boys and four girls, the reality was close to the cultural ideal. Both birth mothers and foster-mothers maintained strong, close relationships. These mothers provided detailed accounts of how they were collaborating in the children's care. For example, they made joint decisions regarding the children's general wellbeing; they conveyed such sentiments as, *'The two of us are in charge of Edith'* and *'One cannot take a decision on the child without the other'* (in Verhoef, 2005, p. 375). They were also in frequent contact with each other; and even though five of these seven pairs of mothers lived in different towns (some in different provinces or countries), they made great efforts to visit or find other ways of exchanging information on a daily or, at least, monthly basis. In these cases, even long distances posed no barriers to some form of contact with the children.

The mothers and foster-mothers in joint venture described themselves as jointly raising all of their collective children – not just the mother's foster-children. As one mother explained, *'We just care for our children together ... I give what I can to help. And when Mom has, she gives'* (in Verhoef, 2005, p. 376). In this type of arrangement, the foster-parents spoke of actively supporting not only the children who lived with them, but also the children who remained with the birth mother. The birth mothers similarly claimed 'contributing' to the foster-mother and her children – sending food and clothes not just to her children, but to all the children in the foster-mother's household. These mothers stressed also the importance of positive social experiences, especially with other children, to the children's socio-emotional wellbeing.

The ambivalent takeover: In nine (45%) of the 20 cases (three boys, six girls), the foster-parents were seen by all involved as having complete authority over and responsibility for the children in their care. Contrary to the cultural ideal, these foster-parents were portrayed as 'the only mother' to the children, particularly those born into or living in what were considered somewhat less-than-ideal circumstances. Four of the children involved had been orphaned; a further four were 'born out of wedlock', typically while their mothers were living with the foster-mothers. The living mothers admitted having a limited say in decisions affecting their children. Unlike the joint venture birth mothers who were in professional occupations or in cash-based trades, these mothers were of a lower status compared to the foster-parents, educationally, financially and in terms of age. Given the cultural context, it is therefore unsurprising that they felt subordinate and were deferential to the foster-mothers in matters affecting their children. In short, in the ambi-valent takeover situations, the foster-mothers saw the children as their 'own' children, and the birth mothers were acquiescent. This does not imply that the children did not know who their genetic mothers were.

Whereas those involved in joint venture cases emphasized children's need for positive social experiences (especially with other children), in the ambiva-lent takeover situation, the focus of both pairs of parents was on stability, access to education, and a generally better standard of living. Although cul-tural norms dictated that the birth mothers exercised very little choice in the arrangement, they unanimously accepted that the children were better off, that if they were left with them their life chances would be seriously com-promised. One may, therefore, question the accuracy or fairness of Verhoef's description of the foster-parents as 'take-overs' or usurpers, especially in view of the cultural context of their actions. Describing them as 'paternal-istic' might be more appropriate. In theory, as well as in reality, they were foster-parents not only to the children, but also to their mothers: four of the children had lost their parents through death; and in the other five cases, the children were born out of wedlock while the mothers (most likely in their early teens) were living with the foster-mothers. As such, the foster-mothers were fulfilling their 'parental' duties and responsibilities as required by Nso culture and other African cultures.

The tug-of-war: In four (20%) of the foster-care arrangements (two girls and two boys), the birth mothers and foster-mothers disagreed on their rela-tionship regarding the children. These arrangements were characterized by ongoing power struggle, open conflict over who should hold responsibility for the children. Unlike the other groups where the pairs of mothers were blood relatives, maternal grandparents or aunts, the foster-parents in this category were related through marriage. These arrangements were much farther removed from the cultural ideal.

All four (tug-of-war) mother–caregiver pairs narrated conflicting stories about the circumstances surrounding the children's living arrangements. The mothers were suspicious of the foster-mothers' motives; they believed that the children were taken by the caregivers to meet their own needs, such as loneliness, grief or just out of disrespect for the birth mothers. The caregiv-ers, on the other hand, contended that the birth mothers were incapable of taking care of their children. Like the ambivalent takeover caregivers, they saw themselves as compensating for incompetent mothers. When these foster-mothers were asked about the circumstances surrounding the children's transition, they rationalized that they were part of the mother's extended family, and senior to the mothers; it was, therefore, their right to raise the children. Although the Nso norm requires that a child be sent to alternative households if that household promotes his/her development better than the birth family's does, in one's view, this situation (the tug-of-war) comes closer to the takeover situation than the second situation does.

What all this amounts to is that we should expect child abuse/neglect to be rare in the Nso community. The community acts as a 'big sister'; any sign of child abuse/neglect, actual or potential, and members of the wider family are ready and eager to come to the child's rescue. If Cameroon may be seen as somehow representative of sub-Saharan African kinship or extended family solidarity and child-rearing, then, the above depicts the extent to which kinship foster-care placement in Africa tallies with the African ideal regarding children.

In Cameroon, Verhoef (2005) reports that the reality today is that parents and relatives consciously or unwittingly juggle the challenges of raising children with extended family politics in the background, and not always to maintain family harmony. The primary motive, however, seems to be to demonstrate who is best suited to meeting and safeguarding the child's best interest, to promote the child's growth and development. This is not a bad thing; it creates more potential 'mothers' for the child. Having many 'mothers' is a culturally valued norm for children. Thus, regardless of family politics, for children wherever this norm prevails, it is a blessing, in that their chances of survival are raised concomitantly with the number of 'mothers' on whom they can count in times of need. Still, Verhoef emphasizes that what appears to be truly valued is how well families cooperate for the betterment of their children. 'A child is a child, *but only if the mothers can truly work together*' (Verhoef, 2005, p. 387). This is an invaluable lesson for agencies and professionals involved in formal foster-care placements in Western societies, working together with the child, the biological parents and foster-parents for the betterment of the child. It might therefore be argued that the interest of the child is paramount, but only insofar as the interest of the family is paramount.

Fostering in East Africa

Talle (2004) sees the act of fostering among the Maasai of East Africa as embodying the collective rights to children and the responsibility to care for them. To the Maasai, children are most valuable gifts from God to be shared by all: '*Children are riches ... not made and owned, but given into human race*' (Lienhardt, 1961, in Talle, 2004, p. 66). To the Maasai, like the Nso and other African communities, a child is a child. Likewise, to a Maasai child, a mother is a mother and a father is a father when it comes to meeting one's needs. Thus, Maasai children address mother, step-mother, maternal aunt and other close female relatives by the common term *yieyio* (mother). Similarly, they use the term *papa* (father) for a category of male relatives of the father's generation. In terms of address, there is no difference between biological parent, foster-parent or step-parent. As far as the child's survival and his/her needs are concerned, one mother or father may substitute for another.

Talle describes the Maasai procedure of fostering from one woman to another as following a general and uncomplicated pattern. A childless woman approaches a pregnant relative, for instance, a co-wife or sister-in-law and asks to be given the child she is carrying. If the latter agrees and her husband consents, the foster-mother takes over all the practical and social responsibilities connected with the birth. She assumes her duties and responsibilities as soon as the child is delivered (if it is a girl – boys are normally not given away easily).

Among the Maasai, as elsewhere in sub-Saharan Africa, children are generally fostered within the extended family, and hardly ever outside the kinship network. As among the Nso in Cameroon and elsewhere, extended family members are willing to take charge of young members in need of care; indeed, they do so as a matter of course. Talle provides an example of a situation in which the mother of the child died and a childless woman in the family readily took charge of the newborn child. Also, as children are 'gifts' to be shared, it is common for women who give birth to twins, which the Maasai regard as a 'luck' beyond all expectations, to give one of them as a gift to a barren co-wife or sister-in-law (Talle, 2004). A true, divine gift and sincere demonstration of compassion!

The Oceanic context

Oceania is a geographical region comprising the numerous islands in the Pacific Ocean. Ethnographically, it is divided into the subregions of Melanesia, Micronesia and Polynesia. For a considerable period now, these regions, especially Polynesia, like West Africa, have been well-known to anthropologists for their high rates of fostering and 'adoption' (e.g., Brady, 1976; Donner, 1987, 1999; Kirkpatrick and Broder, 1976; Treide, 2004). In these regions, like other societies where fostering is normative, the practice does not just serve the purpose of solving a crisis, for example, the loss of a parent(s) or infertility. It rather forms a core element of the culture (Donner, 1999). In these Oceanic societies, the line between fostering and adoption (if the latter exists at all) is extremely opaque. Summarized below is Donner's (1999) description of fostering and its functions on Sikaiana, one of the Polynesian islands. Donner is a veteran anthropologist with extensive experience in the region.

Fostering in Sikaiana

'*You white people do not know anything about compassion.*'
(Interviewee, quoted by Donner, 1999, p. 703)

On Sikaiana, according to Donner, it is expected that, like in West Africa, many children will live for long periods with foster-parents. In three different surveys, carried out between 1981 and 1987, Donner (1999) reported that 40–50 per cent of children living on the island were residing not with their biological parents but with foster-parents. Many foster-children, however, oscillate between the households of their birth parents and foster-parents.

Children are glad to have multiple families, and parents encourage their children to do so. Many adults are equally proud to give a litany of several foster-children whom they have raised (Donner, 1999).

In Donner's view, the deep-rootedness of fostering in Sikaiana and other South Pacific communities is reflected in the way they perceive the act and the words and idioms they use to describe it. Sikaiana people consider the act of fostering, taking children into one's household, to be a clear sign of generosity or kindness. Caring for children, including foster-children, is often described as *deriving from the 'compassion' or 'sympathy', (aloha), for the helpless state of small children* (Donner, 1999, p. 708). Donner underscores the importance of the role of provider for someone else in Sikaiana social relationships. In this community, he informs us, members are praised or criticized for their care of others, especially those who cannot care for themselves, such as older people, children and those with disability. Fostering typically involves undertaking responsibilities to feed, rear and socialize the child. In other words, Sikaiana people follow the scripture as well as the spirit of fostering. It is therefore not surprising that Donner found strong emotional bonds between children and their foster-parents.

The fostering protocol on Sikaiana seems to parallel that of the Maasai. On Sikaiana, Donner informs us, the act of fostering a child is described by the verb, *too*, which means (literally) 'take'. Usually, a Sikaiana person tells a pregnant mother of his or her intention to *too* (or take) the child she is carrying. Since fostering is viewed as a way to construct and maintain close personal relations, Sikaiana parents should not refuse someone's request to *too* the child, nor should parents demand the return of their biological children from a foster-parent without good reason. To do so would be both culturally and socially aberrant. On Sikaiana, according to Donner, such behaviour implies either a lack of trust in the foster-parent or a very rude lack of interest in the social relationship.

In this community, the foster-parent is called the child's *tupuna*, which is also the word for 'grandparent', or, more generally, 'ancestor' (Donner, 1999). Generally, they call the foster-child, *taku tam*, my child, which is the same term used to refer to a biological child. Child-rearing of both foster- and biological children is often described as 'feeding', nourishing children. Similar to the Nso ideal, within a Sikaiana household, all children, both biological and fostered, should be treated equally. Also, in every family, the child who attracts the most interest is the youngest child, be s/he fostered or biological.

Donner is at pains to emphasize that while fostering establishes a strong emotional bond between children and their foster-parents, children still maintain warm and loving relationships with their biological family. Parents and their biological children retain strong obligations for mutual commitment and support regardless of where the child is raised. Both biological and foster-parents assume that the children, upon maturation, will live with their biological parents. Grown-up children provide support for their biological parents, regardless of who raised them.

In the true sense of cross-cultural study, Donner uses his observations and findings from his fieldwork with Sikaiana people to appraise Western conceptions and assumptions about fostering and adoption. He believes that anthropological perspectives offer a comparative viewpoint for examining issues concerning contemporary family systems in both Western and other societies. He believes that comparing different family systems helps us to recognize and analyse many of the implicit cultural assumptions that organize these systems. Through such an analysis, he points out that while Western societies associate fostering or adoption with something gone wrong – orphanage, unwanted pregnancy, infertility, parental abuse or neglect – other peoples, by contrast, prefer that children move between different households. This by no means detracts from the parents' deep and lasting commitment to their biological children; it is simply because they also have interests in extended kin and others that are expressed through fostering.

Fostering on Sikaiana or in Oceania as a whole, like in other regions outside the West, fulfils both extended family and social functions. When, for instance, genealogical ties between two individuals weaken or are perceived to be weak, they take a foster-child to reinforce their kinship relationship. Since fostering in these societies involves long-term reciprocity, after leaving the household, the foster-child normally continues to support the foster-parent (e.g., Alber, 2003; Donner, 1999). Donner quotes an informant:

> I know we are relatives. I reach out and take your child, to live with me. I feed her. She matures and moves to live with her spouse ... But she comes back, and she keeps an eye on me. She comes and visits me. She brings me things, things to eat, other things.
>
> (in Donner, 1999, p. 709)

Such reciprocity is manifested in other ways. Donner noted, for instance, that on Sikaiana, women often foster a child because the child's mother had fostered them. These exchanges of fostering may continue over several generations. Sometimes, however, fostering is used to cement genealogical ties or to establish a new relationship or alliance. Nevertheless, like other South Pacific societies, such as Tahiti (Kay, 1963) and sub-Saharan Africa, Sikaiana people have clear preferences for fostering close relatives.

Donner describes the normalcy and pervasiveness of fostering on Sikaiana. It is not only adults without offspring who take foster-children, but so do most adults with offspring; and so too do many young women before they marry. He reports a conversation with one of his neighbours on Sikaiana about fostering. Noting that fostering was unusual in Western societies, she replied: '*koutou tama maa e he iloa I Le aloha.*' '*You white people do not know anything about compassion*' (in Donner, 1999, p. 703). His interpretation of this reply is that, for Sikaiana people, fostering reflects love and compassion rather than pathology and misfortune. That is, from their perspective, Americans and Europeans, with their emphasis upon the nuclear family and exclusive rearing of children within one family, lack compassion. In other words, Sikaiana patterns of fostering, being inclusive of biological parents, contrast sharply with Western child-rearing. Briefly, Donner sees Sikaiana child-rearing patterns, like those of the Nso and other traditional communities, as providing a clear example of the flexibility and diversity of family relations, and a vantage point for reassessing family relations in Western societies. Many others, especially Stack (1974) have similarly challenged the Western assumption of the family, the nuclear family, and its functions and relations.

Fostering in other traditional communities

This section describes fostering patterns among other peoples, besides those described above. Illustrative cases are selected from North America (USA) and South America (Brazil). In these communities, like other traditional communities, child fostering meets several needs, principally reciprocity and solidarity among kith and kin. As in all societies where fostering is normal, it plays an essential role in these communities. It provides an invaluable mechanism for integration, adaptability and ingenuity upon which members rely to meet their daily needs. Hence, families maintain strong intergenerational relationships by respect for the older generation, especially grandparents. They maintain also social obligations, solidarity and reciprocity. Witherspoon (1975) asserts that solidarity comes from sharing and is the basis of family social structure; without it there is no family. *'Kinsmen are those who sustain each other's life by helping one another, and by the giving or sharing of food and other items of subsistence'* (in Shomaker, 1989, p. 6). Sharing children and other resources provides a mechanism whereby families can respond to physical needs and limited resources in a manner that meets normative expectations of the culture. Children are shared not as one would share material resources, but as highly valuable, divine 'gifts'.

Fostering among the Navajo

Shomaker (1989) portrays the family as characterized by a matrix of intergenerational relationships reciprocally bound.

> The fibre which binds these relationships is established in the earlier generations and woven into the web of subsequent generations through the warp and woof of socialization and kinship. Validation of the web of the fibre is demonstrated by the grandparents when they assume senior roles as caretakers, role models, historians, mentors and chief adjuncts to their children and grandchildren.
>
> (Shomaker, 1989, p. 1)

Shomaker claims that this depiction of the family finds expressive form in fostering among the Navajo. She describes fostering among Navajo people as a traditional 'no fuss' (i.e., informal) transaction between families; that is, it is a culturally sanctioned practice. It occurs in response to one or more needs expressed by either the grandparents or the parents. Historically, according to Shomaker, the grandchild-grandparent caregiver partnership was the strongest bond in Navajo culture; it was a warm association in which perpetuation of traditional teaching could be effected. The foster-child became known to others as the *child of the grandparent*, changing in status from that of the biological grandchild. In these cases, the biological mother abdicated her maternal role and assumed a sororial relationship with her child. Commonly, children fostered by their grandparents lived with them until adulthood.

The following summarizes a study by Shomaker (1989) which examined fostering patterns among Navajo Indians. It involved 98 cases (54 girls and 44 boys) of child fostering by maternal grandmothers. The sample was drawn from Navajo Indians of three locations in the south western United States: Torreon (26 cases) and Alamo (37 cases) in New Mexico, and Tuba city in Arizona (35 cases). The principal question that the study sought to address was the functions that fostering serves in Navajo culture. Shomaker found that, nowadays, the major precipitating factor in fostering out children to grandmothers among the Navajo is the parents' inability to raise their young. This contrasts markedly with historical precedents when, she notes, older grandchildren were given to frail grandparents to assist in household and herding tasks. She identified five themes that emerged from her study. Four of these involved assistance from the grandmothers for solution. These themes warrant describing in detail.

- The closest parallels to fostering patterns of the past were those instances in which the grandmother was given a child as a sign of respect. In addition, six grandmothers had indicated that they were lonely and would like to have a child around for company, that they would like to rear a child.
- The commonest precipitating factor for fostering was a deficit in parenting skills, in situations where a combination of variables, such as alcohol misuse and poverty, combined to create an inauspicious living environment for the grandchildren. The children were seen by the grandmothers as neglected, rejected or abandoned. The parents who recognized the seriousness of the situation often gave one or all of the children to a grandmother. In other cases, their grandmother simply exercised her authority as the older generation and took the children to her home and reared them.
- The next commonest factor leading to fostering concerned changes in the parents' circumstances. Most often it was the death of a parent, migration or remarriage, with rejection of the children by the second husband.
- In situations where the workload was too heavy for the mother, the

grandmother was sought as a resource. In these cases, the parents were teenage mothers, often still in school.
- Grandmothers were also an asset to the mothers who had large families, new twins or fragile children.

Among Shomaker's sample, grandchild fostering involved different arrangements, for example: 1) the child could be temporarily reared by the grandmother with the intent to return him/her to the mother; 2) the child could become a permanent member of the grandmother's household, and be seen as her child, but with no particular message of honour attached to it; 3) it could be given to the grandmother as a symbolic gift, bearing the honour and respect for the grandmother; or 4) it could end in a formal adoption. In two cases, which Shomaker describes as adoption, the mothers of the children died and the children were adopted by their maternal grandmothers. These grandparents described their action: *'It was the natural thing to do'* (in Shomaker, 1989, p. 14).

Does giving a child away as a gift, with or without honour attached, devalue the child; does it imply that Navajo people or the Maasai, for example, treat children as mere objects, that they do not attach the same value to children as do other peoples? On the contrary, in Navajo culture, the golden rule is that the child is only a gift so long as s/he wishes to be with the grandmother; the child is at liberty to leave and return to his/her biological mother, albeit this seldom happens more or less because of the indissoluble bond between maternal grandmothers and their grandchildren, a desired and highly valued relationship. Among Shomaker's sample, in all 'permanent' transfers, including gifts and adoption, the grandchild became known as the offspring of the new mother (i.e., the grandmother) and the biological mother assumed a sororial relationship, that of an older sister. Offering a child to his/her grandmother as a gift was considered the apogee of gifts a daughter could make to her mother, a gift of love, a gift from the heart.

Shomaker found also that, in the grandmother generation, there was a need to continue parenting, and that need was fulfilled by having a grandchild under their tutelage. For some, it was a chance to make up for what they had not been able to do with their own children in earlier times. Shomaker argues that when a mother devalues her child through abuse, neglect or poor parenting, it appears contradictory to the normative Navajo cultural expectations. However, if she turns to her mother for help, or allows her mother to take charge of the child and care for it, it is following the norms established in the Navajo value system. When a mother gives her child to her mother and surrenders her child-rearing responsibilities we may construe that as child-abandonment. Nonetheless, Navajo cultural norms support this practice because the *'mother's mother is an extension of the mother lineage and clanship'* (Shomaker, 1989, p. 19). Shomaker stresses that the principal function of fostering in today's Navajo culture is principally to provide child and family support in response to expressed needs. Where no need is evident, children are not fostered out. In Navajo culture, as elsewhere, fostering occurs because the social structure encourages and supports it. Like Stack (1974), Shomaker describes family support as a process of nurturing, mutual obligations, emotional involvement, reciprocity, advice and feedback, a means of coping during times of crisis. In the case of Navajo fostering, she sees it as also providing a mechanism for integration for the youngest members of the group into the cultural socialization process, especially when the parents are absent or ineffectual.

Shomaker makes an important observation with regard to fostering and identity. She points out that during crisis transition, ambiguity results from not knowing what is to come, so that children caught in this transition are in jeopardy of losing their sense of integration and identity. Transfer to the maternal mother, a very strong identity in Navajo culture, provides for continuity of identity from grandmothers to grandchildren. She argues, therefore, that if a Navajo child were adopted or placed in foster care away from kith and kin, there would be no Navajo mentor to provide for this crucial developmental phase of the child's life.

> A child fostered to its grandmother is never without role modelling in what constitutes a Navajo identity. Even though the child is reared by the grandmother, the child's status is never not Navajo but generations telescope to preserve a mother-child nurturing relationship that integrates the child into Navajo culture. Navajo fostering allows biological and cultural ties and identity to remain intact. Moreover, the ambiguity of transition is minimized because cultural continuity is continued through an extended family, multi-generational relationship.
>
> (Shomaker, 1989, p. 15)

Atwool (2006) notes similar beliefs among Maori people. Namely, within indigenous Maori culture, there was provision with the traditional framework for children to be placed outside their immediate biological family. Fostering was an open arrangement for the purpose of strengthening kinship ties and structures. A central element of this arrangement, Atwool highlights, was that it occurred within the kinship group and ensured genealogical continuity; it allowed children to maintain contact and connections with their birth family and their ethnic group. Today, these structures continue to be significant. Like Nso, Maasai or Sikaiana children, for example, Maori children are not the exclusive possession of their parents; they belong to the extended family, the sub-ethnic group and the ethnic group as a whole. Their identity is inextricably linked to genealogy and this, in turn, links them to specific places, symbolized by mountains and rivers. Atwool emphasizes that, regardless of their residence, local or not, this remains their primary place of belonging, their roots and therefore the seat of their identity. According to this belief, then, a child placed outside the kinship system remains in limbo as far as identity is concerned.

Fostering in urban USA

For a very long time, American and European anthropologists have jour-
neyed to faraway places in search of 'exotic' child-rearing patterns. They
either ignored or forgot to survey their own backyards before embarking
on those journeys. In other words, in the case of American anthropologists,
the fostering patterns they pursued in distant places were (and still are)
also home-grown. Those child-rearing patterns have always been present in
almost every urban area in the USA. Why, then, did American anthropologists show no interest in those families? Put plainly, not only were these
families black and poor, but, more important to white researchers, they were
descendants of slaves. As such, they were considered unworthy of research,
they were of no theoretical or practical value; they had nothing about them
from which 'decent' Americans could learn. Those who 'studied' them (e.g.,
Moynihan, 1965) claimed that their traditions and family structure were
rooted in slavery; that, due to their history of slavery, African-American
families were unsound, chaotic and pathology-ridden.

Such studies spawned a host of misconceptions and preconceptions that
reinforced common and damaging stereotypes about African-American
families. These stereotypes were imported wholesale into the UK and applied
to African-Caribbean families. From the 1960s to the present, African-
Caribbean families in the UK have been described, couched linguistically
differently, by politicians, writers and child welfare professionals – social
workers, schoolteachers, therapists and psychologists – in predominantly
negative terms, as deviant or out of the ordinary, lackadaisical and broken,
among many other things (e.g., Brian and Martin, 1983; Dwivedi and Varma,
1996; Lobo, 1978).

Stack (1974), a white female sociologist, was the exception. She debunked
these misconceptions in a study of African-American families of a USA
ghetto community that she anonymously called 'The Flats'. Living among
the residents, she studied the kinship networks that existed in The Flats, the
support system that family and friends formed to cope with poverty and
racial discrimination. Her study revealed the ingenuity and resilience of the
residents; it showed that families in The Flats adapted to their disadvantaged
circumstances by forming large, resilient, lifelong support networks based
on friendship and family that were very powerful, highly structured and
complex.

As in the societies described earlier, in The Flats, Stack found that parenthood or mothering was not confined to the biological mother. For example, a
female who gave birth as a teenager frequently did not raise and nurture her
firstborn. While she resided in the household and shared the same room with
her baby, her mother, maternal aunt or older sister would care for the child
and become the child's 'mama'. Whichever relative took responsibility for the
child acquired parenthood that often lasted throughout the child's lifetime.
Although the child knew who his/her mother was, his/her 'mama' was the

woman who raised him/her up. Just as among Navajo and Nso communities, in The Flats, very often, young mothers and their firstborn were raised as sisters, and lasting ties existed between these mothers and their daughters. Resulting from a casual sexual relationship did not diminish a child's status in The Flats. '*The offspring of these unions are publicly accepted by the community; a child's existence seems to legitimise the child in the eyes of the community*' (in Stack, 1974, p. 50).

By Stack's account, fostering (or child-keeping) was the norm in The Flats. The families used shared parental responsibility among kin in response to the harsh realities that faced them. Their circumstances dictated that co-resident kin took care of one another's children. There were also situations that required children to stay in a household that did not include their biological parents. The arrangements had historical precedent. Like Sikaiana foster-parents, most of the adults were veteran foster-children themselves, and at the time of the study, some of their own children were or had been kept by kin in the past. Families regarded fostering as part of the flux and elasticity of residence, as a way of spreading parental responsibility as widely as possible in order to make it manageable. A woman who intermittently raised a sister's, niece's or a cousin's child regarded their offspring as much her grandchildren as children born to her own sons and daughters. Thus, from the children's point of view, the more grandmothers, mothers and aunts there were, the better for them; they always had someone to feed, quench their thirst and comfort them.

Stack concluded that the highly adaptive structural features of families in The Flats comprised a resilient response to the harsh conditions of poverty, the inexorable unemployment of black women and men, and the access to scarce economic resources. By such informal circulation of children in The Flats, the poor facilitated the distribution and exchange of the limited resources available to them. Also, aside from functioning as a child and family support system, fostering in The Flats had other in-built functions. For example, Stack found temporary child exchange among kin and friends to be a symbol of mutual trust and a means of acquiring self-esteem. '*People began accepting my trust and respect when I trusted my son with them*' (in Stack, 1974, p. 29).

Fostering among the Brazilian poor

Fonseca (2002, 2003) has made parallel observations about fostering patterns among the Brazilian poor. For example, she describes an interesting case involving a little girl, Claudine. When Claudine was just two weeks old, her mother left her with one of her maternal aunts, Volcira, for a 'few days' because she wanted to spend some time at the beach, to 'chill out'. Volcira, eager to replenish her household because she was occupying an 'empty nest' – her teenage daughter had recently left home – accepted the task. Volcira's younger sister (another maternal aunt), having just given birth, had a plentiful supply of milk, and so offered to wet-nurse Claudine. At the time of the study, Claudine was seven years old and still 'stayed on'; and Volcira was more than happy for her to stay on: *'She's my daughter. She sleeps and eats in my house, and she calls me "mother"'* (in Fonseca, 2003, p. 116).

Being kin and neighbours, the triangular childcare arrangement among the three women endured. How did this arrangement affect the little girl, did it cause her any confusion or psychological harm? *'Claudine'*, called one of the mothers, *'come over here and tell this lady* [the researcher] ... *How many mothers do you have?'* Savouring all the attention she was receiving, the child delightedly answered: *'Three ... The mother who nursed me, the mother who raised me, and the mother who gave birth to me'* (in Fonseca, 2003, p. 116). Fonseca stresses that among the Brazilian poor, children know who the biological mother is among their multiple 'mothers'. She points out also the importance of fathers to the children's definition of personal identity, belonging and integration into social networks.

One of the lessons Fonseca highlights in her studies is that a mother in difficulty, like her counterparts in The Flats, need not necessarily institutionalize her child. Rather, in many cases, she can count on the extended family and social network in which, between relatives, godparents or neighbours, she is bound to find an additional mother for her child. Grandmothers are the first to be involved, and are happy to accept the task. One grandmother explained the kinship terminology used by her different grandchildren:

> He and his sister [grandchildren] call me 'Mother' and refer to my daughter as 'Mother Elsi'. I raised the ... grandson since he was born. My daughter, who was living with me, had to work, and I'm the one who took care of him. When she and her husband moved out, he just stayed on. I'm his mother. He calls my daughter [his mother] 'Aunt Elsi'.
> (Fonseca, 2003, p. 116)

A good number of youngsters in Fonseca's study claimed to have chosen where they wanted to live. For example, a six-year-old child stated: *'Auntie asked me to visit, I liked it, so I just told my mom I was going to stay on'* (Fonseca, 2003, p. 117). As on Sikaiana, among the Brazilian poor, people will include in their own life histories a list of various households in which they lived in their childhood. Children are able to do so because, Fonseca points out, the Brazilian poor, as the communities described above, cherish children highly for the affection and company they provide. People, whether couples with fertility problems, young brides who have not yet become pregnant, women who have recently suffered the loss of a child, or grandmothers whose own children have all moved out, very often look for a baby or child to raise 'as their own'. Thus, a birth mother has every reason to see her child's placement as a 'gift'. Against such a background, Fonseca rightly questions the utility of the nuclear family as an analytical tool for studying families in other cultures.

Summary

One of the most striking features of kinship foster care to emerge from the foregoing review is its universality. Another obvious element is the shared aims or purposes of the practice in spite of the diverse regions where it is a cultural norm, in Africa, North America, South America or Oceania. In these societies, unlike Western societies, the act of fostering is not just a crisis response, but rather a desired mode of child-rearing that meets several needs and desires. Indeed, in some of these societies, such as Baatombu in Northern Benin and Sikaiana in the South Pacific, it is the preferred childcare arrangement (Alber, 2003; Donner, 1999). Many researchers (e.g., Donner, 1999, Fonseca, 2003) suggest that there are lessons, in terms of values and policy, to be learned from fostering in these societies. That is, it provides a perspective for examining some of the fundamental assumptions of contemporary families in the Western world. They argue that despite the differences between, for example, sub-Saharan African societies and Western European societies, fostering in the former suggests some possible alternative avenues for change in family configurations and policy in the latter. Based on his studies in Sikaiana, Donner calls for a broader recognition of the consequences of values and policies that both emphasize nuclear families and at the same time isolate them.

While acknowledging that fostering among kin entails benefits – filial, social, demographic, economic and political benefits – others claim that it cannot be practised everywhere; that is, it requires the right environment. Alber (2003) agues, for instance, that the debates concerning these benefits fail to acknowledge how deeply parenthood and childcare are rooted in social norms. Alber (2003, p. 488) asks: *'if fosterage and adoption solve so many of society's problems, why are there societies like those in Europe and North America where adoption and fostering are the exception?'* Her explanation is that Western European and North American societies do not circulate children among kin, not because those social problems that could be solved or minimized by kinship foster care do not exist, but, rather, because the practice is inconsistent with certain social and cultural norms and ideas regarded as fundamental. She explains further that the cultural beliefs that the biological parents are the best persons to educate a child, and that changes in parenting cause damage to a child's development, preclude people from even the thought of giving a child away or taking in someone else's child.

This does not necessarily refute Donner's argument; in fact, it reinforces it, as Alber's further suggestion indicates. She suggests that a better understanding of the logic of kinship fostering in traditional societies requires a research perspective that also acknowledges the meaning of foster parenthood within the general norms and ideas about parenthood, childhood and kinship in a particular society. She recommends an *emic* perspective for this purpose. She suggests that the relevant norms which we must examine concern the *belonging* of children, since these norms define who has the right to take children, rear them; they also govern issues relating to, for instance, inheritance as well as from whom children may claim food, shelter, attention, education and love.

> [T]he answer to the question of how kinship is structured in society can never consist of a simple dichotomy between 'biological' and 'social'. Rather, we should aim at understanding society-specific ideas about relatedness, or belonging.
>
> (Alber, 2003, p. 489)

As inspection of the literature indicates, in societies where kinship care-giving is a cultural norm, children are regarded as belonging not only to birth parents, but, at least in principle, to their kin group as well; hence, conceptions of 'parenthood' are more inclusive than those of nuclear families. In these societies, as Lloyd and Blanc (1996) argue, motherhood might be central to the female identity, but rarely is it assumed that the birth mother alone can raise competent children. Instead, the 'motherhood' concept allows for various relatives and friends to participate in different aspects of nurturing, socializing or educating children. This is a circumlocutory expression of the Nso proverb, 'a child is only its mother's in the womb'. So, in societies where shared parenthood is normal:

> Grandmothers may be involved in feeding children, older 'brothers' and 'sisters' in instilling cultural values, aunts in introducing them to marketing skills, and wealthier relatives in contributing to their school fees. In this context, it is understandable why the practice of fostering children is rarely questioned – other 'mothers' are merely 'holding', 'minding', or 'taking care of' the family's collective children.
>
> (Verhoef, 2005, p. 370)

Studies on traditional kinship fostering around the world suggest several useful directions for alternative childcare in Western societies where any form of care other than by the biological parents is generally regarded as aberrant; societies that stigmatize children in alternative parental care and make them feel socially and psychologically fouled. Firstly, as several investigators (e.g. Alber, 2003; Donner, 1999; Fonseca, 2002, 2003; Goody, 1982; Shomaker, 1989; Silk, 1987; Stack, 1974; Talle, 2004; Treide, 2004; Verhoef, 2005) have documented, kinship fostering must be seen as an expression of cultural values that emphasize sharing and caring. It involves circulating children among households for extended periods of time, but does not permanently sever the child's ties to his/her biological parents. Second, genetic parents typically select close consanguineal kin to whom they delegate primary responsibility for raising their offspring; maternal grandmothers are, in most cases, the favourite choice. Third, besides grandparents, natural parents typically prefer adults who can offer their children better economic prospects than they can themselves. Finally, birth parents are generally reluctant to relinquish their children to others on a permanent basis; that is, parental investment is not necessarily terminated when fostering arrangements have been completed. Even after their children have left their households, natural parents maintain contact with them, continue to contribute some resources to their care, and retain their rights to retrieve their offspring if they are mistreated.

3 Fostering in contemporary Western societies

In the pre-industrial era, attitudes towards and the motives for adoption and fostering were more or less similar across cultures. Things have changed since then, and continue to change concomitantly with advances in technology and medical science. Consequently, while fostering or caring for children in need of care, such as orphans, was once perceived to be a natural thing to do, this is no longer the case in Western societies. This chapter discusses the consequences of these changes and resultant changes in societal attitudes for children who have lost their parents through, for example, death, or those whose parents, for various reasons, cannot or cannot be expected to adequately care for them. It discusses the factors associated with why even the extended family or kin are reluctant or unable to care for their own or, indeed, are deterred from doing so.

In the societies described in the preceding chapter, there is generally collective ownership of children and shared responsibilities toward them. Wherever children find themselves, they are in the company of familiar relatives and friends. These adults are all equally likely to feed them when hungry, comfort them when in distress, or discipline them when mischievous. If a mother is too ill to take care of her own children, her mother, sister or neighbour will step in and take charge of the children. In these communities, the family is an expandable concept, allowing children to be raised in various households so that the biological family home is but one of several possible homes for the child (Donner, 1999; Isiugo-Abanihe, 1985; Verhoef, 2005). Isiugo-Abanihe (1985) points out that in West Africa, for example, a woman may achieve prestige and recognition by giving birth to a number of children without necessarily raising all of them herself.

Because kinship care plays an important role in the childcare systems of many societies around the world, it does not seem to be compromised in those societies where the Western model of foster care or child placement is introduced; it is not adopted wholly, nor does it supplant the customary system. Instead, it is modified and incorporated into the existing framework. For example, in India (Goriawalla and Telang, 2006) and in Poland (Stelmaszuk, 2006), it is traditionally expected that relatives will provide care, so kinship foster placement caters for a majority of formal child placements. According to Goriawalla and Telang (2006), in Maharashtra, in India, the authorities first try to place children with relatives, neighbours or close acquaintances, whether married or single. It is only where this is not possible that a child is placed with an unrelated or unknown foster-parent.

Similarly, in Poland, the phrase 'foster care' means placement with the child's next of kin or appointed caregivers or guardians by court order (Stelmaszuk, 2006). However, next of kin is always given priority over other potential caregivers. Stelmaszuk points out that it is traditional in Poland for children and young people, irrespective of the social status of their birth family, to live with their grandparents and develop strong bonds between them. If the grandparents happen also to be the foster-parents in the formal sense, they receive state assistance to enable them to care for their grandchildren whom they might otherwise not financially be able to support (Stelmaszuk, 2006). In other words, in Poland, the state encourages and supports kinship care. This explains the reported higher rate (80–90%) of kinship foster care in Poland, compared to the rest of the European Community nations (Greeff, 1999; Stelmaszuk, 2006).

In Argentina, Dezeo de Nicora (2006) describes how the Western philosophy of child protection is modified and incorporated into traditional child welfare systems. She emphasizes that the Argentine child welfare system makes a distinction between foster care and family placement. Foster care in Argentina is viewed as an expression of solidarity within communities. As a part of the child welfare system, it is defined as providing a space in a family, for as long as needed, to children and adolescents who, for whatever reason, cannot live with their own families. As a child and family support system, foster placement in Argentina recognizes the children's stories and identities and allows for reattachment with their origins. Dezeo de Nicora describes the major aims of foster care as: 1) to encourage families to share their homes with children who are not their own, and to train and support such families, and 2) to strengthen and support birth families so that they can continue to have bonds with their children and work together with foster families.

Dezeo de Nicora describes 'family placement' in Argentina, on the other hand, as a protective measure, employed in situations where a child is either separated from their family or excluded from it due to the child's behaviour problems and the parents' inability to deal with those problems. In such situations, the emphasis is on safeguarding the child's wellbeing, so the child's interaction with his/her birth family may be curtailed, if deemed necessary. Foster care does not have this child protection element. Instead, it is a response to a family in need and, as such, acknowledges the family's right to request help or assistance when it is experiencing difficulty. This 'rights' ethos, according to Dezeo de Nicora, encourages the biological family to continue to play a vital role in the child's life, and also to understand its importance to the child and his/her wellbeing.

Dezeo de Nicora draws attention to the guiding principle of foster care in Argentina, that it is a family support service located within the child's community.

> If foster care is not perceived as a means of strengthening families, it runs the risk of continuing to implement programmes that increase family vulnerability. For this reason, the approach must involve all three of the major actors in the foster-care environment: the child, the birth family and the foster family. The participation of these actors in all phases of the foster-care process, from assessment of training to support, must be recognised not only by professional teams, but also by all the other services and systems (e.g., schools, health and care agencies) which interact with the birth and foster families.
>
> (Dezeo de Nicora, 2006, p. 9)

This is clearly in the spirit of traditional foster care. As such, neither 'foster care' nor 'family placement' carries stigma.

The Western context

> Although the caretakers of young children do have goals that are universal (e.g., protection, socialization), there are societal differences in the behaviours of caretakers that are related to the community's ecology, basic economy, social organization, and value systems.
>
> (Whiting and Edwards, 1988, p. 89)

We saw in Chapter 1 that fostering and adoption patterns in pre-industrial Western Europe and elsewhere were pretty similar to those observed in other present-day traditional communities, in those societies described in the preceding chapter. This is no longer the case. In fact, very few people are aware that fostering was once a commonplace practice in Western Europe and served very similar purposes as it does, for example, in West Africa. Through cross-country adoption, adoption, but not fostering, has for sometime now been popularized by Western middle-class families. Media celebrities, such as pop stars, are currently giving it a boost. The question is: Why is fostering rarely undertaken, why does it occur only in exceptional circumstances, and why is it perceived negatively by many? The simplest explanation is that the Western ecology, economy, social organization, including family structure, and value systems today are far removed from what they used to be in days bygone.

Almost half of a century ago, Pareto (1963) argued that the dominant groups in society sing the tune while the masses take up the chorus. In other words, the groups that dominate society set the values and ensure that society is organized such that it facilitates the pursuit of their needs and interests. Hence, since the Industrial Revolution, Western societies have been redesigned; they are organized in a way that revolves around the production of material wealth. This has necessitated a geographically mobile workforce and an emphasis on individualism, hedonism and consumerism. These values have permeated the family system as well as other facets of the culture (Bilgé and Kaufman, 1983; Owusu-Bempah, 2007). A homely example of the extent to which Western cultural values have been turned upside down relates to the family and how children are perceived. Bilgé and Kaufman (1983) draw attention to the glaring fact that family structure is now deeply rooted in the economic system, so much so that any changes in economic structure are reflected in the family. In other words, people rapidly and constantly migrate in pursuit of material wealth. Consequently, the nuclear family has supplanted the extended family; it has become the ideal family configuration.

In today's Western societies, individual families and their individual members are expected to be self-sufficient; independence has replaced interdependence, 'standing on your own feet', 'making it on your own' being a 'go-getter' are considered healthy and sound ideals; individual self-fulfilment has become the maxim (Owusu-Bempah, 2007; Owusu-Bempah and Howitt, 2000b). In terms of functions, Bilgé and Kaufman (1983), for example, see the primary functions of the family in Western societies to be consumption, rearing its own children, meeting the emotional needs of its members, the provision of personal services for productive personnel, and reproduction which provides the future workers and consumers needed to lubricate the system and keep it going. Thus, most family members cut close ties, kith or kin, with alacrity; parents have no room for any child, relative or stranger, other than their own; they are 'on the move' and so have no space for extra baggage, as it were. Indeed, some have described the nuclear family as an increasingly atomized entity (Bilgé and Kaufman, 1983; Donner, 1999; Owusu-Bempah, 2007; Owusu-Bempah and Howitt, 2000b).

Briefly, children in modern Western societies, their parents and grandparents occupy a completely different social, cultural and spiritual ecology from that of their pre-industrial counterparts as well as their peers in other contemporary societies. Extended family or kinship solidarity seems to no longer exist; kinship has become an archaic concept. In fact, today, it would not be a hyperbole to suggest that to the ordinary Anglo-Saxon person in Western Europe and North America, representatives of the Western world, the 'extended family' is alien, something that 'ethnic minorities' or 'native people' have. The question is: What are the implications of this for children whose parents cannot nurture, protect or socialize them? Put plainly, they are more or less on their own; society expects them to 'stand on their own feet', to fend for themselves unless the state comes to their 'rescue'. The state has to come to the rescue because, as Connor (2006) and others have pointed out, even grandparents who would naturally assume responsibility for such children are either discouraged by societal negative attitudes toward grandparenting or even prevented from doing so by the state legislative machinery. Legally grandparents have no rights to their grandchildren. *Inter alia*, these factors destroy or at least threaten grandparents' ability not only to protect their vulnerable progeny, but also to pass on their knowledge, culture and values to them. Consequently, a significant number of children are denied this opportunity. Children in Sweden and the UK are reported to be among those most affected (Greeff, 1999).

This does not suggest that vulnerable children have been completely neglected, that no one has been concerned about their plight since the Industrial Revolution. On the contrary, since then, there have always been concerned individuals and bodies prepared to take responsibility for children in need or find them a home, particularly orphans, abandoned children (or foundlings) and babies of unmarried women. Historically, such bodies were started either by Christian organizations or by the efforts of concerned individuals. In the UK, for example, Dr Barnardo and Thomas Coram are legendary figures in the field of child fostering. Generally, the children were cared for in organized settings, in institutions. Babies who required wet-nursing were placed in foster families until they were about five years old, when they were returned to the institution which had received them for education, training and apprenticeship, in preparation for independent living in adulthood (Molloy, 2002).

Since the institutions were run by Christian organizations, they had a policy of baptizing each child with a new name (Molloy, 2002). Thus, they grew up with no knowledge of their origins. In this respect, at least, their circumstances were not much different from their counterparts who were cared for in orphanages. The orphanages also provided institutional care for affected infants and children. Older children were 'boarded out' as apprentices or domestic servants (Molloy, 2002; Triseliotis *et al.*, 1995). The primary aim of all those institutions, children's homes provided by church organizations and orphanages, was to ensure the physical survival of the children in their charge, and not much else; they did not cater specifically for the children's psychological, emotional or social needs.

Public child care

Child welfare systems in Western societies have improved markedly since the Victorian era, and have continued to improve since the Second World War. Today there exist international policies as well as national laws and regulations governing childcare and child welfare. There also exist various international and national organizations, such as UNICEF, NSPCC (in the UK), and the Child Welfare League of America (in the USA), which seek to promote and safeguard children's rights as well as their healthy growth and development. Notwithstanding, these efforts have not eliminated the need of substantial numbers of children in a given Western society to be cared for away from their biological parents. The home characteristics of most children received into the public care system today often parallel those of their Victorian peers, with the exception that, in most cases, their parents are very often living and known. They come predominantly from socially disadvantaged backgrounds, with all the associated negative developmental implications.

Family backgrounds

Today, child protection provides the main rationale for state care for children requiring care away from their parents. However, in an era of plenty, why do children need protection from their parents? Examination of the home characteristics of children admitted into state care provides some answers to this and related questions. In the UK, for instance, Bebbington and Miles (1989) examined the family backgrounds of children in the public care system. The study involved 2,500 children who were admitted into care in England in 1987. One of the main aims of the study was to quantify the association of material and social deprivation, and entry into care by comparing these children with other children. The study found poverty to be the most significant factor: 80 per cent of the families of the children who went into care were council tenants. The second most significant factors were single parenthood (75%) and poverty – 75 per cent of the children were from families who were in receipt of income support; these were followed by poor housing, where over 50 per cent lived in poor neighbourhoods.

Subsequent international research and commentators reinforce Bebbington and Miles' findings and also add a host of other family characteristics closely linked with a child's entry into the public care system (e.g., Benedict *et al.*, 1996; Dubowitz *et al.*, 1994; Everett, 1995; Ford *et al.*, 2007; Goodman *et al.*, 2004; Hornby *et al.*, 1995; McFadden, 1998; Stelmaszuk, 2006; Vinnerljung *et al.*, 2005). These include alcohol and/or substance abuse; domestic violence; child abuse (physical and/or sexual) and/or neglect; parental mental illness; and homelessness. This means that most children who are taken into care require state intervention for reasons of abuse, neglect, rejection or even separation from their parents prior to state intervention, rather than, for instance, poverty per se. Thus, fostering, as with the rest of the public child welfare system, is in reality a child protection mechanism. Although it may connote fostering as defined earlier, it does not denote it. In other words, it is a response to crisis and not a risk-avoidance mechanism or family support system.

Because fostering is an anomalous childcare practice, state intervention results from not only any of the above home characteristics, but also even in situations where a child is relocated in an innocuous environment, an environment which might be even more congenial than the parents'. For example, the state may intervene if a child is informally cared for by adults other than his/her parents for a 'prolonged' period of time.

> If parents leave a child with other adults (including family) without
> indicating when they will return and without financially providing for

the care of the child, child neglect charges can be levelled against the parent. Court documents may read, for example, that the mother left the child with 'relatives for extended periods of time without making provisions for their care'. Note that these charges do not mean that the children were not cared for, but rather that their care was not formally arranged (or contracted).

(Brown *et al.*, 2002, p. 62)

Paraphrased, this may read: the child was cared for by relatives for what the authorities construed as an 'unreasonable' period of time instead of his/her parents – the nuclear family – therefore, the parent(s) abandoned or neglected the child. May this be taking the importance of the nuclear family too far, a reification of monotropism? Whatever one's answer is, this means that the state could have intervened in the case of Claudine (the Brazilian girl with three mothers), had she been in the USA, for example. Alternatively, how or what would Donner's informant in Sikaiana perceive or say about this kind of mindset? A justification for intervening in such a case could be that, unlike in Argentina (Dezeo de Nicora, 2006), fostering is a protective measure; its principal objective is to ensure the physical survival of children by removing them from the source of danger, from their parents. This, however, does not mean that crisis fostering or state intervention always involves children in danger from their parents or family.

Because it entails the physical removal of children from their family home, very often against the wishes of the parents, fostering usually takes place through state mediation, through a court-appointed child welfare agency. Once a court has authorized the removal of a child from home, the child becomes the responsibility of the state; the state, *de jure* as well as *de facto*, assumes responsibility for not only protecting the child from a dangerous environment, but also for his/her general wellbeing. In short, it becomes responsible for ensuring the child's survival, as well as safeguarding his/her rights and interests. The state usually delegates its duty to the child to other agencies. In the UK, for instance, local authorities (social services) are the primary state agencies charged with this duty. Traditionally, local authorities fulfil this duty in two main ways, either by looking after the children themselves or by contracting other agencies or families to look after them. The former generally involves caring for the children in residential settings or group homes run by the local authority, while the latter necessitates placing them with a foster family, commonly an unrelated family. Until very recently, hardly was placing the child with a relative ever considered as an option, in spite of its naturalness and obvious advantages. In either case, the local authority remains state-appointed *in loco parentis*.

Consequences for the child

Holtan (2008) argues that foster care, as a social welfare measure, is built on the model of the family institution with the purpose of ensuring the wellbeing of children and creating 'decent' individuals who can contribute to society. Similarly, McFadden (1998) points out that the historical developmental of child welfare systems in Western societies has been premised on the use of non-kin or stranger foster care for children in need of care and protection. Consequently, child welfare policies and laws that have evolved relate to central aspects of 'permanency planning'. McFadden describes permanency planning as a concept that includes the nature of foster care, the rights of parents in the nuclear family and the need for a secure legal status formulated to facilitate the child's transition from the 'system' into adoption or return to the biological parents. That is all well and good, but away from their parents, kith and kin and community, how well is the child served? What are the consequences of the public care system for the children caught within it?

Historically, studies have linked the public care system with negative developmental outcomes. The literature is awash with evidence that children growing up in the public care system experience difficulties in almost every aspect of development, mental (or emotional), behavioural, academic and interpersonal problems. It was observing the negative experiences of foster children and adopted children and youth which prompted Shants (1946) to propound his idea of genealogical bewilderment. Bowlby likewise derived inspiration from his clinical work with such children in advancing his (1969, 1973) attachment theory. The literature suggests that not only are the undesirable effects of the public care system on children, including homelessness and poor parenting, enduring, but they are also generationally transmitted. It must be stressed at the outset that these difficulties are not wholly attributable to the care system. Because of their previous negative experiences of abuse, physical, sexual and/or emotional, neglect/rejection, family violence and so forth, most children who enter the care system either already have mental health difficulties or are prone to developing them. For example, Sempik and colleagues (2008) have reported a range of mental, emotional and behavioural problems among their sample of 648 children at point of entry into the care system.

Mental health and emotional problems

Internationally, research into the psychosocial developmental outcomes for children suggests that 45–85 per cent of children in care experience one or more mental health problems. It suggests further that public care in childhood is associated with adverse adult socio-economic, educational, legal and health outcomes in excess of that associated with childhood or adult disadvantages. Briefly, research indicates that, compared to other children, children in care are more vulnerable to mental health, behavioural problems, such as anti-social behaviour, relationship problems and academic difficulties.

The literature shows that the most common emotional and mental health problems that these youngsters exhibit include: anxiety, phobias, depression, conduct disorder and attachment disorder (Beck, 2006; McCann *et al.*, 1996; Meltzer *et al.*, 2003; O'Connor and Zeanah, 2003). Frequently, the feeling of helplessness or despair about their lives or the need to direct attention to their dire predicaments drives many of them to suicide attempts and self-harming behaviour, typically, drug overdose and wrist laceration. Many expose themselves to further risk by absconding and getting involved in drugs/ alcohol misuse, serious crime, promiscuity and prostitution – each of which very frequently results in teenage pregnancy (Corlyon and McGuire, 1999; Coy, 2008; Gallagher, 1999; Knight *et al.*, 2006; Sinclair and Gibbs, 1998). It needs stressing that the mental health problems and other developmental difficulties facing these children are not caused by a single factor. Rather, they are attributable to a complex relationship between the experiences of being in care and the adverse circumstances which led to their admission into care. A further confounding factor is that, while in care, many of them move so often between placements that their lives lose the constancy or stability and pattern that they need in order to thrive.

For a long time now, researchers and clinicians have highlighted the high rate of mental health problems among children living away from their parents (Bowlby, 1944; Goldfarb, 1943; Spitz, 1945). Research continues to show that children in foster care are very much in need of attention by mental health professionals. It shows that children in foster care exhibit a significant number of mental health problems and adaptive functioning deficits far in excess of that expected in the general population. The sheer mass of research in this area defies a summary review. What is presented here is for the purposes of illustration of the extent of the mental and emotional health difficulties facing children in the public care system.

One of the large-scale surveys of the mental health of children in foster care and other types of public care in the UK in recent times was carried out by (Meltzer *et al.*, 2003). The study, a national survey, involved a random sample of 2,500 children, aged 5–17 years, in the care of English local authorities. The survey concentrated on the three most common categories of childhood mental disorders: emotional disorders such as anxiety, depression and obsessions; hyperactivity disorders involving inattention; conduct disorders characterized by awkward, troublesome, aggressive and antisocial behaviours. The study was thorough enough to include questionnaire items related to less common mental disorders such as tics and twitches, pervasive developmental disorders such as those in the autistic spectrum, and eating disorders. Data were also collected from the carers and teachers of those in the sample aged between 11 and 17 years.

Overall, the survey reported the following rates of mental health and emotional difficulties among the sample: 45 per cent were assessed as having a mental disorder, including children who had more than one type of disorder;

37 per cent of these had clinically significant conduct disorders; 12 per cent were assessed as having emotional disorders – anxiety and depression; 7 per cent were rated as hyperactive; and 4 per cent had less common disorders – tics and twitches, and eating disorders. These rates are based on the diagnostic criteria for research using the ICD-10 Classification of Mental and Behavioural Disorders with strict impairment criteria – that is, the disorder causes distress to the child or has considerable impact on the child's day-to-day life (Meltzer *et al.*, 2003).

The results were analysed further according to gender and age, placement characteristics, and emotional disorder by type of placement. The analysis showed that 5–10-year-olds in the sample were about five times more likely to have a mental disorder (42%), compared with their counterparts in the general population (8%). In terms of gender and age, the proportion of children and adolescents with mental disorder was greater among boys than girls: 49 per cent of boys and 39 per cent of girls. Further analysis revealed the following rates: 50 per cent and 33 per cent among 5–10-year-old boys and girls respectively; among 11–15-year-olds: 55 per cent (boys) and 43 per cent (girls); and among 16–17-year-olds the rate was 40 per cent for both sexes.

Regarding emotional disorders, the analysis also revealed a gender and age bias, with 5–10-year-old boys at greater risk of experiencing emotional disorders (13%) compared to children in the same age-group in the community (8%); while 16–17-year-olds were 20 per cent more likely to exhibit emotional difficulties. The analysis showed also that 37 per cent of the whole sample was displaying a conduct disorder. However, boys were more vulnerable (42%) than were girls (31%). Among 11–15-year-olds, the rates were 45 per cent for boys and 34 per cent for girls. Of the sample as a whole, 7 per cent were diagnosed with hyperkinetic disorders.

Placement characteristics

Meltzer *et al.* also examined the association between type of placement or care and mental health and emotional difficulties. The children and young people were, therefore, categorized according to their residence: foster care, parental care, residential care and independent living. The distribution of mental disorders according to type of placement was significantly different. Children in foster care and those in local authority care but living with their own parents were similar with respect to their mental health status (39% and 41% respectively). Sixty-eight per cent of children in residential care, on the other hand, had a mental problem, while 51 per cent of young people in local authority care, but living independently had a mental health problem. The study reported similar findings regarding type of placement and emotional disorders: 29 per cent of children who were placed with foster-carers had emotional difficulties, compared with 28 per cent of children living with their biological parents. The rates were much higher for those in residential care (56%) and those living in independent accommodation (46%). Meltzer and colleagues (2004a, b) conducted two similar surveys: one in Wales, and the other in Scotland. Both of these national surveys reported very similar findings to those of the English survey (see Meltzer *et al.*, 2003, and Meltzer *et al.*, 2004a, b).

In the UK at large, both previous and subsequent research, surveys and reports have reported similar findings to Meltzer and colleagues'. More recently, another team of researchers (Ford *et al.*, 2007) examined socio-demographic characteristics and psychopathology by type of placement among children in the British public care system. The study compared 1,453 children in the care of local authorities with a community sample of 10,428 socially deprived children and socially privileged children. The researchers found higher levels of psychopathology, educational difficulties and neuro-developmental disorders among children looked after by local authorities. They also found an independent association between being in care and all types of psychiatric disorder after adjusting for educational and physical factors. In support of Meltzer and colleagues' findings, they found a particularly high prevalence of psychiatric disorder among those living in residential care and those who had experienced multiple placements. The team concluded:

> Our findings suggest that fewer than one in ten of the children looked after by local authorities in Britain had positively good mental health and that their substantially increased prevalence of psychiatric disorder was at least partially explained because they had also experienced particularly high levels of psychosocial and educational adversity. However, there was also a strong association between psychiatric disorder and care-related variables.
>
> (Ford *et al.*, 2007, p. 325)

The findings of the above large-scale studies reinforce those of several international studies (e.g., Beck, 2006; Brand and Brinich, 1999; Clausen *et al.*, 1998; Farmer and Moyers, 2008; Hill and Thompson, 2003; Hukkanen, *et al.*, 1999; McCann *et al.*, 1996; McCarthy *et al.*, 2003; Minnis, 2004; Nicolas *et al.*, 2003; Richards *et al.*, 2006; Stanley *et al.*, 2005; Stein *et al.*, 1996; Tarren-Sweeney and Hazell, 2006). For example, a Scottish study by Minnis (2004) involving 121 foster families reported that 61 per cent of the children showed symptoms of mental health problems. Of these, 50 per cent had hyperkinetic symptoms; 60 per cent had symptoms of conduct disorder; 45 per cent displayed symptoms of anxiety and depression; while 50 per cent had interpersonal relationship difficulties, particularly with peers. Like many other studies, the study found children who had experienced a high number of placement changes were more likely to have mental health problems.

Behavioural problems

Conduct disorder is reported to be among the commonest internalized and externalized mental health problems in children in care. Externalized mental health problems include fighting, physical aggression, antisocial behaviour (lying and stealing), substance abuse (drinking, smoking and drug abuse), truancy, absconding, prostitution and criminality (e.g., Beck, 2006; Hill and Thompson, 2003; McCann *et al.*, 1996; Meltzer *et al.*, 2003, 2004a, b; O'Connor and Zeanah, 2003). However, these problems coexist with internalized psychosocial developmental difficulties, ranging from phobias, educational difficulties, low self-esteem, poor relationships with adults, self-harming behaviour, social withdrawal, depression, insomnia and loss of appetite to headaches and other psychosomatic symptoms.

Using Achenbach's (1991) Child Behavior Check List (CBCL) standardized assessment instruments, a group of North American researchers (Clausen *et al.*, 1998) conducted a comprehensive analysis of children in foster care in three different counties in California: Santa Cruz, Monterey and San Diego. The variables of interest were behavioural problems, social competence problems, self-concept and adaptive functioning. The sample comprised a total of 267 children and youngsters (aged 0–17 years). The assessment was carried out two to three months after the children's entry into foster care. At two of the research locations, a behavioural screening checklist – a measure for self-concept – was used, and in the third county, an adaptive behaviour survey was used. The results supported previous studies with regard to mental health; there were consistently high rates of mental health problems across the three counties. As regards behavioural problems, the results indicated that the sample was within the clinical or borderline range of the CBCL; the prevalence of behaviour difficulties among the sample was two-and-a-half times that expected in a community population. Intergroup comparisons revealed no significant differences in the rates between the three county foster-care cohorts, despite the different demographic characteristics of the counties.

On the adaptive behaviour scale, the mean scores for the sample were more than one standard deviation below the norm. Clausen and colleagues concluded by highlighting the fact that children entering foster care exhibit a significant number of behavioural problems and adaptive functioning deficits far in excess of that expected in the general population. As previously acknowledged, many children enter care with problems; nonetheless, those problems are very often compounded by certain features of the care system, particularly placement instability or multiple changes and a lack of contact with their parents, siblings, relatives and friends.

A later study (Newton *et al.*, 2000), also in California, examined the relationship between changes in placement and problem behaviours over a 12-month period among a cohort of foster-children. This study also employed the Child Behavior Check List. The sample comprised 415 youths, a part of a larger cohort of children who entered care in San Diego and remained in placement for at least five months. Every change of placement during the first 18 months after entry into the foster-care system was abstracted from case records. The results showed that placement instability was a significant contributory factor in both internalizing and externalizing behaviour of foster-children. The authors stressed the seriously negative consequences of multiple placements for developmental outcomes for children in the public foster-care system. Several other studies have reported similar findings and reached similar conclusions (e.g., Berrick *et al.*, 1994; Dubowitz *et al.*, 1993; Knight *et al.*, 2006; McCarthy *et al.*, 2003).

That multiple placements, an endemic facet of the public care system, very often further compound the adversities, particularly identity and mental health difficulties, with which children enter care, was presaged by the psychologist-cum-philosopher, William James, when he wrote: *'Each of us when he awakens says, Here's the same old self again, just as he says, Here's the same old bed, the same old room, the same old world'* (William James, 1890, p. 334). The reality for many children in care, especially those in non-relative (i.e., stranger) foster care, is often the opposite; their lives lack the stability and pattern required to develop a stable sense of continuity and identity. In other words, while in care, many of them move so often between placements that they become bewildered; they wonder who and what they are and where they belong. As a 16-year-old alumna and mother of one put it:

> They put me in placements but they didn't sit down and say this is what the person's name is ... you don't get to meet the person before you go ... so there isn't any rapport ... or anything so you are just ending up with people you don't know. It's quite distressing actually ... sometimes you get immune to it after a while, but how do they [social services] expect children to be normal and behave well ... they just live in a fantasy world of children who adapt to certain things ... we're not chameleons ... we don't adapt.
>
> (in Knight *et al.*, 2006, p. 60)

The mental health, behavioural and other problems that children in care experience have implications not only for them, but for all in their social environment, especially their caregivers. Unresolved mental health problems, for instance, cause ongoing distress in the children, and very often blight the lives of those who care for them. McCarthy and colleagues (2003), using the Strengths and Difficulties Questionnaire of Goodman (1999), investigated the level of social impairment and distress shown by children with behavioural difficulties in an English local authority. They examined also the duration of the difficulties and their effects on the foster-carers. Fifty-nine per cent of the children displayed symptoms of psychiatric disorder; and 40 per cent had significant problems in three key areas of their lives: home, learning and peer and leisure. Where significant problems were identified by the carers, 65 per cent reported that the problems had existed for over a year.

The carers reported very high levels of negative social impact in several areas, including home life and peer relationships. Almost half of the foster-parents revealed that the children's problems were imposing a significant burden on them, their families and others.

Educational difficulties

Like the effects of mental health problems on a child's overall functioning, the impact of being in care on children's educational attainment and their life chances has, over the years, received special attention from international researchers, for example, from Australia (Cashmore and Paxman, 1996), Canada (e.g., Flynn and Biro, 1998), Sweden (Vinnerljung *et al.*, 2005), the UK (Aldgate *et al.*, 1993; Berridge and Brodie, 1998; Gallagher, 1999; Goddard, 2000), and the USA (e.g., Benedict *et al.*, 1994; Berrick *et al.*, 1999; Courtney *et al.*, 2005; LeProhn, 1994; McMillen *et al.*, 2003). Only a handful of recent major studies in this area are briefly summarized here, starting with a Swedish large-scale longitudinal (retrospective) study.

In Sweden, a group of investigators (Vinnerljung *et al.*, 2005) examined the educational attainments of children who had experienced either residential care or foster care. Data were collected from a national survey of some 800,000 Swedish-born children in eight national birth cohorts (1972–9) still alive in Sweden on 31 December 1999. They were identified in the Swedish Total Population Register. The study was limited to Swedish-born children in order to eliminate the common association between immigrant status (and language limitations) and poor achievement in the Swedish educational system, as in the educational systems of other Western nations. A total of 31,355 met the research criteria. These were compared with their community peers, 744,425 children who had no direct experience with the public care system.

The investigators used logistic regression models to estimate risks of having only a basic education at the time of follow-up, and of chances of having a postsecondary education, controlling for age, gender and parental education. The parents' level of education was included in the analysis because of the link between parental educational background and children's school performance, for example, parents' educational aspirations for their children (including those in foster care) and their capacity to help with school-related activities.

The analysis revealed that, compared with their peers in the general population whose parents were educationally disadvantaged, those who entered care before adolescence or had been in long-term stable foster care had a threefold higher risk of entering adult life with only a basic education. Young people who entered care during adolescence had approximately a fourfold risk of having only basic education at the time of follow-up, compared with their peers. In contrast, their peers from similar socio-economic background were between three and four times more likely to have a postsecondary education. Vinnerljung and colleagues concluded with a plea:

Child welfare clients are – irrespective of issues of causality and regardless of birth parents' educational background – a high-risk group for low educational attainment. Child welfare agencies, in the capacity of *in loco parentis*, should spare no efforts in trying to improve 'their' children's chances of actually getting an education.

(Vinnerljung, *et al.*, 2005, p. 274)

Generally, the causes of the poor academic performance of children in care, like the causes of their mental health difficulties, are complex. Several factors, both endogenous – for example innate ability and health status – and exogenous factors, such as stigma associated with being in care, the care environment (especially residential settings), lack of educational resources or facilities, lack of encouragement and support from significant adults and so forth are involved. All these factors conspire or interact to influence negatively these children's academic ability and motivation. One important exogenous factor is the children's school experiences. For example, McMillen and colleagues (2003) document the school experiences of 262 youth referred for independent living in preparation for their exit from the foster-care system of one Midwestern US county. A majority of the young people reported negative school experiences: 73 per cent of them had been suspended at least once since seventh grade, and 16 per cent had been expelled. In the previous year, 58 per cent had failed a class, and 29 per cent had physical fights with students.

These problems could not have been entirely due to the children's lack of academic ability or motivation, as this and other studies show (e.g., Aldgate *et al.*, 1993; Berridge and Brodie, 1998; Essen *et al.*, 1976; Heath *et al.*, 1994; McMillen *et al.*, 2003). For example, 70 per cent of McMillen and colleagues' sample reported high educational aspirations; they wanted to attend college. Like Vinnerljung and colleagues, McMillen and colleagues concluded by highlighting the educational needs of children in the public care system. They also advocated a system of education in which specialists work to secure and maintain proper education placements for youth in foster care and help them to receive adequate and appropriate academic resources to enable them to unfold their academic potential.

In the UK, Gallagher (1999) reported that 75 per cent of young people left care without educational qualifications, with negative consequences for their post-care lives. The future of children in care in the UK does not seem to have improved since then. Simon and Owen (2006) report on aspects of educational performance of children in care in England and Wales as compared to their peers in the general population. Most young people (16-year-olds) in these countries take their General Certificate of Secondary Education (GCSE) examination, but only 56 per cent of young people in care were found to have done so. From other official data during and before this period, Simon and Owen reported also that 54 per cent of young people aged 16 and over who had left the care system in the year ending 2003 had no educational qualification. At the opposite end of the spectrum, only 8.7 per cent of youngsters in care had attained the desirable standard of success in five GCSE subjects at A*–C grade levels (Gilligan, 2007).

To conclude this section, Trout and colleagues (2008) conducted a thorough review of the literature, with the purpose of examining the status of the published research on the academic and school functioning of children in foster care and those in residential care. The review assessed: a) the characteristics of the children and youth involved in the reported studies examined; b) academic and school functioning areas evaluated by the studies; c) reports of overall academic performance; and d) quality of the studies. Like other investigators and reviewers, they concluded that, overall, children in the public care system demonstrate several academic risks across placement settings and academic areas.

Acknowledging the limitations in the literature, Trout and colleagues stress that, overall, the studies support the general belief that this population is clearly at risk for short- and long-term school failure. They identify specific deficits across subject areas on standardized measures of academic functioning and on indicators of deficit as reported by classroom teachers (e.g., grade scores and teacher ratings). Their suggestion is that intervention programmes that focus only on behavioural and mental health and family functioning of these children and youth at the neglect of their academic functioning may be missing a critical opportunity to improve the academic skills of this population, and to improve short- and long-term outcomes associated with success.

Adulthood

In a substantial number of cases, the negative experiences of being in care do not dissipate on reaching adulthood. In other words, a large number of public care alumni still exhibit many of the negative mental health, emotional, psychological, behavioural and educational experiences associated with the care system (e.g., Barth, 1990; Benedict *et al.*, 1994, 1996; Coy, 2008; Dumaret *et al.*, 1997; Iglehart, 1994; McCarthy, 2004; Minty, 1999; Russell and Taylor, 2005). In a longitudinal study, Russell and Taylor (2005) examined adult socio-economic, educational, social, and mental health outcomes of being in public care. They followed the 1970 British birth cohort (children born in Britain between April 5 and 11, 1970). These children (N=16,567) were then followed at ages five (13,135 children), 10 (14,875 children), 16 (11,622 youngsters), and 30 (11,261 adults). Of the cohort, 9,557 took part in the 30-year follow-up and comprised the sample for the analyses. Cases were defined as those who had ever been in statutory or voluntary public care at five, 10, and 16 years. Amongst the 9,557 respondents, 344 (3.6%) had been in care for less than 17 years. Self-reported adult outcomes (at age 30 years) were: occupation, educational achievement, general health, psychological morbidity, history of homelessness, school exclusion, and convictions.

Controlling for socio-economic status, the results showed that, compared with their peers in the general population, men with a history of public care were less likely to attain high social class and more likely to have been homeless, to have a conviction, psychological morbidity and to be in poor general health. Similar associations were found among women. However, men, but not women, with a history of care were more likely to be unemployed and less likely to attain a higher degree. Being black was associated with poorer adult outcomes of being in care. The study concluded that public care in childhood is associated with adverse adult socio-economic, educational, legal and health outcomes in excess of that associated with childhood or adult disadvantages. In an earlier British survey, Gallagher (1999) reported similar negative outcomes for public care alumni. Seventy-five per cent of youth who had left care at the time of the survey did so with no academic qualifications; 50 per cent were unemployed; 17 per cent of young women were pregnant or already mothers on leaving care or soon after; 20 per cent of the total sample became homeless within two years of leaving care.

International research shows similar patterns among public care leavers. In Canada, Martin (1994, in Tweedle, 2007) reported that 66 per cent of 18-year-old public care alumni possessed no educational qualifications; 38 per cent were unemployed; 50 per cent of the females were mothers; and 7 per cent had been incarcerated (over 50% of these had been in jail since leaving care). Another Canadian study, carried out some ten years later, Rutman *et al.* (2005, in Tweedle, 2007) showed that the circumstances of young people who had been in care had not much improved: 33 per cent were unemployed; over one-third (both males and females) were parents; 30 per cent had changed residence four or more times within 18 months of leaving care; over 50 per cent had concerns about their physical health; 25 per cent reported being concerned about their mental health (commonly, depression). An Australia study (Trocmé, 1999, in Tweedle, 2007) that involved youngsters who left care between February and September 1996 it was found that some 80 per cent left without educational qualifications; 64 per cent were unemployed; 33 per cent of the females were pregnant; 50 per cent had been homeless since leaving care; and 50 per cent had committed criminal offences since leaving care.

The situation for public care alumni in the USA seems to be equally bleak (Barth, 1990; Benedict *et al.*, 1996; Courtney *et al.*, 2001; Roman and Wolfe, 1995; Schneider *et al.*, 2009; Zuravin *et al.*, 1999). For example, Zuravin and colleagues (1999) reported that, for the majority of former foster-children, educational accomplishment was below that of comparison group members (the general population); males appeared to have higher rates of unemployment; and for many former foster-children, employment was low-paid jobs; for males in particular, arrest and convictions rates were higher than those for the general population.

The vast majority of the studies that examined mental health found former foster-children to be doing worse than their counterparts in the general population. A more recent US study (Schneider *et al.*, 2009) compared 368 women aged 18 years and older with a history of foster care with 9,240 women of similar age, but with no history of foster care, on measures of physical and mental health, educational attainment and socio-economic status. The results showed that the former foster-children were disadvantaged in all these areas relative to the comparison group. That is, the results suggested an association between foster care and poor mental physical health, low educational attainment and poverty in adulthood.

In summary, research from across the Western world shows a clear link between the public care system and adult adversities. In their adult lives, compared to their counterparts in the general population, those who have been in care are more likely to be far less educated and to be unemployed or experience employment difficulties; more likely to become parents at a young age; to be involved in criminal activities; to be involved in prostitution; more likely to be homeless; to be at higher risk for alcohol/drug abuse; and to experience mental health problems. This is by no means to suggest that every adult public care alumnus or alumna is at risk, is unable to surmount the adversities presented by the system. A good number of them exhibit admirable resilience and function well in most domains of adult life; they become successful adults and parents. Protective factors associated with the resilience of such children and adults, such as type of placement and social support, form the theme of Chapter 7.

4 Motives for child fostering

The motives for fostering, as opposed to adoption, are diverse and complex, more so from a cross-cultural perspective. For example, we saw earlier that, contrary to Western norms, children are transferred to another person or household in some cultures not because their parents are incapable of caring for them or unwilling to do so, but rather because they are responding to social and cultural norms. Those norms very much govern also who takes a child, from whom and for what reasons. In traditional cultures of North America, for instance, a boy in his late childhood is sent to live in his maternal uncle's household in order to integrate him into the larger community (Payne-Price, 1981). Similarly, Alber (2003, 2004) reports that, in West Africa, there is a general belief that biological parents not only do not 'own' a child, but also they are not capable of guaranteeing their children a good education. Alber (2003) cites Baatombu child-rearing patterns as a case in point.

According to Alber, Baatombu people believe that parents are over solicit-ous towards their own children and so spoil them; that is, they are incapable of disciplining them. Baatombu people, therefore, use fostering not just as a mechanism for caring for children or for cementing kinship relation-ships, but also as a means of ensuring that children are properly socialized and integrated into the community. This cultural belief, as we saw earlier, was once a rationale for out-fostering in Western Europe and the USA. For example, Payne-Price (1981) points out that, during the colonial era in the USA, parents would send their young children to live with relatives in order for the children to receive proper training and to prevent the parents from spoiling them. In many cultures today, children are transferred to relatives or acquaintances for similar reasons, for the purpose of education or training.

Whatever the motives for child fostering or the circumstances in which fostering takes place today, it entails considerable costs or challenges for the caregiver; besides social and emotional costs, it involves costs of nurturing, feeding, clothing, housing and educating other people's offspring. As Silk (1987) points out, if foster-parental resources are assumed to be limited, investment in adoptive and foster-children may be costly because it will restrict parents' ability to invest in their own progeny. So, why do people get involved in it? There may be said to be an element of altruism in kinship or relative foster care, making personal sacrifices in the interest of the survival or continuity of the family, ensuring the perpetuation of the family genes. This, however, is not so in the case of non-relative foster care. Thus, non-relative carers are frequently referred to as 'professional' foster-carers. Indeed, many often question their motives for caring for other people's children: 'What is in it for them?' This chapter examines the reasons why families and individuals are prepared to care for and bring up children who are not their progeny. It examines also the motives for giving up a child to be raised by others.

Theories of fostering

Mainstream psychological accounts tend to conflate adoption and fostering. They tend to equate the motives for and the experiences of fostering with those of adoption essentially because both mechanisms have traditionally been associated with orphaned and 'unwanted' children – abandoned, abused or neglected children – who are often psychologically damaged by their adverse experiences. Hence the adoptive or foster-parents are also presumed to be acting out of altruism. Furthermore, conventional psychosocial developmental theories assume that loving and caring parents do not delegate the care of their children to others, be they relatives or non-relatives, because it is detrimental to the child's wellbeing. Based on such assumptions, psychological explanations for fostering and adoption are couched predominantly in psychoanalytic or psychodynamic terms.

For many researchers and practitioners in the child welfare field today, Bowlby's (1969, 1973) attachment theory has, for a long time, provided off-the-peg explanations for both fostering and adoption. While attachment theory goes some way in accounting for the effects of fostering and adoption on developmental outcomes, it does not explain adequately why parents willingly give up their children for fostering. The converse is equally true; it does not account for why a person or family voluntarily takes in another capable person's offspring to raise. From a psychodynamic perspective, Hegar (1999b) attributes individuals' willingness to take in another person's child to what she claims to be the human impulse to take in and care for a young relative, which, she suggests, is as old as the urge to parent one's own offspring. She interprets this human motive in terms of Erikson's (1968/1980) notion of *generativity*. Although this may apply to grandparent-caregivers, it hardly applies to young foster-carers. Besides, research suggests that grandparental investment or caregiving is not haphazard. In other words, the question as to what specific factors motivate individuals to foster other people's children remains, at best, only partially answered.

Inclusive fitness and child fostering

In recent years, theorists have turned to neo-Darwinism for explanations concerning motives for child fostering in contemporary societies. Studies overwhelmingly show that the task of providing kinship care falls predominantly upon maternal relatives, especially maternal grandparents and aunts (e.g., Euler and Weitzel, 1996; Euler *et al.*, 2001; Fletcher and Zwick, 2006; Geary, 2006; Herring, 2005; Rushton, 2004; van den Berghe and Parash, 1977). We will later see further evidence in support of this claim. The neo-Darwinian notions of inclusive fitness (or kin selection) and paternity uncertainty have been proposed as the main motivating factors in childcare, including fostering.

In its simplest sense, inclusive fitness relates to an individual's degree of success at procreation. According to evolutionary theory, reproductive success is itself ultimately determined by the maximum number or copies of genes a person spreads and leaves behind in the population. In evolutionary biology and evolutionary psychology, however, inclusive fitness refers not only to an individual's own reproductive success, the propagation of his/her genes into the future, but also to the totality of vigour that an individual contributes to or generates in his/her genetic kinfolk. From a selfish gene's (or individual's) standpoint, it is to its advantage to have the maximum number of copies of itself in the population. This is possible only if the individual is able to bequeath the highest number of copies of his/her genes in the population, for instance, by having as many offspring as possible. The literature indicates that, for a long time, this used to be the given, the unquestioned belief among evolutionary scientists, until Hamilton (1964) demonstrated that because close relatives of an individual have closely related genes, a person can also increase his/her inclusive fitness or evolutionary success by promoting the reproduction and survival of these related individuals. This is commonly referred to as the 'Hamilton rule'.

In other words, when an individual's actions enhance or diminish the fitness of other individuals with closely related genes, those actions vicariously affect his/her own fitness. This is claimed to motivate individuals to behave in a manner that maximizes their inclusive fitness, rather than their individual fitness. This can be achieved either directly by mating and caring for offspring, or indirectly by helping relatives (kin) survive and reproduce. Herring (2005) presents this scenario to elucidate the point: in a three-generation family (without identical twins who share 100 per cent of their genes with each other), each parent shares 50 per cent of his/her genes with each of their offspring; siblings share 50 per cent of their genes with one another; while grandparents share 25 per cent of their genes with each of their grandchildren. Hence, for example, an infertile brother or sister, or a grandmother (although no longer fecund) can still increase his/her own inclusive fitness by helping his/her nephews, nieces or grandchildren survive and reproduce.

Many claim that inclusive fitness theory explains nepotism – the tendency to behave more altruistically or favourably towards genetically related individuals than unrelated individuals (Burnstein *et al.*, 1994; Euler and Weitzel, 1996; Euler *et al.*, 2001; Hamilton, 1964; Herring, 2005; Rushton, 2004; Silk, 1987). The Hamilton rule states that altruism involves a donor, a beneficiary, a cost to the donor and benefit to the recipient. In other words, an altruistic act involves the donor giving something of benefit to the recipient, which will enable the recipient to survive and reproduce. In Hamilton's (1964) formulation, altruism increases or decreases in proportion to the degree of genetic relatedness or the amount of genes the donor and the recipient share. A logical assumption from this is that a person will behave more favourably towards close relatives than distant ones for any given act of benevolence. The notion of inclusive fitness (or kin selection) proposes that individuals with a predisposition to favour kin by providing resources that contribute to survival and successful reproduction leave more copies of their own genes, on average, than individuals who somehow lack this disposition.

This theory posits that because kin share a significant percentage of genetic material which varies in a population, they have a genetic interest in ensuring that members of their kinship group survive and reproduce. In this way, an individual increases the likelihood that a significant proportion of his or her own genes will pass to the next generation. Applied specifically to the family structure and childcare, inclusive fitness theory proposes that parents will give the most care, followed by older siblings, then grandparents, aunts and uncles (of both sides of the family), with the most distant relative giving the least care. Parents and grandparents, for instance, will invest the most in terms of time, effort and emotion into their children and grandchildren. This is evidenced by the obvious fact that parents frequently make sacrifices towards their children with the hope that they will carry on the family genes (Geary, 2006).

According to evolutionary social psychology, altruistic behaviours, defined as acts that increase the genetic fitness of the recipient at the cost of the donor may extend to reciprocating non-kin partners (Fletcher and Zwick, 2006; Silk, 1987). Herring's (2005) review of the literature suggests that, as in the animal kingdom, human beings provide more assistance to kin than they do to non-kin, and that individuals tend to provide more assistance to closer kin than they do to distant kin. Nonetheless, he argues that much sacrificial behaviour by humans is generally done in the hope of reciprocity at some point in the future, so that increasing inclusive fitness in humans is not necessarily dependent upon relatedness. Rather, it is commonly based on reciprocal altruism. This means that a person may act altruistically towards a genetically unrelated individual not because there is a probability of shared genetic material between them, but because of the possibility of reciprocation in the future. Such an altruistic act may be seen as an insurance policy, albeit, sometimes unwitting on the part of the donor or helper. Many of the cases described in previous chapters reinforce this proposition.

Paternity uncertainty and fostering

One might hypothesize from the foregoing discussion that kin, both maternal and paternal, would eagerly and indiscriminately provide foster care for a young relative in need, since doing so would enhance their inclusive fitness. There exists abundant evidence refuting such an assumption; it shows that the kinship system is skewed heavily in favour of the maternal side. The concept of paternity uncertainty, which may be regarded as complimentary to inclusive fitness theory, is frequently evoked to account for the asymmetry in the kinship system. Much of the literature reviewed in the preceding and later chapters provides evidence of this lopsidedness, manifest in a variety of domains, including fostering.

Euler and co-investigators (Euler and Weitzel, 1996; Euler *et al.*, 2001) detect the most obvious asymmetry in parental care. They point out (the obvious) that mothers care more for their offspring than fathers do. Thus, they argue that because the average amount of parental care differs between the sexes, that because mothers provide more care than fathers do, it makes a difference to grandparents whether a daughter's or son's parental effort is assisted. In terms of grandparental childcare, they argue that a mother needs more help in direct childcare than a father does. On this basis, Euler and Weitzel (1996) predicted that maternal grandparents would care more for their grandchildren, compared to paternal grandparents.

From an inclusive fitness perspective, a counterhypothesis is that it is equally beneficial to paternal grandparents to bypass their son in his parental effort, or to compensate for his lack of it, in order to continue to propagate their genes, to enhance their own inclusive fitness. Research, however, does not seem to support this assumption. In Germany, Euler and Weitzel (1996) examined grandparental care-giving as rated retrospectively by adult grandchildren. Their final sample comprised 603 cases whose two sets of (putative) genetic grandparents were all still alive when the participants were seven years old. The results confirmed the inclusive fitness theory's prediction about parental differential solicitude: 1) the participants rated the most care from their maternal grandmother; 2) the second most care was rated from the maternal grandfather; 3) the third most care was rated from the paternal grandmother; and 4) the paternal grandfather gave the least care.

Euler and Weitzel (1996) examined also if the sex of the child had any influence on the grandparents' devotion. The analysis showed that the sex of the grandchild mattered little: female grandchildren rated just slightly higher grandparental devotion than male grandchildren did. Residential proximity, however, had a large influence on grandparental care, but the four grandparents did not differ significantly in residential distance. They found also that the age of the grandparent had no significant effect on care; neither did the availability of other grandparents. Euler and colleagues (Euler and Weitzel, 1996; Euler *et al.*, 2001) claim support from comparable studies conducted in European countries and the USA for their findings. Other studies that have examined aspects of grandparental investment, other than child-rated solicitude, point to the general pattern of differential grandparental investment: perception of closeness to and time spent with grandchild; interaction frequencies; gifts received from grandparents; and grandparental mourning after a grandchild's death (Euler *et al.*, 2001). Euler and colleagues explain their findings and those of other studies in terms of sex-specific reproductive strategy and paternity uncertainty.

The concept of paternity uncertainty simply relates to a parent's degree of confidence that his/her child is actually his/her genetic offspring. It holds that, as in other viviparous mammals, women know with absolute certainty, other things being equal, that they are the mothers of their own children (maternal certainty). On the other hand, because of the possibility of female infidelity and its concomitant risk of cuckoldry, men can never be wholly confident that they sired their children (paternal uncertainty). In the case of a grand-father, there are potentially two opportunities for the genetic link between himself and his grandchildren to be dubious: 1) because of female infidelity, the grandfather may not be the biological parent of his son or daughter; and 2) for the same reason, his son may not be the biological parent of his own children. This is often referred to as the 'double whammy' effect (Euler *et al.* 2001). In contrast, a grandmother is 100 per cent confident that she gave birth to her sons and daughters, other things being equal; that she is geneti-cally related to her daughter's children. A grandmother is, therefore, justified in being entirely certain of her genetic link between her and her daughter's children, but she cannot entertain the same degree of confidence with regard to her son's children because of female infidelity.

From an inclusive fitness point of view, the above scenario makes a man's investment in his (putative) children a risky venture; there is the likelihood (however slim) that he might be investing in another man's inclusive fitness, that he might be helping another man to propagate his genes. In fact, some attribute fathers' lesser investment, in terms of time and effort, in their children, compared to mothers', to paternity uncertainty, a man's lesser certainty that his wife's or partner's progeny are his. In the case of paternal grandfathers, this risk is even greater; it is, therefore, not surprising that Euler and colleagues' respondents gave paternal grandfathers the lowest rating in care-giving. In short, the amount of care received by grandchildren is influenced by paternity uncertainty and maternal certainty. In the kinship system, the paternal grandfather is the one who experiences the greatest uncertainty of paternity and, thus, degree of genetic relatedness. According to inclusive fitness theory, he is expected to provide the least investment in grandchildren. In human societies where low paternity certainty is prevalent, men are at risk of such misdirected investment, and so tend to invest more in their maternal relatives, in terms of care-giving as well as inheritance (e.g., Alexander, 1979; Bloch and Sperber, 2004; Geary, 2006; Owusu-Bempah, 2007; Pashos, 2000).

In a comparative study carried out in Germany and Greece, Pashos (2000) tested the paternal uncertainty hypothesis in both rural and urban locations. The study involved 544 adult participants (318 Greeks, 208 Germans and 18 of others origins) who rated their grandparents' care-giving. They were asked to estimate on a 7-point rating scale from 1 (not at all) to 7 (very much) the amount of care they received from each grandparent until the age of seven years (to some degree replicating Euler and Weitzel's 1996 study). Other variables examined were the geographical (or residential) distance to each grandparent, each grandparent's occupation and health status during a participant's childhood. Pashos reported somewhat mixed findings. In all groups, grandmothers were more caring than were grandfathers. However, in Germany and urban Greece, the maternal grandparents were rated as more intensive caregivers than paternal grandparents, in contrast to rural Greek paternal grandparents who provided more care.

Among urban Greeks, the pattern of grandparental devotion was essentially the same as those reported by other studies (e.g., Euler and Weitzel, 1996; Euler *et al.*, 2001; Smith, 1998), but among rural Greeks it differed, especially for male respondents who rated the care given by paternal grandparents higher than by maternal grandparents. One explanation Pashos gives for this difference is the prevailing patrilocality in rural Greece. The claim here is that spouse residential arrangement (the close residential proximity between a wife and her mother-in-law) reduces the possibility of female infidelity and, conversely, increases the level of paternal certainty. Namely, spouses' close residential proximity, husband and wife living in the same household as the husband's parents, enhances the relatives' confidence that the children carry the genetic material of their kin. In other words, the findings support the paternal certainty hypothesis. However, Euler and colleagues (2001) see patrilinearity with preferred investment in paternal grandchildren, especially paternal grandsons, as a more fitting explanation for Pashos' data from rural Greek grandparents.

Regarding the relationship between paternity certainty and fostering, Taylor (2005) investigated parents' preferred foster-caregiver for their children: maternal versus paternal relatives and genetic distance of caregivers. The study was conducted in two rural sites in Thailand. The findings suggest that in environments where high marital stability and paternal certainty prevail, both mothers and fathers prefer close genetic kin from either side as foster-parents for their children. In low marital stability and paternal certainty environments, on the other hand, mothers trust their own side of the family, regardless of genetic distance, more than close genetic kin from the other side. Taylor's findings and other studies may be seen as highlighting the important role of socio-cultural factors in parents' choice of kin to whom they foster out their children, as suggested by many investigators (e.g., Donner, 1999; Goody, 1973, 1982; Oni, 1995; Silk, 1987; Verhoef, 2005). Nevertheless, they also lend support to the paternal certainty hypothesis. With respect to kinship foster care, several studies have found systematic differences in care-giving by blood relatives. On average, maternal relatives provide more care to their young progeny than do paternal relatives.

To recapitulate, both inclusive fitness theory and paternity certainty theory posit that we have a tendency to favour kin over non-kin, and that this disposition is sensitive to degrees of doubt or certainty of relatedness.

This means that, for example, a man's investment in his putative children is determined or at least influenced by the degree of confidence he has that he actually sired them, that he is their biological father. That is to say, if a man has reasons to doubt his paternity, he will be reluctant to invest in his (putative) children. His kin will likewise be less favourably disposed towards the children than they would be in the absence of any doubt about their relative's paternity. Inclusive fitness theory predicts also that acts of altruism decrease proportionally with genetic distance. Euler and colleagues (2001) suggest that combining both theories yields a hierarchical prediction about grandparental investment. In other words, a maternal grandmother should be expected to invest the most and the paternal grandfather the least. The maternal grandfather should be expected to invest more than the paternal grandmother because the former helps a daughter and the latter helps a son, and both have one link of uncertain paternity. The evidence reviewed above seems to support these assumptions.

Traditional communities

Motives for fostering out children

Inclusive fitness theory posits that acts of altruism will be increasingly limited to kin. From this assumption, Silk (1987, pp. 41–42) suggests a number of more specific predictions about the pattern of fostering transactions, including the following.

i.　If fostering transactions have been shaped by evolved behavioural propensities, then these transactions are also expected to be most common among close kin.

ii.　Related adults may be expected to commonly absorb substantial economic costs in raising foster children for which they are not fully compensated, while unrelated adults may be much less likely to incur costs without compensation.

iii.　Since parents are more closely related to their natural children than to their foster-children, conflicts may arise over the treatment of foster- and natural children. In general, kin selection theory predicts that natural children will receive more favourable treatment since they are more closely related to their parents than are their foster-siblings.

Evidence supports these assumptions. The question remains, though, as to why parents who are capable of raising and investing in their children, capable of propagating their genes through their own children, voluntarily foster them out. To address these and related assumptions fully, therefore, we need to examine the motives for willingly giving away one's child for fostering, as well as the motives for fostering or investing in someone's child, for nurturing and promoting the growth and development of another person's offspring.

The anthropological literature reviewed in Chapter 2 suggests that, in some traditional cultures, giving up a child for fostering is perceived as a gift, the finest gift one can give to another person. Most people's understanding of a gift of any kind entails altruism or self-sacrifice; it involves acting in a way that benefits another person at one's expense. Simply put, altruism is the converse of selfishness. The preceding discussion also suggests that because of the costs to the donor, altruistic acts are commonly limited to close relatives, genetically related individuals. The fundamental question is whether voluntarily fostering out one's child to a relative or friend is wholly an act of benevolence, an act from which the birth parents derive no benefit. A broader and closer examination of the literature shows that this is neither always nor necessarily the case. Indeed, much of the evidence indirectly supports both inclusive fitness and paternity uncertainty hypotheses.

In societies where fostering is normal, it often occurs in situations that benefit not only the child, but also the birth parents. Researchers and observers have documented some of the factors that influence parents' decision to foster out their children. These range from marital status, migration and employment or participation of the mothers in the labour force, poverty, the health status of the child, family size and composition to the child's life chances (e.g., Bohr and Tse, 2009; Castle, 1995; Goody, 1982; Lloyd and Desai, 1992; Oppong, 1973; Shomaker, 1989; Silk, 1987; Vandermeersch, 2002; Verhoef, 2005). Regarding marital status, research indicates that remarriage strongly influences the frequency of fostering out children, because women may find it difficult to remarry or incorporate themselves into their new husband's household if they are accompanied by offspring. In other words, lone-parent mothers are more motivated than married or co-habiting mothers to foster out their young children. In such circumstances, fostering out her children frees a lone mother for remarriage and ensures the child's safety and survival.

Research shows that there is a close connection between poverty and child fostering. Various investigators have pointed out that, among families in communities experiencing unemployment, poverty and other hardships, fostering provides a useful coping mechanism (e.g., Brown *et al.*, 2002; Castle, 1995; Fonseca, 2002, 2003, Lloyd and Desai, 1992; Serra, 2009; Stack, 1974; Vandermeersch, 2002). These investigators see fostering among relatives and friends as a mechanism of family survival. Through fostering, they transfer resources and services across households and are able to make adjustments to household size and so forth. In these circumstances, the costs of raising children are rarely borne exclusively by biological parents; rather, as predicted by Silk (1987), they are shared by many people through the extended family and other social networks. This includes cost-sharing within (extended family) households as well as fostering out children to other households. Fostering in such situations appears to benefit all the parties involved in the transaction; it provides a mechanism for coping in hard times as well as for ensuring the survival of the young and the continuity of the family genes.

Evidence suggests migration to be another strong influence on parents' decision to relinquish their children for fostering (e.g., Bohr and Tse, 2009; Goody, 1982, Lloyd and Desai, 1992; Shomaker, 1989; Vandermeersch, 2002; Verhoef, 2005). Apart from enabling migrant parents to maintain links with their place of origin, fostering also enables them, particularly mothers, to combine their reproductive role and their participation in the workforce (Bohr and Tse, 2009; Lloyd and Desai, 1992). A recent study by Bohr and Tse (2009) highlights this. They recognize that an increasing number of immigrants to Western nations send infants thousands of miles back to their country of origin to be raised by their extended families – a culturally sanctioned tradition. After four to five years of separation, the children return to their biological parents to attend school in the adopted country. Bohr and Tse claim that, in North America, this practice is particularly prevalent among immigrants from the People's Republic of China. They cite Sengupta's (1999) estimate that, in 1999, at the New York Chinatown Health Centre alone, 10–20 per cent of approximately 1,500 babies born each year appear to have been sent away, and up to half of all expectant parents at another hospital in the area had stated their intention to do likewise.

Following anecdotal evidence from social workers in Toronto's Chinese community centres suggesting an even higher incidence of temporarily relocating babies, Bohr and Tse conducted an exploratory inquiry (using semi-structured interviews) into the motives of a group of Chinese immigrant parents in Toronto. The parents were considering relocating their young children to be cared for by their grandparents back in the People's Republic of China. Sixteen university-educated parents (12 mothers and four fathers) who had emigrated from mainland China took part in the study. They were aged between 24 and 36 years, and their babies ranged in age from five months to 15 months. The families were relatively new arrivals in Canada; they had been in Canada for one to three years, with an average stay of 18 months.

Bohr and Tse found the following to be the two major motivating factors in the parents' decision to relocate their children: a) their economic and career needs, and b) the desire to preserve their old (original) culture. All the participants perceived parenting by proxy as an economic and career necessity, the necessity to retrain or to develop their careers. Namely, they needed the time, free of their children, to build a career and lifestyle in the new country. Regarding cultural influence, more than half of the parents mentioned that they were themselves fostered by their grandparents, so that they were following a cultural tradition. Bohr and Tse see cultural traditions, rather than selfishness, as playing a crucial role in the parents' quest for solutions to their childcare difficulties. It is clear, however, that there is an element of self-interest in the parents' decision to parent by proxy. This is not to imply that the grandparents do not benefit materially, for example in the form of remittance, from the arrangement or derive no satisfaction or a sense of purpose from playing their cultural role of caring for and integrating their grandchildren into the extended family, connecting them to their ancestral roots.

This study supports previous research by Goody (1973, 1982). In her research with West African mature students in England, Goody observed that a high percentage of West African families either sent their children 'back home' to be cared for by their grandparents or other relatives or, alternatively, boarded them out with English foster-parents. She contrasted this practice with other groups of parents who sent their children to 'nannies' or child-minders on a daily basis. Goody suggested that, like Chinese migrants in North America and elsewhere, the African parents, who frequently worked and attended college or university at the same time, shared a cultural view of parenthood (from home) that is approving of delegating certain aspects of their parenting or child-rearing roles. In both cases, however, enhancing their career prospects was the parents' principal motive for fostering out their young.

Research, especially from West Africa, indicates that parents also foster out their children to wealthier or better-off relatives or acquaintances in order to enhance the children's life chances. In a wide-ranging survey of fostering in West Africa, Goody (1982) has shown that besides its other functions, such as family integration, obligations and solidarity, fostering has become part of an apprenticeship system in urban areas of West Africa. Just as it used to be in olden Scotland, for example, it allows foster-children from rural areas to apprentice in urban skills and trades. In other words, there has been a shift in the direction of requests for fostering. Customarily, foster-parents requested children from the children's biological parents. In recent times, however, biological parents ask relatives in urban areas to take their children so that these children can take advantage of opportunities in urban areas that are unavailable in rural areas. That is, fostering is now an important part of a child's education and moral training (Goody, 1982). Fostering potentially provides the child with a route for social and economic mobility. Thus, children are normally sent to foster-parents who live in larger towns than the natural parents do; the ideal foster-parents are both wealthy and well-educated. Fostering out in such situations is consistent with the inclusive fitness hypothesis, because it potentially enhances not just the child's eco-nomic prospects, but also his/her inclusive fitness and, indirectly, the parents'.

The foregoing discussion suggests clearly that parents relinquish their chil-dren for fostering for a variety of reasons, including altruism. Nevertheless, whatever parents' motivations for relinquishing their child for fostering, they do not ignore or are indifferent to the child's wellbeing. Even in situa-tions where it is done as an act of altruism, as a gift, such as those described in Chapter 2 (Donner, 1999; Griffin, 2006; Shomaker, 1989; Talle, 2004), we must bear in mind that cultural as well as social norms can preclude the retrieval of a gift. Contrary to this norm, Shomaker (1989), for example, stresses that, among Navajo people, a child is given to his grandmother as a gift only for as long as that child is happy and wishes to remain a gift.

Similarly, Goody (1973) has noted that, in Ghana, as in other societies, while parents are generally discouraged from terminating foster arrangements prematurely without due cause, parents may reclaim children who are treated poorly. A child's happiness in the foster home strongly influences his/her parents' decision to leave him/her with the foster-parent.

Alber (2003) and Verhoef (2005) also point out that in traditional societies where collective child-rearing is widespread and accepted, all 'mothers' within the extended family are not equal in the eyes of the biological parents. Beliefs about child development, including what children need at certain developmental stages and how these needs should be met, seem to influence which 'mothers' are considered more or less acceptable foster-parents. Generally, acceptable foster-parents occupy a higher socio-economic status than the birth parents; they are more educated and more affluent relatives. Often, these relatives are not afraid to make children buckle down to learn, and, where the status gap between the child and guardian is great, parents seem willing to tolerate children's endurance of significant 'hardship' so they might have a real chance of success in life (Alber, 2003; Verhoef, 2005). Nonetheless, although such beliefs about adult discipline seem to allow for differential treatment in some cases, rarely will parents foster their children out to potential foster-parents who are thought to be likely to 'maltreat' them. For instance, step-parents, being outside the extended family network of obligations, are generally not seen as acceptable foster-parents. They are not thought capable of having children's best interests at heart, and it is expected that parents who remarry will protect their children from previous unions by finding other relatives to raise them (Verhoef, 2005). This cultural belief reinforces Silk's (1987) prediction.

Undoubtedly, fostering out entails a degree of self-interest, although this is not always obvious to the parties involved. For example, the social and/or economic benefits biological parents expect to gain from the transaction also influence, to some extent, the success of foster arrangements. For example, more foster-children are reared by members of important descent groups than are reared by ordinary individuals (Alber, 2003; Goody, 1982; Serra, 2009; Verhoef, 2005; Verhoef and Morelli, 2007). Natural parents sometimes retrieve their children from foster homes when the desired economic advantages associated with the foster arrangements fail to accrue or materialize. Evidence indicates that parents often terminate foster arrangements upon learning that children whom they fostered out principally to attend school were more actively engaged in non-academic activities (Alber, 2003; Goody, 1973). Even where a child is given away out of 'pure' altruism, as an irretrievable gift, the donor derives satisfaction from the knowledge that his/her action has benefited the recipient. Richard Titmus (1970) made this very clear in his acclaimed book, *The Gift Relationship: From Human Blood to Social Policy.*

Motives for fostering in children

The evidence examined in this and the preceding chapters shows clearly the complexity and diversity of motives for fostering in traditional societies. This is mainly because, unlike its Western connotations, fostering is not necessarily associated with families that are in some way 'disjointed' or 'dysfunctional'. The complexity and diversity of the motives for fostering in these communities may be demonstrated by reference to Stanford's (1971, in Payne-Price, 1981) typology of fostering and Stack's (1974) list of reasons for the practice. Stanford identifies five reasons for fostering, including: 1) child lending – a child is lent to a relative or non-relative who has none and the child is treated as a child of the home; and 2) child employment – ideally the child (as a helper) is treated as a full member of the household, but is kept by strangers, rather than kin. Whereas Stack identified 13 reasons, including: 1) childlessness; 2) love, concern and desire to keep a child; 3) as symbolic and mutual trust between friends; and 4) for children to help out. These reasons suggest clearly that foster-parents benefit from fostering transactions in traditional societies.

There are several benefits, tangible as well as intangible, that may accrue to the foster-parent. Concerning intangible benefits, Goody (1982) and Oni (1995), for example, point out that among some communities in West Africa, such as the Igbo of Nigeria, as also among Navajo people for instance, it is prestigious for a woman to have her grandchildren living with her; it is regarded as a blessing when a woman starts building around her a 'throng' of grandchildren and great-grandchildren. Apart from enhancing her social status and consequently bolstering her ego or sense of purpose, this arrangement has an in-built social and economic support system that comes in the form of regular or occasional visits and gifts of money, foodstuffs and clothing by parents to foster-parents. These form an important part of their resource accumulation. Oni (1995) stresses that wealth flow from parents to foster-parents takes place in the absence of foster-children, but their presence guarantees the regularity of the accompanying visits and the size and variety of goods received. It must be added that these visits and the flow of wealth from the parents to the foster-parents and the children occur irrespective of the distance between them (e.g., Goody, 1982; Verhoef, 2005).

In the West African context, Serra (2009), perhaps unwittingly summarizing Stanford's and Stack's typologies of fostering, identifies the conditions under which all actors involved in fostering, including children, may benefit from the act. She accepts that reasons for fostering include, but are not limited to, strengthening extended family ties, redistributing child labour, making life-cycle adjustments of household size and composition, schooling, apprenticeship and taking advantage of an informal insurance mechanism. She agrees also that fostering a child involves the transfer of resources across households, such as child labour and other services, material goods and claims to future returns from child investment. However, she sees the arrangement as carrying in its train far-reaching implications. She contends that appreciation of those implications is necessary for a proper understanding of the strategies households devise to increase income, smooth consumption over time or insure against contingencies.

On the biological parents' part, Serra agrees with others, such as Goody (1973, 1982), that they foster out their children to better-off households as a means to enhance their children's prospects of moving forward and succeeding in life. That is to say, living in a higher-status home is likely to provide a child with the opportunity to attend a better and more prestigious school than that available in the parents' locality, and to accumulate cultural and social capital by making useful connections with important people. On these grounds, she concurs with previous investigators (e.g., Alber, 2003; Verhoef, 2005) that parents' decision to transfer their child is justified, even if the child may have to work harder than other children in the receiving household. In short, from the point of view of parents who cannot afford education, skills or a promising environment for all of their children, fostering out a child is a rational decision. Given that the children are the future providers for their parents, the parents are investing in their own future through fostering out one or two of their children.

Serra (2009, p. 166) asks: 'Why is child fostering so pervasive in Africa? Why have similar mechanisms for redistributing child labour or providing for child education not arisen in other parts of the world?' Her answer is that child fostering is an efficient way of raising and training children and preparing them for adult life under very specific conditions typical of African societies, particularly in the western region. As we saw in Chapter 2, similar conditions exist elsewhere in the world; they are not peculiar to West Africa. Cultural factors, altruism and inclusive fitness theory combined provide explanations for the normativeness and pervasiveness of fostering in West Africa and other traditional societies worldwide; and also for fostering out children and taking in another person's child.

To summarize, whatever the motives for a given act of fostering in traditional communities, much of the evidence examined so far provides us with an understanding of the practice; it depicts and delineates the elasticity of a family within the context of social networks, *'not fixed sets of abstracts which cannot account for the give and take in everyday living'* (Payne-Price, 1981, p. 140). It provides us with an alternative lens and a means for exploring and working with the psycho-socio-cultural dynamics which exist within a given society. In brief, it puts a break on our ethnocentrism.

> By realizing that fostering and adoption are adaptive mechanisms we can better account for the dynamics of the real world. Awareness of differences in time elements, values and material circumstances is needed in order to report the vitality and plasticity of the family scene. The precise mode of child transfer in each case is the result of the interplay of a rich

variety of forces. The interplay reveals the fluidity by which people cope with life and maintain their concepts of proper family.

(Payne-Price, 1981, p. 140)

Another expression of this is that, in certain circumstances, such as those described by Stack (1974) and Fonseca (2003), child relocation is a reflection of the reality framework in which families operate. *'The reality framework is that of eating and living and responding today, in today's realities, in preparation for tomorrow'* (Haley, 1996, p. 8). Also, in view of the fact that fostering occurs predominantly among kin in these communities, it may be seen as a mechanism for ensuring the family's (or clan's) collective inclusive fitness, a mechanism for ensuring the continuity of the family.

The Western context

Motives for fostering in Western societies

Alber (2003) has examined the arguments that in communities where fostering is commonplace, there are social, demographic, economic and political benefits derived from the practice. She argues that what these arguments fail to consider is how the practice is set within social norms. She asks a similar question to that posed by Serra (above), that: *'if fosterage and adoption solves so many of society's problems, why are there societies like those in Europe and North America, where adoption and fostering are the exception?'* (Alber, 2003, p. 488). She accepts that those problems exist in Western societies. She accepts also that those problems could be solved or minimized through fostering and adoption. Nevertheless, she argues that the fostering or circulation of children among kin is not practised because it does not correspond to certain norms and ideas regarded as fundamental. The belief that the biological parents are the best persons to educate a child, and that changes in parentage cause damage to a child's development, prevents people from thinking of giving a child away or taking a child in. Alber's argument suggests that, to understand the motives for fostering in Western societies, we need to understand both how it is perceived and the circumstances in which is it occurs.

In Western societies, fostering is commonly associated with something gone badly and 'shamefully' wrong, something wrong with the family or the child or both, and never with the social structure. It is predominantly perceived as a child protection service, as opposed to a childcare mechanism; it is hardly regarded as a family or community support system. In short, it is not an accepted way of raising children. So, the motives of individuals and families, especially professional (or non-kin) caregivers, who choose to raise another family's children are often questioned not only by other families, but also by child welfare professionals: 'Are they philanthropists or mercenaries?' In other words, are they acting out of altruism or for financial gain? This is an important question to consider because research (e.g., Beeman and Boisen, 1999; Chipman *et al.*, 2002; Cole, 2005; Dando and Minty, 1987; Proch, 1982) has found caregivers' motives to be influential in the success or failure of placements or fostering arrangements.

Research suggests that the primary motives for undertaking to bring up another family's children, in spite of its economic, social, emotional and psychological costs involved, vary according to the child's relationship with the caregiver, whether the caregiver is kin or a stranger. For example, non-kin caregivers are contractual personnel who provide childcare under agency supervision. Thus, their motives vary from adoption – intention to adopt a child; social conscience – the desire to provide protection and safety to the child; to financial – providing foster care as a job. Relative caregivers, on the other hand, undertake fostering for similar reasons to their counterparts in traditional societies; they provide care for young and vulnerable relatives primarily for familial reasons: as a duty or obligation or simply as the natural thing to do (e.g., Anderson, 2001; Beeman and Boisen, 1999; Cleaver, 2000, Cole, 2005; Dando and Minty, 1987; Sykes *et al.*, 2002). They undertake childcare duties for the love of the children and also because they want to keep the children within the kinship network and out of the foster-care system.

In a study that focused on foster-parents of 10–11-year-old children, Anderson (2001) investigated their motives for becoming foster-parents, which were linked to their family and work circumstances. Among the 21 families involved in the study, Anderson identified four different, but equally frequent, reasons for providing foster care: 1) relatives who feel responsibility for a child; 2) couples who want children and do not think that they can have children of their own; 3) families where the mother wants to be at home taking care of her biological children as well as foster-children instead of having unskilled employed work outside the home; and 4) parents with grown-up children who want to fill the 'empty nest' by becoming foster-parents. The third motive lends some support to Silk's (1987) hypothesis (p. 64).

Previous and later studies generally support Anderson's findings. Cole (2005) examined the relationship between caregivers' motives and developmental outcomes. Specifically, the study concerned the relationship between caregivers' motivation and infant attachment. It involved 46 kin and non-kin caregivers, 98 per cent of whom were female. The results showed that the motives for providing foster care for children varied for the kin and non-kin foster-carers. The three reasons most often reported included: 1) rescuing abused or neglected children; 2) increasing family size (a 'selfish' motive); and 3) social concern. Social concern or rescuing abused or neglected children was a motivator for both groups of carers. However, the strength of the agreement with this reason varied between the two groups of caregivers: 66.7 per cent of the non-kin caregivers as opposed to 38.2 per cent of the kin caregivers strongly agreed with this reason, somehow confirming Silk's prediction. Unsurprisingly, increasing family size was not a strong motive among kin caregivers. A majority of kin (91%) and non-kin caregivers (79.4%) strongly disagreed that financial gain was a reason for providing foster care. Again, this confirms Silk's prediction that kin are more prepared than non-kin to provide care without monetary compensation.

To tap into their unconscious motives, all carers were asked if they had other reasons for deciding to provide foster care. An important motive for kin caregivers in agreeing to care for the children placed with them was not to lose them to the care system. Kin caregivers also saw caring for the infant as a way to give the child a new start in life, or, in Hamiltonian terms, to increase their own inclusive fitness. Cole found that, for kin, rescuing the child and social concern were very strong motivators. This finding is interesting, given that one of the main objections among policy-makers and professionals to kinship care concerns intergenerational child abuse or neglect.

It is a well-established fact that fostering provides a convenient route to individuals and families wishing to adopt a child. Gillis-Arnold and colleagues (1998) examined the attitudes and motivations of potential adoptive and foster-parents towards parenting and foster-parenting. Their sample comprised 44 female adoptive and 149 female non-adoptive foster-parent trainees toward parenting and foster-parenting. They found that the intention of the potential adoptive foster-parents was to ultimately adopt the child, whereas the non-adoptive foster-parent trainees wanted to look after the child on a temporary basis. There were significant differences between the two groups on both measures: parenting attitudes and motives for fostering a child. For example, the adoptive trainees were found to be more motivated than the non-adoptive trainees in the following areas: 1) rescuing a child; 2) companionship for adult; 3) replacing grown children, and 4) companionship for own child. The first three reasons might be construed as fostering a child out of self-interest. That would not in itself be morally wrong, if it ultimately benefits the child.

Much of the research concerning foster-parents' reasons for providing care tends to concentrate on the caregivers, to the virtual exclusion of the views of the other parties involved, the children and professionals. One of the most frequently cited investigations into foster-parents' motives from the perspective of other actors was carried out by Beeman and Boisen (1999). The study examined caregivers' reasons from the viewpoint of urban, metropolitan and rural childcare professionals – social workers in three Minnesota counties, USA. The analysis compared the professionals' views regarding kin and non-kin motives for being foster-parents. Many of their findings support Silk's predictions. The reason most given by workers for kin choosing to become foster-parents was 'family responsibility' or 'to keep the family together' (68.6% of respondents). The second most frequently given reason was 'to help or care for the children' (15.9%); a third reason given was money (11.7%). In contrast, when asked why non-kin chose to become foster-parents, 57 per cent of the respondents believed that their major motive was 'to help children', followed by money (18.4%), 'social responsibility' or 'for the good of the community' (9%), and 'because they like working with kids' (6.9%).

The respondents were also specifically asked reasons for choosing to become foster-parents, for example: 1) why they thought kin become foster-parents; 2) what their perceptions of kin functioning as foster-parents were; and 3) how they thought children in kinship foster care fared. Just over 83 per cent of the professionals agreed that kinship foster-parents are more motivated to provide care by their strong desire to hold their family together, and 63 per cent believed that kinship foster-parents provide care because of family expectations. Only 11.6 per cent stated that kinship foster-parents are motivated by money.

Because adoption has been identified as a major motivating factor in fostering, the professionals were asked about their views on kin's interest in adoption. Over 62 per cent of them believed that kinship foster-parents do not feel adoption is necessary because family ties already exist; and 67.8 per cent agreed that kinship foster-parents do not want to adopt because they believe that adoption would cause conflicts in their relationships with the child's biological parents. Approximately 34.2 per cent agreed that kinship foster-parents show little interest in adoption.

We know that individuals may be motivated to foster a child for a number of reasons: altruism, the desire to have a child of one's own to raise, the sense of duty or obligation experienced by many kinship carers and, in a few cases, the desire to improve their own condition through fostering. On the whole, however, Beeman and Boisen's study supports the cultural belief that the primary motivating factor in kinship foster care relates to familial obligation and a desire to preserve the family, rather than money. Thus, they encourage child welfare agencies to acknowledge the uniqueness of kinship agreements and the role of the kinship caregiver. They also urge workers to clearly lay out the expectations and objectives that exist from the agency's perspective, since there is often a mismatch between caregiver and agency objectives.

Subsequent studies reinforce Beeman and Boisen's findings and suggestions. For example, a Canadian study by Shorkey and Mitchell (2003) reported that grandparents take children into their homes in order to avoid the child's entry into the public care system. Similarly, Gordon and colleagues (2003) found that grandparents frequently assumed responsibility for their grandchildren prior to the children's arrival in their home on a permanent or semi-permanent basis. In other words, grandparents often worry about the children and so take them in to provide a safe place for them. Grandma to the rescue! Regarding agency expectations, Chipman and colleagues (2002) also note that the primary objective of the agency is different from that of the caregiver. The agency's mandate is the physical safety and protection of the child, manifested as 'permanency' status for the child. In contrast, they argue that caregivers often have love and moral guidance as their goal which frequently manifests as appropriate behaviour, school performance and happiness for the child.

Other studies suggest that not only are kin keen to keep the child out of the care system, but also they are highly committed to the child's wellbeing, so much so that they put the child's needs before their own (Altshuler, 1999; Brown *et al.*, 2002; Farmer and Moyers, 2008; Lindheim and Dozier, 2007; Messing, 2006; Pitcher, 2002). This represents a clear evidence of Hamilton's (1964) notion of inclusive fitness. Such studies show that kin caregivers, especially grandparents, are generally persevering – they are determined not to give up even when problems arise, for example, when the child shows very difficult behaviour. In short, they are highly motivated to be in an enduring relationship with the children and to ensure their general wellbeing.

Proch's (1982) study is worth highlighting because of its uniqueness. It is unique in that it involved children who experienced both fostering and adoption by the same family. Proch solicited the perceptions of 29 adopted children who were initially fostered by their adoptive parents and their motives of their adoptive parents (N=56). The results showed that the adoptive parents' main motives were: to increase family size, followed by companionship for their own children, to care for children as a job and to help other children. On the basis of the results and findings, Proch (1982) pointed out that the goals (case plan) for the child and the motivations for some people who are becoming foster-parents conflict with the accepted goal of foster care, which is to provide temporary care for children until they can be reunited with their biological parent/s or placed for adoption. Hence, pre-empting later investigators (e.g., Beeman and Boisen, 1999; Chipman *et al.*, 2002; Pitcher, 2002) she stressed the need for careful interpretation of the purpose of foster care to potential foster-parents and for child welfare workers to be more careful in distinguishing the differences between foster care and adoption.

Proch also found that companionship for self was a major motive reported by the participants. For example, adoptive parents may be more motivated to initially foster a child in the hope of adopting that child, to provide companionship for their own child if they cannot have any more children and do not want their own child growing up as an only child. She suggested that those who wish to adopt generally want to add more children to their family. On the other hand, non-adoptive caregivers are more motivated than adoptive caregivers to foster for financial gain. In other words, Proch found wanting to care for children as a job to be one of the main motives for providing foster care.

Overall, there is a disparity not only in patterns of fostering, but also regarding the motives for providing foster care between Western societies and other societies. The societies of sub-Saharan Africa and Oceania, for example, seem to have very little in common, other than the frequency with which parental responsibilities are delegated to others. In these societies, caring for a related or unrelated child is a conventional, socially supported practice. Indeed, in these societies, fostering is predominantly a private affair, a private arrangement between families who are very often related. As such it is mainly undertaken for familial and social reasons. In Western societies, in contrast, caring for any child who is not one's biological child is neither conventional nor socially sanctioned. In fact, it is regarded as something to be avoided. Thus, apart from kin, those who go into fostering other parents' children often do so for personal reasons, typically as a job or to meet their own emotional needs.

5 Public care and kinship care

When does kinship care become public care? Addressing this question is important because in many societies today, particularly in Western societies, children who need care away from their biological parents are cared for by the state. In the UK, for instance, local authorities are the primary state agencies charged with the duty to promote their development and welfare. In fulfilling their statutory duty towards these children, as mentioned earlier, local authorities either care for the children in residential settings or recruit and pay foster families to care for them. These children become state responsibility so that local authorities become involved even in the care of those who are cared for by relatives, such as grandparents, an uncle, an aunt or even an older brother or sister. There are other children cared for by relatives whose living arrangements are 'unknown' to local authorities. Since local authorities are not 'aware' of these arrangements, the caregivers do not receive any support from them, even though they perform the same care duties as professional foster-carers. This gives rise to a dichotomy of kinship foster care: formal (or public) and informal (or private) kinship foster care. This chapter examines the implications of this dichotomy for the children and families involved.

We saw in previous chapters that the placement of children with relatives and friends is among the oldest and commonest traditions in child-rearing; in most contemporary societies, it remains second nature. So, why is there so much fuss about kinship foster care in Western societies? Why, until recently, have childcare agencies and professionals been reluctant to promote and support this 'natural' form of childcare? For instance, in the UK, in a review of foster care, Berridge (1997, p. 78) commented: *'In the light of its success it seems curious that such arrangements (kinship foster care) are not common.'* Indeed, both researchers and childcare practitioners frequently describe the practice as a new phenomenon (e.g., Altshuler, 1998; Berrick *et al.*, 1994; Boada, 2007; Broad, 2004; Connolly, 2003; Dubowitz *et al.*, 1994; Everett, 1995; Farmer and Moyers, 2008; Flynn, 2002; Goodman *et al.*, 2004; Greeff, 1999; Hegar, 1999b; McFadden, 1998; Scannapieco and Hegar, 1999; Sykes *et al.*, 2002). Nonetheless, they acknowledge that, as an organized social service, there has been an exponential increase in kinship care in recent years.

In the USA, it is estimated that, on average, kinship care accounts for some 35 per cent of child placements (e.g., Berrick *et al.*, 1994; Hegar, 1999a, b; Winokur, *et al.*; 2005). In New Zealand, kinship care accounts for 32 per cent of placements (Connolly, 2003). In an international survey, Greeff (1999) reported that, although the UK was among those nations with the lowest proportion of kinship foster care, kinship care accounted for 23 per cent of all child placements. In subsequent surveys, this figure continues to rise (Broad, 2004). In Australia, Spence (2004) reported that, in 2003, 57 per cent of all indigenous children in care were in (formal) kinship care placements. Spence acknowledges that, as in other nations, there exist no official data on the number of children living with relatives informally. He claims, however, that it is generally believed that there are many more children in informal than there are in formal kinship care.

Reasons for kinship care

In spite of the apparent increase in kinship care in Western societies, it is still comparatively uncommon, relative to other societies. This is largely because it is considered out of the ordinary for children to spend any part of their childhood away from their biological parents. Thus, while acknowledging its emergence as a viable childcare arrangement, we must consider the impetus for it. Evidence indicates that kinship care has surfaced within a wider philosophical, policy and financial child welfare policy context (Greeff, 1999; McFadden, 1998). What precisely is this context? Put more plainly: What are the reasons for this change of attitude? Researchers have suggested several factors associated with the exponential increase in kinship foster care in Western societies, especially in the USA (e.g., Broad, 2004; Dubowitz *et al.*, 1994; Everett, 1995; McFadden, 1998; McFadden and Downs, 1995). These include the philosophy of family preservation, dwindling foster care resources, legislation and policy, an increase in parental substance misuse, and poor outcomes for children leaving care.

In Western societies, kinship care provides a safety net for a category of children in need. In support of inclusive fitness theory, grandparents, particularly maternal grandparents, occupy this role. In the USA, the 2000 census estimated that 2.4 million grandparents were responsible for most of the basic needs of their co-resident grandchildren (Goodman *et al.*, 2004). According to these researchers, grandparents typically assume care informally for children in response to the parent's needs or incapacity, particularly as a result of parental death, substance abuse, child neglect, mental instability, or financial need. In a study involving 373 grandparents who informally provided full-time care for their grandchildren and 208 grandparents awarded custody through the child welfare system (public kinship care) Goodman and colleagues examined the context in which kinship care takes place. In confirmation of McFadden's (1998) analysis, they found that public (formal) kinship caregivers were 2.7 times more likely to provide care as a response to crisis, because of parental drug use and almost 60 per cent more likely because of child neglect. Private or informal kinship caregivers, on the other hand, had provided care for a longer time and were more apt to share decision-making with the child's parent. However, a significant proportion of informal grandmother-caregivers (over 40%) assumed care because of parental drug use or neglect of their grandchild.

Concerning legislation and policy, these appear to be more explicit in some countries than in others. Nations reported to have explicit legislation and policy on kinship placement include: Poland (Stelmaszuk, 2006), the Netherlands (Strijker *et al.*, 2003), and also New Zealand (Atwool, 2006; Swain, 1995), Australia and Canada (Connolly, 2003) in relation to indigenous children. In the Netherlands, for example, Strijker and colleagues (2003) point out that, before the 1970s, kinship foster care was predominantly a family affair. Changing legislation has, however, resulted in a growing number of formal placements in kinship families. They report that in the most densely populated region of the Netherlands, kin provide 55 per cent of foster placements. Researchers have reported that, following the practices of indigenous Pacific Islanders, the government of New Zealand has established policies that include members of extended families in making decisions about a child's welfare (Atwool, 2006; Connolly, 2003; Swain, 1995).

When kin become strangers

The differentiation between public (or formal) and private (or informal) kinship foster care clearly indicates that there exist two forms of kinship care. The pertinent question is what is the difference between the two, given that the primary function of both forms of placement is to provide care and protection for a child? Put differently, given that kinship care has been an important childcare mechanism across cultures and for millennia, when or under what circumstances does kinship care become public care or stranger care (as it is commonly referred to in the UK)? This is tantamount to the question: When does a grandparent, an aunt, uncle, or even a sister or brother with whom the child is familiar, become a stranger? It is strange, as Everett (1995) has perceptively observed, that while kinship care has now become an integral part of the formal child welfare system, states and child welfare agencies continue to struggle where to draw the boundary between public responsibility and family duty.

Kinship care: definitions

Many may see ambiguity in the lack of a universal definition of kinship care. Basically, kinship care is any living arrangement whereby a relative or someone else familiar to the child (e.g., a friend, neighbour or godparent) takes primary responsibility for rearing or caring for that child. Kinship care, therefore, poses no conceptual ambiguity. Curiously, however, there is an unwarranted variability with respect to how this ancient and natural childcare mechanism is defined in modern Western societies. For example, the Child Welfare League of America (1994) defines kinship care somewhat ambiguously as the full-time care, nurturing and protection of a child by relatives. Consequently, according to investigators, for instance Connolly (2003) and Winokur and colleagues (2005), approximately half of the states in the USA define kin only as those related by blood, marriage or adoption, while others go beyond this to include family friends, neighbours and godparents. In the UK, the phrase in vogue is 'family and friends care'. This comes closer to the traditional understanding of kinship care, in that it offers a broader interpretation of who constitute kin. That is, it is inclusive of fictive kin – friends and neighbours. The alternative foster-care arrangement is termed 'stranger care'.

In bygone years, there was just one type of kinship care, a childcare arrangement between the birth parents and the foster-parents and the child (if older). This is still the case in traditional communities, including those (ethnic minorities) in Western nations (Berrick *et al.*, 1994; Broad, 2001a, b; Iglehart, 1994; Richards, 2001; Scannapieco, 1999). McFadden (1998), for example, points out that, besides African-Americans, other groups in the USA, such as American-Indians, Hispanics and Asians have extended family networks and multi-generational families that are instrumental in child-rearing. She highlights also that in Northern European nations, kinship care used to be the predominant childcare arrangement before industrialization and its accompanying social mobility, urbanization and immigration affected extended family structures (McFadden, 1998). To a lesser extent, kinship foster care is still evident in these regions.

In recent years, however, a new kind of kinship care has evolved in Western societies. The new type, often referred to as 'formal kinship care', has not supplanted the old type which is commonly referred to as 'informal kinship care'. Instead, they coexist. In both types of childcare, care is provided by kin. One may, therefore, wonder what actually distinguishes one from the other. McFadden (1998, pp. 14–15) tries to differentiate them:

> The term 'kinship care' may refer to the *informal family* arrangements which take place outside the child welfare system and the jurisdiction of the courts, or the *formal* arrangements which are arranged and approved by child welfare agencies following court adjudication of children as dependent or neglected.

In other words, formal kinship care is located within the public arena, while informal kinship care takes place in the private domain. As Scannapieco and Hegar (1999) highlight, the difference between the two types of kinship care is a legal matter; that is, it depends on who has legal custody of the child. Informal kinship care arrangements, on the other hand, are made privately between family members, and the children remain in the legal custody of their parents, though they are living with relatives. In plain language, formal kinship placement is care provided by relatives for a child who is in the legal custody of the state, and whose care is overseen by the state via welfare agencies. In this type of arrangement, children removed from the custody of their parents by the state, as a result of a complaint of abuse or neglect, are placed with kin in a supervised foster care arrangement (Gibbs and Müller, 2000).

In formal kinship care arrangements, custody is not transferred to the relatives who are looking after the child; rather, the state child welfare agency (in the UK, a local authority) assumes custody. As Greeff (1999, p. 1) defines it, formal kinship care *'is the situation where relatives or others who have a kin relationship with a child or young person are caring for a child in partnership with the state, and where social workers therefore play a key role'*. Broad (2001a, b) sees Greeff's definition as incomplete, in that it masks kin, particularly grandparents, who are caring for children under a residence order. Broad notes another important distinction between formal and informal kinship care, which is that kinship caregivers may not necessarily be 'approved' or 'licensed' as foster-carers and the placements may not be the subject of a formal fostering agreement, despite the involvement of the state.

What all this amounts to, in a nutshell, is that the distinction between the two forms of kinship care is a legal one. As such, as we will soon see, it has implications for the children as well as the caregivers. Nonetheless, outside the legal arena, from a theoretical perspective, the notion of socio-genealogical connectedness (Chapter 6) reinforces Tapsfield's (2001, p. 85) contention that kinship care is kinship care. Namely it *'is not a local authority service. Kinship care is a feature of the way in which families operate and can be supported and encouraged by local authorities, or it can be unsupported and undermined'*. A later section of this chapter considers the consequences of 'unsupported and undermined' kinship care for the children and the caregivers.

Legal and policy issues in kinship care

In situations where state child welfare agencies try to support kinship foster care, the tendency is to try to mould it around contemporary foster care, on care provided by a nuclear family (paid foster-carer) unknown to the child. This creates difficulties for all parties, the children, the caregivers and professionals (social workers). McFadden (1998, p. 9) aptly puts it: *'Trying to fit contemporary kinship care into the rigidly defined patterns of American policy on foster care might be compared to the proverbial attempt to put a "round peg into a square hole".'* In the context of the USA, her explanation for this state of affairs is that the historical development of the American child welfare system has been premised or based upon the use of non-relative foster care for children in need of care and protection. Hence, the notion of permanency planning has underpinned childcare generally. McFadden views permanency planning as a Western concept, a concept which includes the nature of foster care, the rights of parents in the nuclear family and the need for a secure legal status that will facilitate the child's transition out of the care system into adoption or return to the biological parents. She accepts the general perception that long-term stay in care or foster-care drift is languishing and so is considered an inferior permanency option. Nonetheless, like other investigators and commentators, she underscores the fact that many of the kin providing care for their young relatives plan to do so on a long-term basis and are willing to raise the child to adulthood, if need be.

Holtan (2008) is in agreement with McFadden that foster care, as a social welfare measure, is built on the model of the nuclear family, the objective of which is to ensure the wellbeing of children during childhood and to create rounded individuals capable of contributing to society. However, if kinship foster care does not fit into the contemporary foster-care model, then, how should it be provided? The answer seems to be in taking cognizance not only of the different ways in which the two types of foster family are constituted, but also of their dynamics. For example, Holtan stresses that kinship foster family and professional foster family are different in their features, that the professional foster family differs from the kinship foster family in several key ways, including: 1) the kinship foster family is characterized by permanent relationships, whereas the professional foster-home arrangement is temporary for the child; 2) the internal life of the kinship-foster family is private, whereas the professional foster-home arrangement is part of a public care provision; 3) whereas children generally have a life-long membership in the kinship network, those in professional foster care have a care contract with the child welfare agency. Many share Holtan's views (e.g., Mosek and Adler, 2001).

Holtan makes a further distinction between non-relative foster homes and kinship foster homes. She points out, for instance, that the former lack traditions, language, and models for how members perceive themselves as individuals and what they should mean to one another. In this child placement arrangement, a contract from a public authority gives associations linked with paid employment, so that, in effect, the family becomes a public employee. In kinship foster homes, in contrast, the children are emotionally tied to their kin, giving an association of obligations and solidarity. In this respect, Holtan is right in arguing that kinship thrives on cultural notions regarding solidarity, love, confidence and durability. She acknowledges, though, that the closest kinship ties (or relations) are negotiated in interactions connected with reproduction and upbringing which entail close contact over time with people with whom one lives. Thus, in line with the evolutionary psychological notion of inclusive fitness, concerning altruistic behaviour, she points out that kinship obligations pale with genealogical distance. This notion proposes that when kinship is based on an indirect or weak connection, the relationship becomes weaker and the basis for solidarity is weaker, as is the case with persons related by marriage and those with whom you have not lived. Without disagreeing with Holtan, this raises the question of how genetically close a person must be to qualify as kin for the purpose of providing foster care to a dependent relative. For example, should we consider a step-parent or a person with whom the child has a warm and close relationship for the task? The traditional sense of the concept suggests that we should.

Nevertheless, in most Western jurisdictions, regardless of genetic distance, no one but the genetic parents has parental rights or a say in decisions affecting a child. Grandparents and other close relatives have no legal rights regarding decisions affecting their young relatives. Typically, in child custody cases for instance, they are considered 'third parties' with no inherent rights to seek custody. So, as commentators (e.g., McFadden, 1998; Pitcher, 2002) have noted, many kinship caregivers find the potential threat posed by the foster-care system – in seeking termination of parental rights and placement of the children for adoption outside the kinship system, as mandated by a restricted reading of permanency planning – mystifying, upsetting, disempowering and emotionally debilitating. Grandparents believe that as family members and the ones closest to the child, *de facto*, they, and not the foster worker or courts, should be the decision-makers for the child's future. Most believe also that it is unnecessary (if not unnatural) for them to adopt (for permanency purposes) their grandchild whose parents are still alive (Beeman and Boisen 1999; Chipman *et al.*, 2002; Farmer and Moyers, 2008; McFadden, 1998; Pitcher, 2002; Sykes *et al.*, 2002). This is partly because, unlike non-relative foster-carers, kin have a pre-existing bond with children which is culturally sanctioned, naturally enduring and has its own existence independent of legal status. A grandmother expressed this natural belief and her frustration thus:

> This child is my grandchild now and forever. He calls me 'grandma', and I call him 'my baby'. I don't need a court to tell me what to do. I'll be here for him as long as he needs me. If some social worker tells me I have to adopt my own grandchild I'll tell her she's crazy. I'm his grandparent, not his parent. It would just confuse everything to pretend I'm his parent. We couldn't be any more 'permanent' than we are now. I don't want to take away my son's parental rights ...
>
> (in McFadden, 1998 p. 10)

Donner's (1999) Sikaiana informant would certainly share this grandparent's frustration and sentiments; so would many a grandparent in a similar situation anywhere.

In Scannapieco and Hegar's (1999) view, much of the confusion surrounding kinship foster care resides not just in its definition, but, more importantly, in how it is perceived or approached in policy and practice. They raise the question: '*How should formal kinship foster care differ from informal kinship foster care arranged by families themselves?*' (p. 5). This is analogous to the question raised previously: When does kinship care become stranger care? Scannapieco and Hegar raise further questions concerning such matters as selection, certification or approval, supervision and payment of kinship foster-parents, as well as about efforts to effect reunification of children with parents or to achieve other permanency plans. They stress that they raise these questions not to provide answers, but to add fuel to the debate and to acknowledge the dilemmas that practitioners face in trying to work with kinship foster families. Briefly, trying to fit kinship family (a square peg) into the nuclear family framework (a round hole) is fraught with many difficulties.

Scannapieco and Hegar try to deal with the question of when kinship foster care becomes stranger foster care or 'out-of-home care' by raising a further issue as to whether kinship foster care is childcare provided outside the extended family. In their view, the answer is straightforward:

> 'Kinship foster care is out-of-home care when the child is in court-ordered state custody; otherwise, it is a branch of services to children in their own homes, whether before state intervention in the parent-child relationship or after it (informal care, guardianship or adoption by relatives as part of permanency planning).'
>
> (Scannapieco and Hegar, 1999, p. 5)

Broad (2004) describes informal kinship care in a similar vein. He defines it as a full-time childcare arrangement known to social services and which is provided by a member of the child's extended family or a friend. The arrangements may be either initiated by social services or via a relative or friend, and involves some sort of assistance or arrangement, including making decisions about legal orders, financial and social work support.

However kinship care is defined, like Holtan (2008) and other writers, O'Brien (2000) stresses the need to appreciate kinship foster families' uniqueness. Without diminishing the importance of safeguarding the wellbeing of children placed with kin in the same manner as any other child in care, O'Brien contends that it is irrational to place kinship caregivers in the same category as non-relative foster-carers, as strangers, or to expect them to alter their pre-existing relationships with the child, for instance, through adoption. In other words, a kinship foster home is a family home, a natural home for the child to grow up in, particularly so when the child is living with his/her grandparents. To put it more strongly, a grandparent cannot be a stranger to his/her grandchild. There is abundant evidence that kin have an innate interest in the wellbeing of their children. As we will see later, in a large number of cases where children need protection from their parents, it is relatives or friends who put themselves forward as carers, even though they are often not considered by social workers as potential caregivers. O'Brien rightly emphasizes that although kinship caregivers want support with the task of parenting their relative's children, they do not see themselves as agency clients. Their self-perception is that of a relative who stepped in to provide care. This, notwithstanding, provides no justification for denying them financial support and services to carry out their childcare duties and responsibilities.

Kinship families: their characteristics and consequences for the children

> When the differences between kinship and foster care are aggregated, it is hard to escape concluding that a two-track system of substitute care is emerging in the United States ... Children in kinship care live in poverty or near-poverty, and lack adequate financial support from the state that assumed responsibility for their care.
>
> (Brown and Bailey-Etta, 1997, in Hegar, 1999a, p 234)

There exists ample evidence supporting this claim. Such evidence shows that kinship care, formal or informal, differs in several respects from non-relative foster care. Concerned researchers and practitioners have argued that these differences combine with inequalities and inflexibility of existing child welfare policies and practices which leave kinship foster-parents at a significant disadvantage relative to non-kin foster-parents.

'When one finger is sore, the whole arm hurts' (a Chinese proverb). The moral here is that whatever inequalities or disadvantages that kinship caregivers face directly and indirectly affect the children in various ways. We therefore require awareness and understanding of the characteristics or circumstances of kinship foster families in order to appreciate the effects of the added social inequalities they experience, in terms of financial assistance and services, on the children. Research from almost every Western nation shows that the differences and inequalities between non-relative and kinship foster families are stark and relate to the circumstances of the two types of foster family. The volume of the international literature concerning kinship foster care and the difficulties that face kinship foster families in Western nations precludes an exhaustive review. Thus, for the purposes of illustration, this section examines only a handful of evidence from the USA, the UK and Spain indicating the disparities between kinship caregivers and their non-relative counterparts.

The USA

Researchers and practitioners in the field will be familiar with USA research which, over the years, has consistently reported glaring disparities between kinship foster families and non-relative foster families, in terms of the characteristics of both the carers and the children (e.g., Beeman *et al.*, 2000; Berrick, 1997; Berrick, *et al.*, 1994; Dubowitz, *et al.*, 1993; Gibbs and Müller, 2000; Grogan-Kaylor, 2000; Hegar and Scannapieco, 1999; Iglehart, 1994; McFadden, 1998; Scannapieco and Jackson, 1996; Stack, 1974). Such research unanimously indicates that kinship care in the USA is predominantly provided by ethnic minority families, especially African-American families. It shows also that these families face several adversities, particularly social and economic adversities. Indeed, the inequalities and disadvantages that kinship foster families in the USA experience, *vis-à-vis* non-relative foster families, are glaring enough to prompt many researchers and practitioners alike to charge the public care system with racism. For instance, Gibbs and Müller (2000) argue that because African-American children are much more likely than all other children to be placed in formal kinship care, inequalities in policies and practices applied to kinship care are just a new system of the injustice and discrimination African-Americans have suffered within the child welfare system since its inception.

In the USA, kinship care is used predominantly by African-American families, because they regard it as essential for family preservation. In the 1960s and 1970s, many saw the African-American extended system as an irrefutable sign of inherent defect within those families. Following Stack (1974), however, researcher and child welfare professionals now seem to regard it as a positive way of valuing the strengths of families and maintaining cultural continuity. Moreover, they actively promote it as a family preservation strategy, though some argue that the current development of kinship foster care in the wider community was, to some extent, forced upon the public services, owing to a shortage of non-relative foster-care providers (e.g., Hegar, 1999b; McFadden, 1998; Scannapieco and Jackson, 1996).

Other differences between kinship foster-care providers and non-relative foster families relate to age, gender, education and employment. Internationally, the general profile of kinship caregivers is one of older women, predominantly maternal grandmothers and aunts who are caring alone. Studies consistently show that these women, grandmothers in particular, tend to be in poorer health, with fewer financial resources, fewer employment prospects and living in a poorer physical environment than other foster-carers. In an extensive review of the literature, Scannapieco (1999) found that women are the most frequent kinship caregivers, grandparents providing more than 50 per cent of the care. Aunts provide a further 30 per cent of kinship placements. These carers also receive lower levels of state support in the way of finance, training and social work visits (Berrick *et al.*, 1994; Dubowitz *et al.*, 1994; Gebel, 1996; Iglehart, 1994; Hayslip and Kaminski, 2005; Scannapieco, 1999).

Most of the studies briefly summarized above relate to kinship foster care in the USA. The remainder of this section examines some of the few studies carried out outside the USA. It concentrates on studies conducted in two separate Western European regions, the UK and Spain. Kinship foster care as a part of the public care system is a more recent development in Western Europe as a whole than it is in the USA.

Kinship foster families in the UK: their characteristics

In the UK, the 'official' phrase for children in the care system generally is 'children looked after', and the phrase for kinship foster care is 'family and friends' placement, while 'stranger foster care' is the phrase used to describe non-relative (or non-kin) foster family placement. Flynn (2002) reported that, in England, in the year ending March 2000, 6,300 'looked after' children and young people were cared for by kin, representing almost 11 per cent of all children looked after and over 16 per cent of those in foster placements. In Wales and Scotland, respectively, the percentages of those looked after by kin were 14.1 per cent and 9 per cent of all looked-after children. Researchers have noted the absence of national data regarding the profile of children in kinship foster care or the families who provide it. Nonetheless, a few studies have found the majority of carers to be maternal grandparents and aunts (e.g., Aldgate and McIntosh, 2006; Broad 2001 a, b; Farmer and Moyers, 2008; Pitcher, 2002; Sykes *et al*, 2002; Waterhouse, 2001).

Broad (1998) was among the first to carry out a specific and systematic study of kinship foster families in the UK, albeit on a comparatively small scale. Broad's initial study was conducted over a four-year period (between 1992 and 1996), and involved a London borough. It focused on 60 place-ments made with relatives or friends where none of the children had 'looked after' status, but the Borough Council (or local authority) was in some way involved in their care. The study found a different pattern of placement for non-Caucasian children and Caucasian children. Sixty-two per cent of the placements were with families of non-Caucasian origin, whereas only 27 per cent were with families of Caucasian origin; a further 11 per cent of the families were classified as 'other'. Specifically, 31 per cent of the children were of African-Caribbean or Guyanese origin; 31 per cent were of other non-Caucasian origins (mainly Chinese and South Asian families); and 27 per cent were of English, Welsh or Scottish origin. Broad reported that the local authority statistics for 1997 also showed that 33 per cent of black children (not defined) were placed with extended families, compared with 24 per cent cared for by the local authority.

Broad suggests that his findings imply favourable use of relative care, since it kept children out of the 'looked after' system and with their families. However, he is quick to point out that a number of interpretations could be made of the statistics and that they need further exploring. One interpretation he offers is that black families are being deliberately or unwittingly encour-aged to provide this kind of care, but are at the same time being denied other services or the kinds of support offered to non-relative carers in the way indicated by US research. Broad argues that this would be a negative finding, assuming that to be the case. Significantly, the caregivers also described feel-ings of isolation and a need for increased financial support (Broad, 2001a).

Broad's findings (1998, 2001a, b) are reinforced by a more recent study by Farmer and Moyers (2008). In Farmer and Moyers' study, the carers who were experiencing the greatest financial hardship were those who had in the first place agreed or were compelled by circumstances to take in the child of a relative or friend informally, that is, without social services involvement. In these cases, social services took the view that the children were not their responsibility and so refused financial assistance and services when the carer later requested help. One such case involved a grandmother who was caring for her three granddaughters, due to their mother's drug dependency and resultant incarceration. Social services refused to assist this caregiver, although it was blatantly obvious that she could not cope financially.

Another study by Richards (2001) obtained information through questionnaires and focus groups comprised of six African-Caribbean grandparents, 30 Chinese grandparents, 11 Pakistani, and 38 Indian Sikh and Gujarati Hindu grandparents. The grandparents were caring in a range of circumstances and for various reasons. Among other findings, Richards reported that African-Caribbean and Caucasian grandparents were predominantly caring for their grandchildren following family crises, and the children were under care or residence orders with them. In contrast to the African-Caribbean and Caucasian grandparents, none of the Chinese and South Asian grandparents had been involved in court proceedings at all. Rather, they were caring for their grandchildren to enable their parents, their own children, to work, or because it was an expected part of their role, a cultural norm.

Like Broad (2001a), Richards points out that on the surface, this could look like a very good case of keeping children out of the public care system, but it could also easily reinforce the stereotype of 'they look after their own' and that these families therefore have no need of public services. On the contrary, a closer look at the findings reveals unmet needs in respect of both the carers and the children. For instance, the grandparents were generally older and in poor health. Many of them reported difficulties in accessing support for their health and practical needs predominantly due to lack of understanding of agency functions and 'language barriers'. These grandparent-caregivers stated that they would use social services and other support systems, if they could access them. Richards found that many of these caregivers, regardless of ethnicity, had no support outside the immediate family and that this was negatively affecting their ability to care for the children on a long-term basis.

Still in the UK, Sykes and colleagues (2002) tested the hypothesis suggested by international research that although kinship foster-care providers are a valued resource, they are less supported by agencies than non-relative foster families are. This large-scale study was carried out in seven local authorities in England: two London boroughs, a metropolitan district council, two shire counties and two unitary authorities (city councils). Using postal questionnaires, the investigators collected data from 944 foster-parents. The results showed that the kinship foster-parents were socio-economically more disadvantaged than the non-relative foster-carers. In keeping with international research findings, significantly fewer kinship-carers were educated beyond compulsory education – 67 per cent and 36 per cent of kinship carers and non-relative carers respectively had no educational or professional qualification. They were also much more likely to have partners, but their partners were more likely to be unemployed (43% and 20% respectively). In terms of family support, twice as many kinship foster families reported receiving no support from immediate family.

Sykes and colleagues recognize the striking similarities between their findings and those from the USA. In both the USA and the UK, foster-children come from disadvantaged groups; and those who are cared for by relatives are doubly disadvantaged by the fact that, as research suggests, kinship foster-carers are more disadvantaged than unrelated foster-carers. In Sykes and colleagues' study, kinship carers appeared to have lower levels of formal education and were much less likely to have an adult partner who was in paid employment than non-relative foster carers were. On average, fostering appeared to have a greater impact on the financial and housing situations of these carers than it did on non-relative foster-carers. Despite these difficulties, as in the USA, they received, on average, less training, lower levels of financial assistance and less back-up from social services than non-relative foster families did.

Nonetheless, Sykes and colleagues found that the kinship foster-carers in their study differed in three ways from those in the USA, and also those in Broad's (1998, 2001a, b) study: 1) they were not more likely than non-relative carers to come from ethnic minority backgrounds; 2) they were not, on average, older than non-relative carers; and 3) they were not likely to be lone parents, though their partners were more likely to be unemployed. Still, Sykes and colleagues suggest that kinship foster-parents should be seen as comprising a heterogeneous group, not just with regard to their demographic characteristics, but also in terms of their needs and wishes. For example, they found that while some wanted to be treated as carers, as providers of a public service, and therefore entitled to similar levels of financial reward and also in need of training, others saw social services involvement as 'intrusive' and regarded themselves as qualified by experience to care for their young relatives. Sykes and colleagues found that, regardless of their feelings towards social services (child welfare agencies), and despite their limited financial resources, as a group, kinship carers were willing to continue to care for their young relatives without monetary compensation, reinforcing Silk's argument.

It needs stressing that kinship carers' willingness to care for their kin without financial reward does not mean that they should be taken for granted, nor does it mean that they should not be supported as fully as possible to enable them to provide adequate care for the children. As other researchers have pointed out, agencies should recognize the heterogeneity of kinship carers, so that, as a group, they require careful assessment, training opportunities, authoritative back-up, flexibility in practical and emotional support, and fairness in financial compensation (Broad, 2001a, b; Farmer and Moyers, 2008; Pitcher, 2002). There appears to be reluctance on the part of agencies to acknowledge this obvious fact. In this respect, as in other respects, the UK is similar to the USA. Although (formal) kinship foster-parents are subjected to the same regulations as unrelated foster-carers are (Berridge, 1997; Hunt, 2003), this in many situations masks the reality in terms of practice. In other words, as Hunt (2003) and several others have stressed, there is evidence of a two-tier system. In actuality, there exists a three-tier system: a system that treats non-relative, formal and informal foster families differentially.

Spain

Boada (2007) underscores the embeddedness of kinship foster care in Spanish culture. He points out that when children need care away from their biological parents for whatever reason – parental death, illness, abuse or neglect – the tradition has been for relatives to assume responsibility for raising them. He points out also that, until very recently, the decision to keep the child in the extended family has always been a private rather than a public one. In other words, as in other Western societies, kinship foster care in the formal sense, as part of the childcare system, is a recent phenomenon in Spain. According to Boada, this new development dates back only about 20 years. He emphasizes also that kinship foster care is now being promoted by state child welfare agencies as a valuable, but scarce, resource alongside residential childcare and non-relative foster care. He recognizes that, in Spain, as elsewhere, social factors have contributed to the promotion of the tradition of kinship care as a valuable public service. These factors include the rapid decline in the number of non-relative foster-care families available.

Despite being a firm institution in Spanish culture, kinship care in Spain today bears striking resemblance to kinship care in other Western societies. That is, the characteristics of both the recipients and providers of kinship care in Spain parallel those of their counterparts in other Western nations, notably the UK and the USA. Boada (2007) and Montserrat and Casas (2006) independently provide evidence for this suggestion. Boada carried out a study in Catalonia and the city of Barcelona. It involved a total of 6,152 children and young people for whom the General Directorate of Child and Adolescent Care was responsible. Of these, 34.9 per cent were in the care of their extended family, just 8 per cent were in non-kinship foster care, and 25 per cent were cared for in residential settings. These represent a total of some 4,177 children who were cared for away from their birth parents. Regarding kinship care, the 117 families were made up of 183 caregivers and 153 children not younger than eight years old.

The results revealed that the characteristics of the caregivers and the circumstances under which they assumed care duties were analogous to their peers elsewhere. Half of the fostering cases dated back to the birth of the child or during the first few months of the child's life. The principal reason for fostering was the parents' drug dependency, including alcohol misuse. As regards the children, their commonest experience was that of neglect. Like other studies in the field, the study found that the majority (63%) of the caregivers were predominantly maternal relatives, mainly grandparents (73.5%), followed by aunts and uncles (18%).

In 70 per cent of all the cases, the proposal for caring for the child formally was initiated by the extended family. The caregivers fell into more or less the same age category as that reported by other studies: their mean age was 56.72 years and ranged from 46 years to 65 years. In terms of socio-economic status, half of the caregivers had only primary education, and 18 per cent had no formal education at all. Almost half of the households were headed by a lone parent – lone women – who tended to be advanced in years. In 60 per cent of the households, there was no caregiver who was employed outside the home, and in 76 per cent of the families, financial help was required from the child welfare agency in order to make ends meet. In highlighting the implications of his findings, Boada draws particular attention to the lack of support, in terms of policy as well as resources, for kinship foster-care families. Indeed, he stresses that formal kinship foster care is currently provided in an extemporary manner. Farmer and Moyers (2008) made a similar observation in their study of kinship foster care in England.

Boada's study parallels an earlier longitudinal research by Montserrat and Casas (2006) not only in terms of its findings, but also as regards the characteristics of the families involved in formal kinship foster care in Spain. Unsurprisingly, they emphasized the paucity of financial assistance, support and training they received from child welfare agencies. In spite of the difficulties facing them and the lack of assistance and support from the child welfare authorities, a number of the grandparents highlighted the sense of meaning in life that they had while caring for a grandchild or a nephew and the satisfaction with helping a child.

To summarize international research, kinship foster-care providers and the children in their care tend to live in far less auspicious circumstances than do other families, including non-relative foster families. Typically, reinforcing the paternity uncertainty hypothesis, they are female (maternal grandmothers and aunts), older and experience age-related health problems. Additionally, they tend to have less education, and consequently less financial resources, and to live in less desirable accommodation in less desirable areas, especially those in urban areas. In essence, as evidence suggests, kinship foster families in Western societies constitute a neglected social group. In the case of those children who were 'rescued' because of parental abuse or neglect, this represents a double whammy. What an irony that is!

In their conclusion of the evidence of the many socio-economic and demographic difficulties facing kinship foster families, and the lack of financial support and services for these families, Scannapieco and Hegar (1999, p. 9) raise serious concerns about the existence of a two-tiered (or three-tiered) and segregated child welfare system. They emphasize their concern with the question: '*Is kinship foster care the newest way to leave society ... to care for their own willing but poorly resourced extended families and communities?*' The answer to this question lies not just with policy- and decision-makers; it lies with society at large.

Needs, support and services

One of the arguments advanced in this book is that kinship foster care is an ancient practice and, as such, rooted in the culture of every human society. In other words, there is nothing novel about grandparents, aunts, uncles, older siblings and other relatives, friends or neighbours assuming responsibility for children when their parents are unable to care for them. Nevertheless, in contemporary Western societies, the practice is generally perceived not just as a new phenomenon, but rather as an anomaly. Although kinship care is gaining currency among childcare agencies and professionals, it is not placed on a par with 'professional' (or non-relative) foster care. In order to be recognized and valued as a childcare resource, kinship care has to be formalized or 'legalized'. This has created two spurious types of kinship foster care: formal kinship care and informal kinship care. The legal or policy distinction between the two is that in the former type of arrangement, although relatives are looking after the child, the child welfare system has legal custody of the child. The child is in the custody of the state because welfare authorities have removed him/her from his/her biological parents. In informal kinship care, on the other hand, child welfare agencies have 'no' involvement in the care of the child, because often it was relatives, instead of the state, who removed the child from his/her parents for the same or similar reasons.

This contrived split entails adverse implications not only for the children, but also for their caregivers, particularly with regard to financial assistance and services. As we have seen from the literature summarized above, kinship foster-care families across Western nations are socially disadvantaged *vis-à-vis* non-relative foster families. The disadvantages they face are further compounded by the discriminatory treatment they receive from the child welfare system as a whole (Benedict *et al.*, 1994; Berrick *et al.*, 1994; Boada, 2007; Connolly, 2003; Courtney, 1994; Dubowitz, *et al.*, 1994; Hayslip and Kaminski, 2005; Hegar and Scannapieco, 1999; Iglehart, 1994; McFadden, 1998; Schwartz, 2002). It is an irony that financial assistance and other support and services provided by child welfare agencies are skewed against kinship caregivers; evidence shows that they have greater needs than non-relative foster-care families. These needs relate not just to their age-related ill-health, but also to their limited financial resources. Although kinship caregivers within the formal foster-care system generally have fewer financial resources than foster-parents, many receive significantly lower rate of payment or nothing at all.

Exacerbating the situation further for them is the fact that, despite their increased needs, kinship foster families and the children frequently do not receive the services and financial benefits to which they are entitled. McFadden (1998), among many others, calls attention to this fact. Besides financial assistance, she underlines kinship caregivers' need for a wide range of support and services, such as medical care, adequate accommodation, transport, respite care and so forth to enable them to better care for their young charges. That is, they are aware that the children have unmet needs and are concerned about how to access services to meet the children's needs. McFadden stresses that, although informal kinship caregivers have similar (if not the same) needs to their formal counterparts, their circumstances are less favourable. Since they fall outside the mainstream care system, they often receive neither financial assistance nor support or services from child welfare agencies. This state of affairs seriously undermines their efforts to provide adequate care for the children.

Effects on the children

In kinship care, the child's relationship with his/her caregiver is umbilical, so that the caregiver's adverse socio-economic circumstances and other characteristics directly affect the child, especially in material terms. Scannapieco and Hegar (1999, p. 5) straightforwardly ask: *'Should children in kinship foster care live in poverty?'* As the literature reviewed so far suggests, kinship caregivers differ substantially in their characteristics from unrelated foster-parents. To reiterate, they are likely to be older women; socio-economically, they are less likely to be married or employed outside the home, and more likely to have lower educational attainment, and, consequently, are poorer, compared to unrelated foster-care parents. Indeed, many rely for their own support on state benefits (Broad, 2001a, b; Scannapieco and Hegar, 1999; Sykes *et al.*, 2002).

In short, international research overwhelmingly shows that not only are kinship foster families less financially well off, but also they receive fewer services from child welfare agencies, relative to unrelated foster-parents. This suggests that the children's needs are unlikely to be fully met. This has prompted many to conclude that the caregivers who are most in need are the least likely to receive adequate financial support when they take kin's children into their homes. Scannapieco and Hegar (1999) point out the paradox in addressing the financial needs of children in kinship care and their caregivers. Namely, the children can obtain an adequate standard of living *only* if they are removed from their parents' custody, an action that often results in the severance of the child's contact with his/her parents and extended family, a consequence which the system, paradoxically, claims to seek to avoid.

Some solutions

Hegar (1999a) has suggested three things which could prevent kinship foster care from being the most residual feature of the already residual child welfare system: 1) the role of the state in safeguarding the rights of parents, children, and relatives who provide kinship foster care; 2) adequate state funding; and 3) state oversight to ensure quality of care and provide supportive services. Likewise, Hunt (2003) and other researchers have identified the provision of the following as a means to rectify this unfair situation: greater access to social work services; assistance with costs; the guarantee of initial start-up funding; respite care; housing needs assistance; transport assistance; improved information, advice and advocacy; networking opportunities (e.g., grandparent groups); mentoring; childcare training; children's support group; assistance for birth parents and help with birth parent-kinship carer relationship; and enabling responses from services underpinned by a family strengths perspective and an overall valuing of the family. It stands to reason that carrying out these and other suggestions would improve the circumstances of kinship families and thereby enhance the social, behavioural and psychological functioning of the children. The resultant benefits to society would likewise be noticeable.

6 Public care versus kinship care
Psychosocial developmental outcomes

Evidence intimately linking the public care system with negative psychosocial developmental outcomes is firmly established. Both research and anecdotal evidence suggests that, compared to children cared for by their biological parents, those in public care exhibit an array of developmental difficulties: emotional and mental health problems, identity problems, behavioural, relationship, educational difficulties and so forth. There is also evidence that the influence of the care system on developmental outcomes is not uniform across placement settings. This chapter discusses traditional theoretical explanations for the children's vulnerability. It also discusses professional interventions derived from these theories that attempt to help these children to surmount those difficulties. The chapter further discusses the limitations of these theories and interventions. It then presents the new theory of socio-genealogical connectedness. This new theory compliments existing developmental theories, notably attachment theory, and contributes towards a fuller understanding of these children's difficulties. A better understanding of their developmental difficulties is needed in order to design effective interventions to deal with those problems, and to promote the children's growth, development and life chances.

Mental health

The commonest negative developmental outcomes associated with the care system relate to mental health symptoms, including anxiety, depression and conduct disorder. Internationally, epidemiological data suggest that 29–96 per cent of children in care experience one or more mental disorders (Brand and Brinich, 1999; Clausen *et al.*, 1998; Dubowitz *et al.*, 1993; Ford *et al.*, 2007; Garland *et al.*, 2003; Hill and Thompson, 2003; McCarthy *et al.*, 2003; McMillen *et al.*, 2005; Meltzer *et al.*, 2003; Rubin *et al.*, 2007; Simms *et al.*, 2000; Stanley *et al.*, 2005; Stein *et al.*, 1996; Tarren-Sweeney and Hazell, 2006; Tweedle, 2007). For example, in the UK, Meltzer and colleagues (2003) conducted a national survey of the mental health of children and young persons (5–17-years old) in the public care system in England. The survey involved 2,500 children and adolescents randomly selected from national data. It concentrated on the three most common groups of childhood mental disorders: 1) emotional disorders such as anxiety, depression and obsessions; 2) hyperactivity disorders; and 3) conduct disorders characterized by awkward, troublesome, aggressive and antisocial behaviours. In this study, 45 per cent of the children and young persons were assessed as having a mental disorder, including those who displayed more than one type of disorder. Thirty-seven per cent of these were assessed as having clinically significant conduct disorders, while 12 per cent were assessed as having emotional disorders.

Among other findings, further analysis revealed that the 5–10-year-olds among the sample were about five times more likely to have a mental disorder (42%) compared to their peers in the general population (8%). Similarly, the 11–15-year-olds were four to five times (49%) more likely to have a mental disorder. Genderwise, the proportion of children and adolescents with a mental disorder was greater among boys (49%) than girls (39%). Later national surveys conducted in Scotland and Wales reported very similar findings to those of the English survey (Meltzer *et al.*, 2004a, b).

In a more recent study, Ford and colleagues (2007) examined the relationship between socio-demographic characteristics, type of placement and psychopathology. They compared a sample of 1,453 children in the British public care system with 10,428 children growing up outside the system. The results showed that children in care had higher levels of not only psychopathology, but also educational difficulties and neuro-developmental disorders. The analysis indicated also that being in care was independently associated with nearly all types of psychiatric disorder after adjusting for these educational and physical factors. The prevalence of psychiatric disorder among the former group was particularly high among those living in residential care and those with many recent changes of placement. In their conclusion, Ford and colleagues draw attention to their finding that less than 10 per cent of their in-care sample had positively good mental health; in other words, more than 90 per cent of them had mental health problems. They emphasize also that the substantially increased prevalence of psychiatric disorder was partially explained by the fact that the children had also experienced particularly high levels of psychosocial and educational adversity. However, there was also a strong association between psychiatric disorder and care-related variables.

It goes without saying that the mental health problems which children in the public care system commonly experience have ramifications for other domains of their functioning, particularly their behaviour or interpersonal relationships and academic performance. Almost every study that has examined the effects of the care system, like other forms of childhood separation, on the developmental outcomes has identified these domains of functioning as particularly problematic for the children involved (e.g., Barth, 1990; Beck, 2006; Berrick *et al.*, 1994; Brand and Brinich, 1999; Courtney *et al.*, 2005; Dubowitz *et al.*, 1993; Elliot, 2002; Gilligan, 2007; Iglehart, 1994; Knight *et al.*, 2006; McCarthy *et al.*, 2003; Meltzer *et al.*, 2003; Rubin *et al.*, 2007;

Tweedle, 2007; Trout *et al.*, 2008; Vinnerljung *et al.*, 2005). Frequently, it is the children's behavioural problems (internalizing and externalizing behaviour) that signal their mental health and educational needs. The children's behavioural problems range from noncompliance, antisocial behaviour – stealing, lying, smoking, drug/alcohol misuse, absconding, promiscuity, prostitution, teenage parenthood to self-harm and suicidal attempts (Coy, 2008; Cusick, 2002; Gallagher, 1999; Knight *et al.*, 2006; Richardson and Goughin, 2002; Simms *et al.*, 2000; Sinclair and Gibbs, 1998; Wolkind and Rutter, 1973). Research has also identified their challenging behaviour as a clear predictor of placement instability (e.g., McCarthy *et al.*, 2003; Rubin *et al.*, 2007).

Educational problems

Given the myriad mental health problems as well as the behavioural difficulties that children in care experience, it is not surprising that, compared with children living with their biological families, their educational attainments fall below par, as international research suggests (e.g., Barth, 1990; Courtney *et al.*, 2001; Dubowitz *et al.*, 1993; Elliot, 2002; Gallagher, 1999; Gilligan, 2007; McCarthy *et al.*, 2003; McMillen *et al.*, 2003; Meltzer *et al* 2003; Rubin *et al.*, 2007; Trout *et al.* 2008; Vinnerljung *et al.*, 2005). For example, a UK national survey by Gallagher (1999) reported that a worrying 75 per cent of young people left care without educational qualifications. More recent surveys show that the attainments of young people in the British public care system have not much improved (e.g., Gilligan, 2007; Meltzer *et al.*, 2003, 2004a, b; Russell and Taylor, 2005; Simon and Owen, 2006). Simon and Owen (2006) compared the academic achievements of children and young people in care in England and Wales to those of their peers in the general population. The analysis revealed that although most young people (16-year-olds) in these countries take their General Certificate of Secondary Education examination, only just over a half of those in care did so. In his review of the literature, Gilligan (2007) points out that some 54 per cent of young people aged 16 and over who had ceased to be in care in the year ending 2003 had no educational qualification, and only 8.7 per cent of youngsters in care had attained an average or above average standard of academic success.

Other European studies have reported similar findings. In Sweden, for example, Vinnerljung and colleagues (2005) examined the scholastic attainments of young people who had had experience of the pubic care system – residential or foster care. Using national data for nearly 800,000 Swedish-born young people in eight national birth cohorts, the investigators compared a total of 31,355 public care alumni with 744, 425 who had not been through the care system. The results showed that, compared to their peers from similar socio-economic backgrounds who had no experience of the care system, children who entered care before adolescence or had been in long-term stable foster care had a two- to threefold elevated relative risk of entering adult life with only a compulsory education. Youth who entered care during adolescence had approximately a fourfold risk of having only basic education. Their community peers from similar backgrounds were between two and six times more likely to have a postsecondary education.

Western European findings mirror those reported by North American studies (e.g., Barth, 1990; Courtney *et al.*, 2001, 2004, 2005; Flynn and Biro, 1998; McMillen *et al.*, 2003; Trout *et al.*, 2008). In the USA, Courtney and colleagues (2005) compared the scholastic attainments of 603 19-year-olds who had left (or were leaving) care with those of 502 19-year-olds from the nationally representative National Longitudinal Study of Adolescent Health. The results showed that over a third (> 33%) of the care group had no high school Graduate Equivalency Diploma, compared to less than 10 per cent of their peers in the general population (in Gilligan, 2007, pp. 137–8). In a previous analysis, Courtney *et al.*'s (2004) team, based at the Chicago Public School System, found that most of the youth in care had high educational aspirations; the majority of those interviewed (aged 17–18 years) hoped and expected to graduate from college eventually. The reality, however, was that a large number of them were experiencing significant academic failure and would almost certainly fall far short of meeting their goals. Courtney concluded that academic, emotional and behavioural difficulties clearly stand in the way of school success for children in care.

Prior and subsequent research and reviews have reached similar conclusions (e.g., Elliot, 2002; McMillen *et al.*, 2003; Trout *et al.*, 2008). For instance, McMillen and colleagues (2003) detail the school experiences of 262 youth referred for independent living preparation from the foster-care system of one Midwestern US county. Of the youth, 73 per cent had been suspended at least once since seventh grade, and 16 per cent had been expelled. In the previous year, 58 per cent had failed a class, and 29 per cent had had physical fights with students. Those in residential care and family settings often had school problems. Yet, the group reported high educational aspirations: 70 per cent wanted to attend college. To provide a favourable school environment for children in care, in order to improve their academic performance, the authors called for a system of education advocates who work to maintain appropriate education placements for youth in foster care and help them receive the academic resources they need.

In a more recent and extensive review of the literature, Trout and colleagues (2008) conducted a quality-assurance exercise on the published research concerning the academic and school functioning behaviours of children in care. They examined: a) the characteristics of the children and youth involved in the reported studies; b) the academic and school functioning areas evaluated by the studies; c) reports of overall academic performance; and d) the quality of each reported study. Their analysis showed that, overall, children in care exhibit several academic risks across placement settings and academic areas. Trout and co-authors identified truancy, grade retention and multiple placements among the factors that contribute to the poor academic performance of the public care population.

Long-term effects

Research suggests also that the negative consequences of being in care do not disappear on attaining adulthood. In other words, the care system is also associated with adverse adult socio-economic, educational, legal and health outcomes in excess of those associated with adult disadvantages generally (Anderson, 1999; Barth, 1990; Coy, 2008; Dumaret *et al*, 1997; Gallagher, 1999; McMillen, *et al.*, 2005; Simms *et al.*, 2000; Taylor, 2005; Wolkind and Rutter, 1973). One such survey (Gallagher, 1999) found that, apart from the high proportion of young people leaving care without educational qualifications; 50 per cent faced chronic unemployment; 20 per cent became homeless shortly after leaving care; 17 per cent of the young females soon got pregnant or were already mothers when they left. More recent surveys reinforce Gallagher's findings (e.g., ONS, 2006; Russell and Taylor, 2005).

In a longitudinal study, Russell and Taylor (2005) examined the adult socio-economic, educational, social and mental health outcomes of being in public care in childhood by following the 1970 British birth cohort at ages five, ten and 30. Cases were defined as those who had at any time been in statutory or voluntary public care at five, ten, and 16 years of age. Using these criteria, they identified a total of 343 cases. Categories of self-reported adult outcomes were occupation, educational achievement, general health and psychological morbidity, history of homelessness, school exclusion and convictions. Controlling for socio-economic status, the results showed that men with a history of public care were less likely to attain high social status, more likely to have been homeless, have a conviction, have psychological morbidity, and to be in poor general health. Similar associations were found in women. However, men, but not women with a history of care, were more likely to be unemployed and less likely to attain a higher degree. The results showed also that being non-Caucasian, regardless of gender, was particularly associated with poor adult outcomes of being in care. Russell and Taylor's firm conclusion is that public care in childhood is associated with adverse adult socio-economic, educational, legal and health outcomes in excess of that associated with childhood or adult disadvantages.

In all the domains of functioning discussed above, research has consistently identified male gender as an additional risk factor (Gallagher, 1999; Rutter, 1991, 1994, 2000; Simms *et al.*, 2000; Tarren-Sweeney and Hazell, 2006; Wolkind and Rutter, 1973; Zuravin *et al.*, 1999). However, an area where women who grew up in the care system are at greater risk is prostitution or commercial sex. Based on her examination of the literature concerning commercial sex as well as her long experience as residential social worker in a therapeutic children's home for young women (12–17-year-olds), Coy (2008) claims that women and young women who grew up (or are growing up) in public care are at particular risk of falling victim to the sex industry. Besides UK research, she cites several studies from other Western nations, for example, Canada, the USA and Australia, to support her claim. Her examination of such studies suggests that, in Western countries, women with public care backgrounds are overrepresented in and outside the sex industry. In other words, public care alumnae are highly vulnerable to sexual exploitation in the sex industry.

Coy attributes their shared patterns of vulnerability to their negative experiences of the care system, especially multiple placements. She quotes a 21-year-old informant: *'The only reason I'm out on the street now is cos I was in care. They let you down. They say they are gonna do that and they're not'* (p. 1414). A 19-year-old informant explained her life on the street: *'I never got nothing, no money, so I had to turn to the game ... because of the life I've been through, it is all I could turn to'* (p. 1414). Briefly, all the women in Coy's study, aged between 17 and 33 years, had backgrounds of public care and involvement in the sex industry. The length of time they spent in care varied from 18 months to 16 years. In Coy's view, the women saw being in care as the primary focus that shaped their lives and, crucially, linked events and emotions of their care experiences in a way that suggests that being in care itself plays a role in the path to prostitution.

Placement type: kinship versus non-relative foster care

That the public care system is intimately associated with adverse psychosocial developmental outcomes is well documented. Historically, the system (residential care and foster care) has been closely linked with negative developmental outcomes (e.g., Bowlby, 1944, 1969, 1973; Goldfarb, 1943; Robertson and Robertson, 1971; Shants, 1964; Spitz, 1945; Tizard and Hodges, 1978; Tizard and Rees, 1975). Various studies show also that not only are the undesirable effects of the care system on children, such as poor parenting skills, child abuse, substance abuse and homelessness enduring, but also they are generationally transmitted (Bowlby, 1973; Coy, 2008; Lataianu, 2003; Quinton and Rutter, 1984). A contentious issue relates to the type of placement that may either compound or ameliorate the children's difficulties. For a proper understanding of the children's social, emotional and psychological difficulties, and in order to better help them, it is essential to address this and related questions, particularly in view of the fact that not every child who experiences public care is adversely affected by it, or is unable to surmount those adversities.

The literature suggests that the developmental problems associated with being in care vary by type of placement (Anderson, 1999; Berridge, 1994; Holtan, *et al.*, 2005; Sallnäs *et al.*, 2004; Tarren-Sweeney and Hazel, 2006; Tizard and Hodges, 1978). In the UK, for example, a series of national surveys of children growing up in the care system (Meltzer *et al.*, 2003, 2004a, b) reported that 39 per cent of those who were living with foster families had emotional problems; 46 per cent of those living independently had emotional problems, while 56 per cent of those in residential care had emotional problems, compared with children living with their biological families (28%). Considering that not all foster-parents (and biological parents for that matter) seek appropriate medical or mental health services for their children, estimates of mental health problems among children in foster care may be best regarded as conservative.

Children are vulnerable in all placement settings. However, virtually every study that has examined the developmental outcomes for children in residential care and those in foster care has reported worse outcomes for those living in residential settings than for those living with foster families (e.g., Anderson, 1999; Berridge, 1994; Dubowitz *et al.*, 1994; Hukkanen *et al.*, 1999; Hussey and Guo, 2002; Jackson, 1994; Keller, *et al.*, 2001; Little *et al.*, 2005; Sallnäs *et al.*, 2004; Tizard *et al.*, 1971; Tizard and Hodges, 1978; Vorria *et al.*, 1998). It is recognized that, because of their previous negative experiences, most children enter the care system having already developed emotional problems or are at greater risk of developing them while in care. Nonetheless, being in care is likely to aggravate or worsen, rather than improve, those difficulties. Thus, finding the right care option, the setting most likely to alleviate the child's difficulties, a placement most suited to promoting the child's overall growth and development, thereby improving his/her life chances, becomes paramount.

Clearly, foster family placement is preferable to residential placement; nevertheless, evidence shows that psychological and behavioural problems are more common among children cared for by strangers than those cared for by relatives. For example, Rowe (1984) reported that children fostered by relatives fared better in virtually all aspects of functioning than those fostered by strangers. Still, studies that have directly compared the wellbeing of these two groups of children remain rare. In fact, Holtan and colleagues (2005) highlight the absence of such studies from the European literature. The few that have been done elsewhere, predominantly in the USA, tend to report somewhat conflicting findings. In the main, though, they tend to support Rowe's claim; they suggest that children in kinship care fare better compared with children in non-relative foster care (Aldgate and McIntosh, 2006; Berrick *et al.*, 1994; Courtney, 1995; Cuddeback, 2004; Dubowitz and Sawyer, 1994; Dubowitz *et al.* 1993; Everett, 1995; Greeff, 1999; Hayslip and Kaminski, 2005; Iglehart, 1994; Jendrek, 1993; Landsverk *et al.*, 1996; McFadden, 1998; Simms *et al.*, 2000; Solomon and Marx, 1995). The following section summarizes a handful of recent studies and reviews in this area.

A Norwegian study by Holtan and colleagues (2005), using Achenbach's (1991) Child Behaviour Check List (CBCL), compared child psychiatric problems and placement characteristics of children living in kinship and non-kinship foster care. The sample comprised 214 children, aged 4–13 years old. Data were obtained on 110 kinship foster-children and 89 non-relative foster-children. The children's foster-parents completed the questionnaires. The results revealed that, of the non-kinship group, 51.8 per cent scored above the borderline on the CBCL Total Problem score, while only 35.8 per cent of the kinship group did so. On the Total Competence and School Competence scale, the kinship foster children scored significantly higher than the non-kinship group and lower on the CBCL scales for Total Problems, Withdrawn Behaviour, Social Problems, Attention Problems and Delinquent Behavior. In both groups, however, boys in both kinship and non-relative foster care scored significantly lower than girls on Total Competence, School Competence and Social Competence and higher on all CBCL scales except for Somatic Complaints, Anxiety/Depressed Behavior and Sex Problems.

The researchers attributed the better mental health status of the children in kinship foster care to the fact that they had fewer previous placements, were more often fostered in their community and had more contact with their biological parents. Several studies have reported significant associations between these variables and positive placement outcomes, in terms of placement stability as well as the children's wellbeing (Berridge and Cleaver, 1987; Rowe, 1984; Solomon and Marx, 1995; Tarren-Sweeney and Hazell, 2006). On the basis of their findings and examination of the literature, Holtan and colleagues recommend placement in kinship foster care above other placement options.

In New South Wales, Australia, Tarren-Sweeney and Hazell (2006) conducted an epidemiological study that compared children in non-relative foster care and those in kinship foster care on measures of mental health and social competence. The placement of both groups of children was court-ordered. This study also employed the Child Behavior Check List, and involved a total of 314 children, aged between four and nine years. The results indicated that, in comparison with their peers in the general population, both groups fared far less well on the measures of interest: mental health and social competence. The prevalence of emotional disturbance and behavioural difficulties among the children was found to be in excess of all prior estimates. However, considering type of placement, rates of disturbance for children in kinship care were high, but within the acceptable range of previous estimates.

Tarren-Sweeney and Hazell's results suggested that there were clinically meaningful differences between the two groups of children. In their discussion of the results, they ask: '*What then might account for the differences between these groups?*' (p. 95). They see the children's current placement settings as the obvious explanatory factor. They argue that growing up within one's extended biological family is a protective factor that mitigates the children's past family adversities, as well as providing them with a protective experience, '*possibly for reasons to do with identity formation and familial bonding*' (Tarren-Sweeney and Hazell, 2006, p. 95). In the investigators' view, kinship care protects children from developing attachment problems and other developmental problems, independent of their exposure to other pre-care and in-care risk factors. In their conclusion, Tarren-Sweeney and Hazell rightly point out, in relation to mental health service delivery, the complexity of the mental health problems facing children in care. They also highlight our poor understanding of those problems. The next section of this book discusses an alternative explanation for the observed differences.

These investigators claim that although the psychopathology of children in care is complex and poorly understood, its core features include disturbances in attachment behaviour. They argue further that for many of these children, disturbances in self-concept and relationships capacity are intertwined with their experiences of anxiety and depression, and with their defiant and aggressive behaviour. They highlight that, despite the complexity of the children's difficulties, interventions are typically based around the construct of discreet disorders, rather than a complex biopsychological phenomenon. '*Hence, we see children in care referred to multiple clinical services, leading to multiple (and in some cases conflicting) diagnoses, and being offered treatments that address discreet set of symptoms*' (Tarren-Sweeney and Hazell, 2006, p. 96). That is to say, because of our limited grasp of these children's difficulties, clinicians often provide inappropriate (and sometimes dangerous) solutions to these problems, including medication.

It was pointed out earlier that research comparing the effects of the two major forms of foster care is scant. However, while some such research tends to report favourable findings for kinship care, other studies report, at best, only tentative findings. A study by Strijker and colleagues (2003) provides an example from the Netherlands where, until the 1970s, kinship foster care was an informal (traditional) childcare practice. Among the hypotheses derived from the literature that the study tested was the assumption that children in kinship foster care function more optimally, in comparison with children in non-relative foster care. It examined also the family dynamics and profile of both types of foster families. Both parents and caseworkers completed questionnaires for the purpose of this study. No statistically significant differences were found between the two types of foster families on all the variables measured. In other words, the results provided no support for the proposition that kinship foster care is superior to non-relative foster care.

Given the serious misgivings expressed by many concerning the characteristics and qualifications of kinship caregivers, and the efficacy of kinship care as an alternative to non-relative foster care, the scarcity of research comparing adult outcomes of kinship placement and non-relative placement is remarkable; it is curious that 'serious' researchers have not jumped into the ring to settle the score, as it were. For instance, Simms (1991) argues that in spite of its ideological appeal in terms of stability and continuity for the child, kinship placement is likely to compromise the quality of care the child receives. Dubowitz and colleagues (1993, p. 154) argue more forcefully against kinship placement: '... *children are being placed with close relatives in the same families that have reared a parent now deemed unable to care for the child.*'

One of the few studies that has compared the adult wellbeing of formal kinship foster care and non-relative foster care alumni was carried out by Benedict and colleagues (1996). The study was conducted in Baltimore, USA, and explored associations between these types of placement and selected outcomes in adulthood. The 214 participants, aged between 19 and 31, were foster-care alumni. Fifty-five per cent of the total sample was female and predominantly African-American (87%). Forty per cent of them had been cared for mainly by kin. The median length of time they spent in care was 12 years. Social services records showed significant differences in the participants' functioning while in care. That is, there were differences between the children in kinship care and those in non-relative family foster care.

It was, therefore, hypothesized that those who were cared for by kin should be faring better in adulthood than those who were cared for by strangers. Through self-report questionnaires, the participants provided information on their current functioning, including education and employment, physical and mental health, stresses and supports, and risk-taking behaviours. The result showed that, although the social services records reported significant differences in functioning while in care, only a few differences remained between groups in the adult outcomes studied. In young adulthood, both groups were functioning similarly in their current lives in terms of education, current employment, physical and mental health, risk-taking behaviours, and the stresses and supports in their lives.

In view of previous studies suggesting that children in kinship care fare better than those in non-relative placement, Benedict and colleagues (1996) drew only a tentative conclusion from their findings. They explained their inconclusive findings in definitional and methodological terms. For instance, they suspected that their definition of kinship care failed to capture the essence of that experience as compared to the non-relative experience. Acknowledging that, it may be suggested that, conceptually, exploring the participant's placement experiences as well as their relationship with their birth parents or relatives while in care and out of care might have yielded more conclusive results.

Zuravin and colleagues (1999) considered these factors in their critique of the literature concerning the consequences of kinship care versus non-relative care for adult wellbeing. The main aim of the study was to assess adult quality of life of former children who grew up in kinship care and those who grew up in non-relative foster families. The studies reviewed together examined a wide range of adult characteristics. In the interest of simplicity, Zuravin and colleagues divided those variables into four categories: 1) adult self-sufficiency (education, employment and economic wellbeing, housing); 2) behavioural adjustment (criminality and substance use); 3) family and social support (marriage and cohabitation rates and outcomes, parenting outcomes, family support, and general social support); and 4) personal wellbeing (physical health, mental health and life satisfaction).

Summarized, their results regarding education, employment, homelessness, criminality and mental health showed that:

- for the majority of former foster-children, educational accomplishment was below that of comparison group members (the general population);
- males appeared to have higher rates of unemployment than comparison group members, and for many former foster-children, employment was low-paid jobs;
- for males in particular, arrest and conviction rates were higher than those for the general population;
- a vast majority of the studies that examined mental health found former foster-children to be doing quite a bit worse than their comparison group counterparts.

Regarding self-sufficiency, the findings with regard to former kin and non-relative foster-children suggest a consistent pattern of poor self-sufficiency for the non-relative subjects compared to the kin-care subjects. Zuravin and associates (1999) found that former non-relative foster-care children were more likely to have been homeless, and their current material levels of living were lower than those of the comparison group. In the domain of family and social support, the analysis revealed no clear differences between the two groups. However, the scale tilted somewhat in favour of non-relative foster care; the results showed that the former kin-care foster-children might have been more socially isolated than their non-relative care counterparts; they had fewer close friends and belonged to significantly fewer voluntary groups than their comparisons. Regarding family support, they were not significantly more likely to be co-habiting than living in a legally sanctioned relationship.

Zuravin and colleagues reached a fairly clear conclusion in support of kinship care. They also made explicit suggestions with regard to policy, especially service provision, and future research. For future research, they presaged Tarren-Sweeney and Hazell's (2006) concern and urged that research should seek to address the question: '*What accounts for the variation in functioning seen among former foster children?*' (p. 221). Although research concerning the impact of kinship care versus non-relative care on adult overall wellbeing is scarce, and the findings of the very few done are tentative, on the whole, the literature indicates that there are significant differences in their impact on child, adolescent and adult functioning. Thus, the next section conceptually pursues the important and related questions raised by Tarren-Sweeney and Hazell and Zuramin and colleagues.

Both the clinical and professional literature is replete with evidence indicating clearly the detrimental effects of the public care system on the children within it. Nevertheless, what research has not provided, so far, is a full answer to the question concerning why the care system has such negative effects. An equally important question is what is needed to alleviate the problems of those children who are damaged or whose problems are worsened by being in care. Full answers to these questions will be helpful in guiding us towards finding means for avoiding those problems and, where they cannot be avoided, towards designing efficacious interventions to alleviate them.

Psychological explanations

Attachment theory and interventions

Clinically, the quest for answers to the questions raised above seems to have been begun by pioneers in the field of child psychopathology (e.g., Bowlby, 1944, 1969, 1973; Goldfarb, 1943; Spitz, 1945). Of these pioneers, it is Bowlby's ideas concerning separation and loss, popularly termed 'maternal deprivation' or attachment theory, that continue to exert a profound and global influence on research, childcare policies, professional practice and child-rearing practices. Bowlby employed the term 'attachment' essentially to characterize the unique relationship between an infant or child and his/her mother or primary caregiver.

Attachment theory postulates that humans, particularly infants and young children, have an innate proclivity to seek proximity to others, especially the primary caregiver (in most cases, the mother) for their survival. In the context of the present work, the most pertinent aspects of attachment theory are its emphasis on the relationship between the 'mother'-child dyad and mental health; and the notion of internal working models. Attachment theory posits that the nature of the 'mother'-child relationship is the determining factor in the child's present and future mental health and interpersonal relationships. Indeed, Bowlby (1969) argued that failure to form a secure attachment or an affectional bond in childhood invariably renders an individual particularly vulnerable to psychiatric or emotional disorders. He attributed failure to achieve this to negative experiences, a disturbance of bonding in childhood. He therefore recommended it as a guideline for the routine management of individuals with psychiatric or mental health needs. This suggests that, from infancy and throughout the life cycle, an individual's mental health is cast in his/her attachment relationships.

Many investigators (e.g., Bretherton and Munholland, 1999; Howe, 1995; Rutter and O'Connor, 1999; Zimmerman, 1999) agree with Bowlby's (1969, 1973, 1980) claim that attachment theory accentuates the central role of relationships in mental health and psychological functioning. According to Bowlby (1969, 1988), infants whose early needs are fully met form secure attachment to their caregivers. It is the foundation for trust that is essential for forming relationships throughout life. Thus, children who lack the experience of loving relationships with parents and, so, lack trust (often the case of many children in care) may be unable to establish healthy relationships with new caregivers. For the child to achieve optimum attachment, Bowlby, in his initial formulations of attachment theory, claimed that certain ingredients must be present in the mother-infant/child relationship; that is, 'mothering' or care-giving must occur under certain conditions. The infant/child must experience a loving, warm relationship, an unbroken relationship that provides adequate stimulation, and in which the mothering is provided by one person (usually the mother), and in which mothering occurs in the child's own home.

These conditions mean that attachment develops through being cared for and responded to continuously, consistently and positively by the attachment-figure. This is believed to enable the child to develop adaptive internal working models or internal representation of the attachment-figure, the firm belief that the caregiver will always be available to appease and comfort him/her for all time. Owusu-Bempah (2007) has suggested that 'an unbroken relationship' and 'mothering in own home' imply temporal continuity and spatial continuity respectively. He suggests further that, together, these notions may be conceived as genealogical (or familial), cultural and ethnic continuity or connection, as opposed to the narrow meaning traditionally attached to these concepts.

Bowlby saw the main function of internal working models as to enable the person to develop foresight and plan his/her life and organize his/her behaviour accordingly. In other words, as Bretherton (1991) and Howe (1995) argue, the models help children to understand how others perceive them, how they view themselves, how they might perceive others, and how the relationship between self and others might best be interpreted. '*Once the inner working models become established, they are increasingly likely to define social experience rather than be defined by social experience*' (Howe, 1995, p. 71). This means that the type of internal working models, steady or shaky, that a child develops in infancy and childhood forms the template for later relationships, and determines how they may be maintained or modified. Namely, one's internal working model shapes one's expectations about new relationships and, consequently, one's behaviour within them. In other words, the child generalizes his/her early experiences to later relationships and social situations. The type and quality of the working models which children develop of their attachment-figures are believed to exercise a profound and lasting influence on their future, and on their relationships throughout the rest of their lives.

A further feature of attachment theory which Rutter and O'Connor (1999) highlight is that it distinguishes between attachment and other components of relationships. [Main (1999) draws our special attention to this]. That is to say, attachment does not constitute the whole of relationships. This aspect of the theory, Rutter and O'Connor point out, later became overlooked or neglected owing to the theory's success and its unquestioning adoption by enthusiasts or zealots. Other writers have made a similar observation (Arredondo and Edwards, 2000). According to Rutter and O'Connor, '*What is special about attachment theory, in this respect, is that it offered a* compelling explanation *for the feelings associated with the "trauma" of separation and loss – fear, anxiety, anger, sadness, and despair – and for their disruptive effects on personality development*' (pp. 824–5, emphasis added). This may be so, but how much farther does it go? This is one of the key questions that this book seeks to address.

It is not the purpose of this book to provide a comprehensive critique of attachment theory and its enduring and pervasive influence on clinical research and practice, notably psychiatry and psychotherapy. Suffice to say that the literature in this area is sated with suggestions that childhood separation or maladaptive attachment, or maladaptive working models, is implicated in almost every mental disorder. So much so that both the *Diagnostic and Statistical Manual of Mental Disorders* (DMS-IV, American Psychiatric Association, 1994) and *International Statistical Classification of Diseases and Related Health Problems* (ICD-10, WHO, 1992) include attachment disorders of childhood in their classification systems. Consequently, since its inception, it has influenced child-rearing practice, research, childcare policy and professional practice worldwide.

Psychological interventions

The literature, as we have seen, shows that a large number of children in foster care have histories of adversity and display higher rates of behavioural and emotional difficulties, relative to their counterparts in the community. It indicates also that, in many cases, these problems do not dissipate on reaching adulthood. Rather, leaving care exposes them to significant risk of unemployment, homelessness, chronic mental health problems, unplanned pregnancies, substance abuse, antisocial behaviours, criminality and so forth. In other words, on leaving care, they are faced with a 'double whammy'; that is, the difficulties they had in adjusting to placement continue to influence their adult lives such that they experience difficulties in adjusting to life post-care.

There exists a wide range of psychological intervention models designed to help these children and youngsters 'adjust' to placement and, hence, to mitigate their past and current traumatic experiences, such as disruption of attachment to biological parents; neglect and/or abuse; disruption of placement and accompanying need to adjust to a new foster-care environment. Racusin and colleagues (2005) have grouped the predominant models into two broad categories: 1) those which focus on treatment for symptoms in the child; and 2) those which manipulate systems (agencies, services, etc.) to effect interventions. The first include behavioural, cognitive-behavioural, and attachment-based therapies. Of these, Racusin and colleagues describe attachment-based approaches as the most conceptually appealing to therapists and social workers because the target of intervention is the child, and not the system. Typically, the target of intervention is the child's putative disturbed attachment relationship with his/her biological parent(s). This is presumed to be at the root of the child's emotional and behavioural difficulties, often described in the clinical literature as 'attachment disorder'. (For a detailed discussion, see, e.g., Barth *et al.*, 2005; O'Connor and Zeanah, 2003; Racusin *et al.*, 2005; van IJzendoorn *et al.*, 1995.) Attachment disorder is a generic term for a whole range of psychosocial developmental problems associated with adoption and fostering.

To reiterate, attachment theory emphasizes the potential risk of childhood separation and experiences of multiple or transient caregivers; it stresses the importance of warm relationships with attachment-figures in infancy and childhood to personality development. It emphasizes also the risk of prolonged disruptions of the child–attachment-figure relationship to the child's emotional wellbeing and adult mental health. Consequently, child-care professionals frequently use attachment concepts not just to explain the mental health and other developmental difficulties that children in care experience, but also to design and use attachment-based interventions in efforts to help them to surmount their early negative experiences (e.g., Barth *et al.*, 2005; Cairns, 2002; Dozier, 2003; Howe and Fearnley, 1999). Despite the exponential popularity of attachment-based approaches, many researchers and writers claim that there is very little empirical support for them (Barth *et al.*, 2005; O'Connor and Zeanah, 2003; Racusin *et al.*, 2005; van IJzendoorn *et al.*, 1995; Zeanah *et al.*, 2002). Still, in dealing with the emotional, behavioural difficulties and other problems that children in care exhibit, attachment theory appears to be dazzlingly irresistible not only to childcare professionals but also to family lawyers and courts (Arredondo and Edwards, 2000). Rocco-Briggs (2008), a psychotherapist with long experience of working with children in the care system, confirms Arredondo and Edwards' observation. She reports that child welfare agencies (social services) frequently refer children placed '*with foster families for individual therapy with an expectation that, by offering the child psychotherapy, the child's overt difficulties will disappear*' (p. 197). Namely, those involved with these children habitually try to understand and address their difficulties by resorting to attachment concepts, and often recommend psychotherapy for them.

Under the attachment therapy umbrella are a range of approaches. Nonetheless, as many have argued, they all tend to see the child as the primary target of clinical intervention; they see the child as suffering from attachment disorder. Evidence suggests that, among fostering and adoption workers and parents, holding therapy, which is claimed to be attachment-based, appears to be the currently favoured treatment for attachment disorder (Barth *et al.*, 2005; Cairns, 2002; Dozier, 2003; Howe (1995); O'Connor and Zeanah, 2003; Racusin *et al.*, 2005; van IJzendoorn *et al.*, 1995). Such evidence shows that the use of holding therapy goes beyond fostering and adoption. For example, a Finnish study by Sourander and colleagues (2002) found that, of the treatment models for child and adolescent inpatients, including medication, holding therapy was the treatment method used in 26 per cent of cases, especially with those under 13 years old, those with attachment disorder and those with autism.

Bowlby (1969, 1988) emphasized infants' need for a secure base through having their needs fully met by their primary caregivers. He described this as the bedrock upon which later relationships are founded. This implies that children who lack the experience of loving relationships with their parents (a frequent pre-placement experience) may be unable to establish healthy relationships with new caregivers. Holding therapy is essentially based upon this idea; the assumption that the children have an unmet emotional need, a pent-up rage, as a consequence of their earlier negative relationship experiences, and that this hinders their formation of trusting relationships. The core objective of therapy, therefore, is to teach the child that the new caregivers are trustworthy, reliable, loving and caring parents. The following section summarizes reviews expressing misgivings about attachment-based therapies with adopted and foster-children.

Limitations

Various investigators and childcare professionals have expressed concern and scepticism about attachment-based therapies for adopted children and children in care on theoretical, therapeutic and ethical grounds (Arredondo and Edwards, 2000; Barth *et al.*, 2005; Belsky, 2006; Dozier, 2003; Eagle, 1994; Green, 2003; Leiberman and Zeanah, 1999; Mercer, 2001; O'Connor and Zeanah, 2003; Owusu-Bempah, 2007; Sroufe *et al.*, 1999, 2006; van IJzendoorn *et al.*, 1995; Zeanah *et al.*, 2002). Theoretically, Barth and colleagues (2005), for example, have argued that the scientific base of attachment theory is limited both in terms of its ability to predict future behaviours and its use as the underpinning theory for therapeutic intervention with children experiencing conduct problems. Hence, they call for a critical examination of the role of attachment theory in child and family services and highlight the need to consider its place among other explanation for children's disturbing behaviour.

Sroufe and colleagues provide a succinct summary of attachment theory's limitations in predicting and explaining childhood psychopathology:

> Early experience does not cause later pathology in a linear way; yet it has special significance due to the complex, systemic, transactional nature of development. Prior history is part of present context, playing a role in selection, engagement, and interpretation of subsequent experience and in the use of available environmental supports. Finally, except in extreme cases, early anxious attachment is not a direct cause of psychopathology but is an initiator of pathways probabilistically associated with later pathology.
>
> (Sroufe *et al.*, 1999, p. 1)

Sroufe and colleagues go on to point out that studies have found little or no evidence of a link between psychological problems in older adopted children and insecure attachment relationships in infancy. They argue, therefore, that higher rates of psychological and academic problems among adopted children cannot be traced to insecure attachment patterns between adoptive mothers and children in infancy; and that attachment theory cannot be used with any confidence to predict how children will develop over longer periods of time. Hence, Sroufe and colleagues (2006) counsel attachment researchers to be the first to acknowledge that early attachment experiences are not (and should not be) related to any and all outcomes. Owusu-Bempah (2007; Owusu-Bempah and Howitt, 1997) concurs with Sroufe and colleagues in arguing that attachment theory does not provide a be-all and end-all explanation for the mental health and other problems facing separated children, such as adopted children and those fostered.

Regarding the efficacy and ethics of attachment-based interventions, a number of researchers and professionals have clearly expressed their misgivings about these approaches, especially holding therapy (e.g., Barth *et al.*, 2005; Dozier, 2003; Mercer, 2001; O'Connor and Zeanah, 2003; van IJzendoorn *et al.*, 1995; Zeanah *et al.*, 2002). For example, O'Connor and Zeanah (2003), in their detailed and well-considered review of the theoretical and clinical literature, argue that, among other concerns, there exists no consensus or protocol for assessing attachment disorder or related symptoms. As such, there exists no accepted treatment for children with attachment disorders. They question also the empirical and ethical basis of such interventions; they claim that no treatments have been shown to be effective for children with attachment disorders. Mercer (2001) also points out that there is little evidence of the usefulness of the treatment.

O'Connor and Zeanah emphasize their doubts about the efficacy and appropriateness of interventions derived from attachment theory by drawing our attention to the adoption literature suggesting that attachment disorder behaviours persists, even following adoption into stable, loving and caring families for a period of many years. Thus, they stress that, in line with existing clinical, ethical standards and other considerations, psychological interventions for children with attachment disorders should be advanced only when they are evidence-based. Barth and colleagues (2005) have similarly warned: *'There is a risk that adoption workers will miss out on new developments because of their immersion in attachment language and concepts. This appears to be excluding them and their clients from benefiting from a wider range of theories and approaches to treatment'* (Barth *et al.*, 2005, p. 265). This echoes Rutter's (1991) warning regarding our overzealousness about attachment concepts.

Summary

The foregoing discussion raises two contentious, but important, matters:

- Attachment theory provides an incomplete explanation for separated children's poor developmental outcomes.
- Accordingly, attachment-based interventions are inefficacious or limited in solving the problems of separation and loss associated with fostering and adoption.

Hence, some researchers and professionals (e.g., Arredondo and Edwards, 2000; Barth *et al.* 2005; Owusu-Bempah, 2006, 2007; Owusu-Bempah and

Howitt, 1997) have called for a fresh perspective. Arredondo and Edwards (2000, p. 110) summarize the rationale for this call: *'Attachment and bonding have evolved as concepts that focus on security-seeking ... to the relative seclusion of other critically important aspects of human relationships in the context of development.'* They argue that we need to accept that children can, do and should have relationships with more than one caregiver or sets of caregivers, in order to consider dyadic relationships in terms that go beyond attachment concepts, and also to consider social systems that extend beyond dyads. Owusu-Bempah (2006, 2007; Owusu-Bempah and Howitt, 1997) advances a similar argument; that attachment theorists, researchers and practitioners tend to overemphasize the dyadic nature of relationships, to the virtual exclusion of the wider system of relatedness which is an essential building block of family, kin and personal identity. Namely, the notion of attachment principally refers to the security- or proximity-seeking aspects of a child's relationship to a caregiver. It does not pay sufficient attention to the wider context in which the child's developmental needs are met.

Over fifty years ago, Spitz (1945) concluded from his observations of institutionalized children that providing only for a child's physical needs is not sufficient for normal development. Although, most foster families in contemporary western societies seek to provide for more than just the physical needs of children in their care, in most circumstances, especially in non-kin placements, they are unable to meet the children's need for a sense of connectedness or continuity and personal identity. The next section presents the notion of socio-genealogical connectedness. It is the kind of new perspective which some (e.g., Arrendendo and Edwards, 2000; Belsky, 2006; Miller, 1999) have requested.

Socio-genealogical connectedness: a new perspective

> Where the resemblance and continuity are no longer felt, the sense of personal identity goes too.
>
> (William James, 1890, p. 335)

Given the claim that attachment theory, the dominant theory in this field, provides only a partial explanation for the difficulties facing children in care, the basis of their vulnerability remains unclear. Since not all children in care are damaged, and many succeed extremely well, even though they enter care from similar family backgrounds and with a similar history of adversities (e.g., Bebbington and Miles, 1989; Simms *et al.*, 2000), it is important to pinpoint the characteristics of high-risk children. That is, we need to go beyond attachment concepts for a fuller understanding of their vulnerability, in order to develop new theories and approaches that will benefit child welfare workers and these youngsters and their families (biological and foster). This requires a shift of focus, that we must expand our conceptual horizon.

The idea of socio-genealogical connectedness offers such a focus; it is a novel approach proposed to compliment attachment theory in order to develop a deeper insight into the developmental needs of these children, and thereby promote their growth and development.

In an earlier book, Owusu-Bempah (2007) considered the developmental difficulties facing separated children – children of lone-parent families, adopted children and the offspring of donor insemination – from this perspective. A common and principal characteristic of children separated from kith and kin is either the severance of their socio-genealogical roots or diluteness of their sense of connectedness. From this perspective, the principal objective of the present book is to address the following important questions:

- Why does the public childcare system have negative effects on children, given that neither the historical nor contemporary anthropological literature (reviewed above) documents any link between fostering and developmental problems, such as mental health and behavioural difficulties?
- In Western societies, the literature indicates disparate outcomes between children in kinship care and those in non-relative foster care. What factors explain this disparity?

The next chapter employs the notion of socio-genealogical connectedness to address these questions. Meanwhile, the following section summarizes the main assumptions upon which the idea is based. (See Owusu-Bempah, 2007 for detailed discussion.)

Socio-genealogical connectedness: assumptions

This new idea proposes that a sense of socio-genealogical connectedness is an essential factor in children's adjustment to separation, and forms the basis of their emotional and mental health and, consequently, their sense of completeness. More specifically, socio-genealogical connectedness refers to our ability and willingness to accept and integrate our biological, social, cultural and ethnic roots. In other words, the notion relates to the extent of our knowledge about our hereditary origins and the degree to which we internalize or assimilate that knowledge. It concerns one's knowledge of, and belief in, one's genetic and cultural heritage and the role this information plays in one's general wellbeing.

Socio-genealogical connectedness postulates that our psychological integrity depends very much upon the degree to which we identify with our origins, how firmly we feel linked to our genealogical chain. As such, it seeks to address questions related to our self-concept or personal identity. It tries to deal with such important fostering and adoption-related questions as those raised by Tizard and Phoenix (1989): for example whether adopted or fostered children's internal working models of their social parents are affected by the knowledge that they are not their genetic parents; and, if so, how this, in turn, affects the meaning of their 'relationship' with the biological parents they have never seen, or rarely see.

Theoretically, as some have pointed out, a person may choose either to accept and incorporate or to reject socio-genealogical knowledge (e.g., Carsten, 2007, Giddens, 1991; Owusu-Bempah, 2007; Owusu-Bempah and Howitt, 1997). If the information is favourable, the person is likely to accept it. Conversely, if it is damaging or threatening to the self, the person may try to reject it, at a psychological cost. However much a person may wish to reject it, complete denial of parental information is not easy to achieve. As Carsten (2007) and Triseliotis (1973), for example, have highlighted, the process operates very much at an unconscious level, so that it is still possible for the individual to incorporate it to an extent without his/her knowing or being conscious of it. In other words, *'however successful the person's efforts may be to repress that knowledge, it is very likely to come to the fore, however fleetingly, at some stages in his/her life – at random moments in the day'* (Carsten, 2007, p. 406). This is likely to happen especially in times of crisis (Baran and Pannor, 1993; Erikson, 1968; Triseliotis, 1973).

Hypotheses

With respect to children specifically, socio-genealogical connectedness concerns the extent to which they integrate (or are allowed to integrate) into their inner worlds their parents' biological, cultural and social backgrounds; it relates to the degree to which a child sees herself or himself as an offshoot of his or her biological parents' backgrounds. It is based upon the following tested assumptions (see Owusu-Bempah, 1995, 2007; Owusu-Bempah and Howitt, 1997, 2000a):

• The quantity and/or quality of information children possess about their biological parents determines the degree to which they integrate the parents' backgrounds and ancestral roots.
• Children who possess adequate and favourable information about their biological parents have a deep sense of connectedness.
• Conversely, children who possess no, or inadequate, or damaging information about their parents are less likely to integrate it and, therefore, have a shallow sense of connectedness.
• Children who have a deep sense of connectedness are better adjusted than those who have no or only a shallow sense of connectedness.

These assumptions suggest that socio-genealogical connectedness is about one's self-identity: one's self-worth, one's sense of psychological wholeness and one's mental health. It follows, therefore, that the potent driving force behind all human activities is the need and quest for self-knowledge, the need to know who one is; to be able to answer questions directly related to 'self': 'Who am I?' 'What am I?' 'Whence did I come?' 'Where do I belong?' Regarding psychological functioning, the main functions of a sense of socio-genealogical connectedness, therefore, concern one's general wellbeing: self-identity, mental health, and sense of psychological wholeness.

Owusu-Bempah (2007) has contrasted this notion with established developmental theories: psychoanalytic theory, learning theory, Erikson's psychosocial developmental theory and Bowlby's attachment theory. Particular emphasis was placed on attachment theory. To summarize some of the distinctive features between socio-genealogical connectedness and attachment theory, attachment theory hypothesizes that if specific attachments are to develop with respect to individual persons, those persons must have actual or face-to-face contact with the child over a prolonged period of time on the grounds that the development of attachment is a long-term process. Socio-genealogical connectedness, on the other hand, does not construe physical presence or actual contact as a prerequisite for a child's sense of being linked to his/her biological parents or relatives. Socio-genealogical knowledge, the amount and/or quality of it, does not have to be provided directly by the parents themselves. For example, in an extended family or a traditional collective community, such as those described in Chapter 2, where linkage is usually to the whole group or clan rather than to biological parents solely, the child's interpersonal relationships transcend the immediate family. Thus, the information the child requires to achieve a sense of connectedness, relatedness or belonging and identity is more or less public property, it is readily available through the extended family and the community as a whole.

Another distinction between attachment theory and the notion of socio-genealogical connectedness relates to bond, a central concept within attachment theory. Ainsworth (1989) describes attachment bond as distinct from attachment behaviour. While the latter relates to (physical) proximity-seeking to the attachment-figure, Ainsworth sees the former as a time-enduring affectional tie. She stresses that an attachment bond is not restricted to any two specific individuals, but rather a characteristic of the individual, *'entailing representation in the internal organization of the individual'* (Ainsworth, 1989, p. 711). This suggests that a child can develop an attachment to another person who does not or cannot reciprocate; thus the existence of bonds cannot be inferred from the presence or absence of attachment behaviour (Fahlberg, 1991). Similarly, attachment bond is considered to exist consistently over time, whether or not attachment behaviour is present (Ainsworth, 1989; Baran and Pannor, 1993; Fahlberg, 1991). A clear conclusion from these two propositions is that children can feel consistently and over time psychologically or emotionally close to and a part of a person, even a parent from whom they are separated, as in fostering or even through death. Rutter (1991) came to a similar conclusion in suggesting that separation need not involve bond disruption, so that the two should not be regarded as synonymous. He decries the taken-for-granted belief that separation per se has detrimental effects. He points out that this belief has for a long time distracted researchers from other factors that may be intrinsic in separation. He stresses that separation may or may not be harmful depending on its effects on bonds and on attachment behaviour.

Granted, the psychosocial mechanisms involved in children's adjustment to separation and loss are complex. It is one of the principal objectives of this book to shed some light on this theoretically thorny question in relation to fostering. It seeks to address the apparent paradox of a bond or affectional tie that a child may develop not only to an abusive parent or a parent from whom they are separated. Briefly, it is a sound proposition that the strength of the bond between a foster-child and his/her genetic parents, or the child's yearning for the parent(s) may weaken over a long period of separation. Nevertheless, it would be fatuous to conclude from this that the psychological significance of the parent(s) to the child dissipates completely.

In his incisive critique of Bowlby's notion of 'maternal deprivation', Rutter (1991) argues also that the average child must separate from his/her parents sometime in their lives if they are to develop independent personalities. For him, therefore, the question is not whether children should separate from their parents, but rather when and the manner in which separation should occur. He reinforces this by drawing attention to research findings showing that certain sorts of happy separation may actually protect young children from the adverse effects of later stressful separation. We will see instances of this in the next chapter. From a socio-genealogical connectedness perspective, and following Rutter's suggestion and the literature reviewed in the preceding chapters, the next chapter examines two types of separation: 1) separation with loss – non-kinship foster care, and 2) separation with or without minimal loss – kinship foster care.

In Western societies, the seat of attachment theory, children are born into a nuclear family and are expected to form attachment or bonds exclusively with their parents. In other cultures, in contrast, children are born into and treasured, treated as valuable, and shared by the extended family and the community as a whole. Hence, the meaning of attachment or bonding is very different; bonding is seen as taking place between a child and multiple members of the extended family and, oftentimes, beyond. Thus, it may be argued that it is misleading and unhelpful to concentrate on relationships between two people (mother and child), ignoring the socio-cultural milieu in which development occurs (Belsky, 2006; Bronfenbrenner, 1979, 1992; Owusu-Bempah, 2007; Valsiner, 2000). Bronfenbrenner (1992) stresses that the developmental setting depends on the extent to which third parties present in the setting support or undermine the activities of those actually engaged in interaction with the developing child. As we saw in Chapter 2, in terms of internal working models of relationships, a key concept in attachment theory, in traditional societies, the child develops an inclusive internal representation, working models that transcend the parent-child dyad. The socialization process encourages the child to believe in the dependability and trustworthiness of kin and the community as whole. Belsky reinforces Bronfenbrenner's position:

> An ecological perspective on human development ... which underscores the fact that the parent-child dyad is embedded in a family system, which is itself embedded in a community, a cultural, and even historical context suggests that if one wants to account for why some infants develop secure and others insecure attachment to mother, father, or even child-care worker, then there is a need to look beyond the proximate determinants of mothering and temperament.
>
> (Belsky, 2006, p. 90)

This is just what the concept of socio-genealogical connectedness seeks to do; it seeks to go beyond the child's immediate and present milieu to include his/her past (ancestors) towards a proper understanding of psychosocial development. Unlike in traditional developmental theories such as attachment theory, a person's psychological wellbeing is, in large measure, contingent upon one's experience of belonging, upon the degree to which one feels connected to one's kin and ancestral roots. Socio-genealogical connectedness theory argues that this may be achieved not solely through one's biological parents, but also through the extended family, grandparents being the richest source of the necessary material, parental or socio-genealogical information.

7 In the interest of the child
Kinship care

The principal objective of this chapter is to address the crucial question: What type of placement best serves the child's interest? In so doing, it considers the questions raised in the preceding chapter (p. 113). Extant research does not deal specifically with these questions. For example, it provides no clear explanation for the observed disparity in psychosocial developmental outcomes between kinship placement and non-kinship placement. Instead, some investigators raise it as a matter for future research to pursue (e.g., Holtan, 2008; Tarren-Sweeney and Hazell, 2006; Zuravin *et al.*, 1999). Others try to address it by resorting to the features of the two forms of child placement. In other words, while some tend to emphasize the benefits of kinship foster care, others stress its risks or disadvantages based on the characteristics of the caregivers.

Concerns about kinship care tend to relate more to policy and practice matters than to psychosocial developmental outcomes. Such fears, as research shows, predominantly relate to the profile of the caregivers, their age and health status, their less-than-desirable financial circumstances, their presumed inability to protect the child or the less-than-adequate assessment, training, monitoring and support they receive from child welfare agencies, relative to non-relative foster-carers, (Bartholet, 1999; Berrick *et al.*, 1994; Broad, 2001a, b; Dubowitz, *et al.*, 1994; Everett, 1995; Farmer and Moyers, 2008; Hayslip and Kaminiski, 2005; Jendrek, 1993; Johnson-Garner and Meyers, 2003; Solomon and Marx, 1995; Sykes *et al.*, 2002). The following section examines some of these concerns.

Disadvantages of kinship placement

Of the identified disadvantages of kinship placement, it is the notion of family pathology or generational child abuse and/or neglect that most deters child welfare agencies from seriously considering kinship foster care as a viable placement option (Brown *et al*, 2002; Farmer and Moyers, 2008; Jackson, 1999; Peters, 2005). This idea is anchored in the belief or presumption that parents whose children need alternative childcare were themselves raised by abusive and neglectful parents (e.g., Dubowitz *et al.*, 1994). In other words, inadequate and harmful parenting is an inherent feature of the whole family, such that extended family members, be they grandparents, aunts or uncles, pose an equal risk to the child. For example, Gray and Nybell (1990, in Gibbs and Müller, 2000) found that child welfare workers sometimes removed children from the entire extended family network because they attributed failure of the parents to the failure of the grandparents or the extended family network.

In a USA study, Peters (2005) elicited the beliefs and attitudes of social workers from seven rural social-work teams regarding kinship foster care. The workers were overwhelmingly positive towards kinship placement, particularly with regard to the developmental benefits that the child derives from being cared for by relatives. Nonetheless, some 80 per cent of them endorsed the old maxim that 'the apple does not fall far form the tree'. The other 20 per cent couched their misgivings in a more subtle language; they expressed reluctance to place children with kin because of dysfunctional family traditions or because kin may have poor parenting skills [or] outdated beliefs around discipline. Put explicitly, the workers feared that the family would use corporal punishment as their preferred mode of discipline, if they placed a child with kin; in short, they would abuse the child.

Evidence questions this belief, but because of its roots in attachment theory, especially as promulgated by Goldstein and colleagues (1973), it is hard to set aside. For example, Zuravin and colleagues (1999) reported that children placed with relatives were at less risk of maltreatment than those placed in non-relative foster-homes. Similarly, Berrick and colleagues (1994) draw attention to empirical research which indicates that the incidence of substantiated maltreatment reports for children in formal kinship care is lower than in non-kinship foster care. Indeed, they found that 31 per cent of the kinship caregivers in their sample actually initiated contact with child protection agencies. Subsequent international studies have reported similar cases. Gibbs and Müller (2000), although tentative in their conclusion of their examination of the literature, argue that child welfare workers' scepticism about the capacity of kinship caregivers to protect the child from maltreatment and abuse is unwarranted.

Recent research supports kin caregivers' capacity, commitment and willingness to care for and protect their progeny in need (Aldgate and McIntosh, 2006; Altshuler, 1999; Brown *et al.*, 2002; Chapman *et al.*, 2004; Farmer and Moyers, 2008; Holtan, 2008; Messing, 2006; Peters, 2005; Pitcher, 2002; Sykes *et al.*, 2002). In most of these studies, it was found that not only were the children living with relatives, especially grandparents, prior to their coming to the attention of child welfare agencies, but, more importantly, they initiated the move from their parents. In many other cases, it was a relative who alerted child welfare agencies to the child's need for alternative care; and having done so, they fought the system to keep the child in the family. '*I didn't want them to go homes, I didn't want them all split up*' (Aunt, quoted by Farmer and Moyers, 2008, p. 184). Farmer and Moyers also quote a grandmother's views on kinship care: '*I just think that if a child's taken and they have experienced something traumatic, the first thing they are looking for is comfort and friendly faces, people that they know, people that they can turn to*' (p. 184). In another UK study, Pitcher (2002) reported that 25 per cent of the grandparents caring for their grandchildren were deeply perturbed to hear that their grandchild had suffered abuse. Another 40 per cent said they knew 'everything' or 'almost everything', and several of them described their difficulties in trying to get professional agencies to listen to their concerns. A number of such cases came to light in the Victoria Climbé Inquiry (see, e.g., Batty, 2003; Gillen, 2002; Owusu-Bempah, 2003).

The experiences of participants in a USA study (Brown *et al.*, 2002) clearly demonstrates kin commitment to providing care and protection for their children, that they will go to any length to protect the children and keep them within the family.

> [Well], it wasn't that simple ... they were with me, and that seemed to be okay at first. But the [social] worker at the time felt that somehow the girls were in some sort of danger staying with me ... So they snatched the girls up and took them and placed them in a foster home. And so I went to court ... *It took me a year* ... but eventually they thought there was no reason, no real reason why they should keep the kids from me, so they let me have them.
>
> (in Brown *et al.*, 2002, p. 64, emphasis added)

Another grandmother describes her struggle with the child welfare system in her efforts to rescue her grandson from the public care system.

> [T]hey took the baby away from them [the parents] for four months. And I was on vacation. And my son called me in Texas where I was to let me know that they were taking the baby ... I shortened my vacation, came home and called the system ... to find out where the baby was and if I could get it back. And with the procedures, they gave him to me at six months. He is been here since.
>
> (in Brown *et al.*, 2002, p. 63)

In brief, evidence generally contradicts the family pathology hypothesis. It shows also that, in many cases, relatives actually pursue custody of the child, often overcoming obstacles in the child welfare system. For example, Pitcher (2002) reports that many grandparents caring for their grandchildren were prepared to endure financial hardship and other difficulties in order to keep the child in the family fold. For instance, they refrained from seeking help or services, even when they desperately needed help, for fear that if they appeared in any way 'demanding' of help, social services would deduce that they could not manage and, so, would place the child elsewhere.

Besides, we saw in the preceding chapter that the idea of generational transmission of attachment patterns, upon which the claim of family pathology is based, is not entirely sound (George and Solomon, 1999; Poehlmann, 2003; Rutter, 1991; Sroufe *et al.*, 1999). For example, Poehlmann (2003) argues that, although such risks as substance abuse and maltreatment tend to run in families, family members may follow diverse developmental trajectories and experience opportunities that may either enhance resilience or increase risk. In other words, negative childhood experiences do not necessarily result in psychopathology, neither are they automatically transmitted. Herring (2005), from an 'inclusive fitness' perspective, likewise warns of the influence of the family pathology approach on child placement decisions that discriminate against potential kin caregivers. It is worth quoting one of Pitcher's participants to reinforce Herring's argument: *'She is ours. She is part of us'* (in Pitcher, 2002, p. 8).

Advantages of kinship placement

This section examines the main features and benefits of kinship foster-placement that are claimed to cushion children from the trauma of separation and the effects of their past adversities, factors which enable children in kinship care to develop resilience and adjust to placement better than do their peers in other placement settings. The literature lists far more advantages of kinship foster care than for non-relative foster care. Specifically, according to the Child Welfare League of America (1994), kinship foster care can meet the child's need for emotional nurturance, safety and continuity by:

- enabling children to live with persons whom they know and trust;
- reducing the trauma children often experience when they are placed with strangers;
- reinforcing children's sense of identity and self-esteem, which flows from knowing their family history and culture;
- facilitating children's connections with their siblings;
- encouraging families to consider and rely on their own family members as resources;
- enhancing children's opportunities to stay connected to their own communities and promoting community responsibility for children and families; and
- strengthening the ability of families to give children the support they need.

Aside from the evidence examined in the preceding chapters, other research endorses and adds to this list (Aldgate and McIntosh, 2006; Broad, 2001a; Brown *et al.*, 2002; Chapman *et al.*, 2004; Dubowitz *et al.*, 1994; Everett, 1995; Farmer and Moyers, 2008; Hegar, 1999a, b; Holtan, 2008; Iglehart, 1995; Johnson-Garner and Meyers, 2003; McFadden, 1998; Mosek and Adler, 2001; Peters, 2005; Pitcher, 2002; Scannapieco and Hegar, 1999).

Such research shows that not only are kinship placements more stable than non-relative placements, but equally importantly, the children are cared for by committed caregivers who love and value them. These factors plus a sense of belonging and continuity resulting from the children's contact with their parents, the extended family and the community facilitate and enhance their sense of group and personal identity and, ultimately, their mental health.

Socio-genealogical connectedness hypothesizes that children cared for by relatives, particularly grandparents, function psychologically better than those in other placement settings because they have fuller biographies and, so, a deeper sense of connectedness. One of the characteristics of kinship care is that the children are included as full family members by the extended family. A child in Brown and colleagues' (2002) study provides a clear example: '*I always visit my relatives on my grandma's side. Like family events and things like that, and they always come over here ... I love spending time with my relatives ... My aunties, practically everyone ...*' (p. 69). Almost all the grandparent caregivers in the same study attested to the children's claim about their feelings of belonging or connectedness.

Out of their own mouths

Several investigators have noted the paucity of research concerning the views of children in the foster-care system, and how their experiences may differ according to the type of placement in which they are growing up. This is curious, given that understanding how children feel about their lives is an important part of research which aims to improve services for them and their families. For instance, Messing (2006) argues that speaking to children in kinship care and their caregivers about their experiences and needs is essential for gaining an understanding of this population. Often, studies which include the perspectives of the children in their design elicit the children's views as a secondary objective. Thus, they interview a subsample, often unrepresentative, of their larger sample. In other words, the children's views are often pursued extempore or as an adjunct to their main objectives. The few studies (e.g., Altshuler, 1999; Brown *et al.*, 2002; Chapman *et al.*, 2004; Messing, 2006; O'Brien, 2000; Rowe *et al.*, 1984) that have specifically explored the perspectives of children in kinship care on their relationships and sense of security have found these to be generally positive.

The views reported in three of such studies are illuminating and worthy of note. In the first of these, Brown and colleagues (2002) carried out a detailed examination of the role of the extended family in the lives of 30 youths, aged 9–17 years, who were residing in kinship care households at the time of the study. They represented 25 families, and the caregivers were also interviewed. In the second study, Altshuler (1999) conducted in-depth, open-ended interviews with African-American children aged 10–15 years. The interviews covered general topic areas: 1) the children's definition of family,

2) their understanding of why they were living with kin instead of their birth parents, 3) the changes they needed to make when they moved, 4) how decisions regarding those changes were made, 5) their perception of permanence, 6) advice for caseworkers, and 7) their overall experience of living in kinship foster care. In the third study, Messing (2006) used focus groups to provide a descriptive analysis of kinship care from the child's perspective. Eight focus groups of 40 children, aged 10–14 years, were conducted. The topic of discussion centred on: 1) transitional issues, 2) family relationships, 3) the stigma of being in care, and 4) the children's perceived stability of their placement. Excerpts from these studies are presented thematically below.

Trauma

Transition of any kind is stressful; it is particularly distressing for a child, so that anything that allays a child's anxiety and gives reassurance to a child in transition is welcome. Consequently, the literature is replete with conjectural claims that placement with kin reduces the trauma of transition or separation from biological parents. The studies summarized above lend some empirical support to this claim. For instance, a 14-year-old female participant in Messing's study described her feeling of her move into her maternal grandmother's care:

> I called my grandma and asked her if she could come and pick me up, and she said yes, and I was like, 'it ain't for the weekend,' and she was like 'alright,' and then I said 'okay, okay,' and then she said 'alright' and then she had my auntie come and pick me up, and then she came [and] picked me up [from my aunt's], and then I move in with my grandma ... I don't want to take nothing [with me]. I wanted to start over.
>
> (in Messing, 2006, p. 1423)

One of Brown and colleagues' participants, asked how he and his brothers and sisters came to live with their grandmother, answered:

> Well, when we was living ... and my mom was like, well she would always leave and don't come home, and we would have to call them, and my grandmother lived down here, and we had to call them, and ask to bring food up. So then once my gran told those people (Child Protection Services). Then they took us to my grandmother's ...
>
> (in Brown *et al.*, 2002, p. 65)

Asked how he and his siblings felt about moving in with his grandmother, this respondent answered simply: '*I felt great because we had something to eat*' (in Brown *et al.*, 2002, p. 65). One is inclined to describe this as a separation without loss.

In Messing's study, things were not so clear-cut for some of the children.

While many children said that they felt good or happy about moving in with their caregiver, others said they were sad (or missing their mothers), confused or angry about the transition. However, Messing concluded that, overall, the adjustments to kinship foster care did not seem to have taken too much of a toll on them. In fact, she argues that moving in with their extended family network facilitated their adjustment to the move. For many, Messing claims, it was not such a big leap, since they had enjoyed visiting their caregivers before they moved in with them. She quotes the experiences of several of her participants prior to their eventual move to their caregivers. For example, one boy stated: *'I was happy* [to be moving in because] ... *when I lived with my mom, I used to like going over to my grandma's house all the time 'cause it was fun over there'* (in Messing, 2006, p. 1424). Another boy spoke fondly about his living arrangements before moving in with his grandmother: *'See I go to my grandma's house and I stay there for a while. Then I go back to my mom's house. I keep switching around ... it feels good sometimes because I like being with both of them. I felt like I was wanted all the time'* (in Messing, 2006, p. 1424). Most children stated unequivocally that they were not scared of moving in with a relative: *'I was living with my grandma, there ain't no reason to be scared about it'* (p. 1424).

Messing suggests that being in an extended family seems to make things easier for children in kinship care. She sees the child's access to kinship networks as key to an easy (or less traumatic) transition: *'You're happy for your grandma that she came, she took you in, because you want so you can see all your family members and stuff. Because if I had gone to foster care, I wouldn't have never saw my cousins or nobody'* (in Messing, 2006, p. 1424).

Involvement in the family

The literature also suggests that being a full member of the extended family is an important factor in the wellbeing of children in kinship foster care. Again, Brown and colleagues' and Messing's studies provide empirical support for this claim. Many of the children in both studies described family relationships as an important element in their resilience. Also, they mentioned family members, more often than friends, when they were asked with whom they shared their most personal feelings. For example, asked about his favourite uncle, one boy in Brown and colleagues' sample replied:

> He is just, it's just because he's hecka sweet. It seems like, you know, you can't go sit down and talk to your mom or your grandma about something? You can always go and talk to him about it, because he always makes you feel good about it ... Say I went to him and I was like, 'Uncle S--, I have a problem.' He'll say, 'Well, let's sit down and talk about it.' And then when I sit down and talk about it, when I first go in, I feel bad, but when I come out, I always feel good ... And then he gives you advice. You don't have to take it, that what's he always say, 'You don't have to

take it, but if you want to, you could,' and it always be good when you take it, you always come out better.

(in Brown *et al.*, 2002, p. 69)

Another interviewee identified his older cousin as his confidant:

My cousin, T-- ... maybe from a baby to like four or five, and he's older than me. And one day, they decided to move out here, and his mom, they talked to my grandma, and she said it was fine, and she picked them up at the airport, and me and him, we was talking, and we just started getting that bond with each other. So we kind of got close to each other. And we are the closest cousins out of the whole batch.

(in Brown *et al.*, 2002, p. 70)

Altshuler (1999) provides further examples of the extent to which the extended family networks serve as a support system of which children in kinship care avail themselves:

It's like, hard, with my grandparents, like about teenage stuff. You know, 'cause they're stuck in the old days, so I go to my mom about it and one of my aunties. My youngest auntie, or my next youngest auntie, they're real cool ... My auntie 'Mary,' [she's my buddy]. I love her. My aunt Latanya, all of them cool except for Sherrell.

(10-year-old girl, quoted by Altshuler, 1999, p. 224)

According to Altshuler, the stories from her respondents varied in scope; all the children described their experiences of being loved and being cared for by their kinship caregivers. She sees the children's experiences, including academic improvement, friendship and connections with extended family, as contributing to their development and the maintenance of their wellbeing.

Regarding contact and relationships with their biological parents, Messing found that the children in her study generally had contact with their mothers. However, their feelings towards them were mixed. Some of them were ambivalent towards their mother, mainly due to the mother's unreliability and unwillingness to give them attention or spend time with them. Messing points out that, in spite of their ambivalence, relationships with their mothers were certainly important to them and played a large role in their lives. However, most children's relationships with their mothers were stable and positive. For example, they could talk to their mother about personal matters, such as love interests or difficulties with friends. Indeed, many stated that they told their mothers more about their personal lives than they told their caregivers. One boy in a legal guardianship situation stated that this was *'because I don't feel comfortable talking with my grandma about sexual things'* (in Messing, 2006, p. 1425).

Messing's respondents also described their relationships with their fathers.

She found that the children's contact with their fathers was generally sporadic or occurred only on special occasions. Although one or two stated that their fathers were more constant in their lives than their mothers were, several of them equated their father's behaviour with their mother's – *'My mom calls, say she is gonna do something, she doesn't do it … My daddy doesn't do it either'* (in Messing, 2006, pp. 1426–7). Still, many of them (especially boys) longed to have a relationship with their father. A male respondent understood the difficulties of not having a father present in his life, and hoped that his brother would not have to go through the same ordeal: *'I don't want my brother to be just like me, you know, without a dad. Because he doesn't know what it means to have a dad either … But I have pictures of my dad'* (in Messing, 2006, pp. 1426–7).

Caregivers, often grandparents, are the most constant persons in the lives of children in kinship placement. It is not surprising, therefore, that the children tend to reserve their deepest and warmest sentiments for them. Messing observed this in her study; she found that her respondents genuinely appreciated the warmth, love and care they were receiving from their kinship caregivers. One of the participants in her study, a boy who was under the legal guardianship of his grandmother, expressed his appreciation movingly. It is worth quoting in full.

> She gets kind of sick sometimes and I love taking care of her. And sometimes I mess up and I get mad at myself because, you know, I don't want to make mistakes. But, and she – when she gets too sick she told me to take care of her. So, you know, I love taking care of her since she is taking care of me. You know in the future when I go to college and stuff I become whatever I wanted and, I'll start taking care of her, you know. Returning the favor. Because she said, she said the reason why she took us in is because she loves us. And I say when I grow up the reason I'm taking care of you too is because I love you. The reason why I want to return the favor. So, I just know when I grow I'm going to return the favor and everything is going to be nice. But I still know I am going to be making mistakes. Like I said, it's still kind of stressful.
>
> (in Messing, 2006, p. 1427)

Stability versus reunification

Scrutiny of the literature reveals that 'stability' and 'reunification' with birth parents constitute the golden rule of professional foster-care practice. As previously pointed out, kinship placement offers greater stability and sense of security for the child than does non-relative foster placement. Ironically, however, child welfare professionals tend to see these aspects of kinship care as negative. This raises several pertinent questions, for example: 1) To what degree does the child's perception of these terms coincide with that of professionals? 2) In most cases, as we have already seen, the children initiated the move from their parents so, who should decide where they are better off, they or we? 3) Why, as in traditional communities, can they not live and grow up in any welcoming unit of the extended family system of which the birth family is but a part or subsystem? We seem to lack answers to these questions because, often, we do not listen to the children or, when we do, we ignore their views, in spite of the philosophy of the paramountcy of the child's views to which we claim to subscribe.

The story of a 14-year-old female respondent in Altshuler's (1999) study illustrates clearly the need to listen to children and respect their views and wishes. Altshuler describes her story as unique among the children she interviewed because the police had asked her, as a nine-year-old child, with whom she would like to live. None of the other children reported that their input had been actively sought during the placement process. Altshuler retells this girl's story:

> When my father changed [and became involved in my life], and wanted to get custody, they asked me, do you want to live with him? 'No, not really,' I said. They also asked me, 'did I have any problems, did I want counselling about my mother, if she was gonna try to get me back.' I answered, 'No I don't really have any problems with my mother. *I love her, and I don't want to live with her.*'
>
> (in Altshuler, 1999, p. 228, emphasis added)

With respect to placement stability or continuity, Messing (2006) found that her sample fell in various places along a continuum. At one end of the continuum, the children hoped to join their parents soon; at the other end were children who stated that they did not want to live with their parents. According to Messing, these children based their decision on a realistic appraisal of their options. An 11-year-old girl's decision to remain with her maternal aunt provides a case in point: '*I think* [where I live is] *good because my mom, she had me, she had four girls and one boy ... I don't think it's fair because she only took one of her daughters and you gonna make your sisters take care of your kids*' (in Messing, 2006, p. 1429). A substantial proportion of Messing's sample perceived their living arrangements as permanent; they believed that they would live with their caregivers until they moved out on their own. Generally, they were confident that their family members would care for them, though they were not always sure if it would be their current caregiver, another relative or their parent. Whatever the case might be, they trusted the extended family to continue to look after them.

An important question that Messing asked all her respondents was whom they would like to live with, if they could choose to live with anyone. Many of the children preferred to continue to live with their current caregiver: '*My grandmother ... because she is really nice to me and she's my grandmother ... when she moves, I'll go with her*' (in Messing, 2006, p. 1429). For those who had never lived with their mother, or did not remember it, living with their grandmother or caregiver seemed 'natural'; they could not imagine doing anything else. Many of those who had memories of living with their parents stated unequivocally that living with their caregiver was better. One female under the legal guardianship of her grandmother stated: '*My grandmother is much* [more] *fun to be around ...* [she is] *always teasing, always coming up with jokes, when I'm bored and stuff she* [will] *just do something silly to make me laugh*' (in Messing, 2006, pp. 1429–30).

The experiences of the children involved in the above studies seriously question child welfare professionals' (social workers') unquestioning belief in the concepts of 'reunification' and 'permanency'. Indeed, kinship care clearly serves the dual purpose of placement stability or continuity and reunification or family preservation. In other words, most children in kinship care, especially those cared for by loving and committed grandparents, do not make a split between biological family and extended family. Rather, they perceive the former as a part of the latter, so that they do not regard being cared for by a relative, a grandparent, as unusual. Mosek and Adler (2001) suggest that, in their Israeli study, it was the stability and continuity perceived by the adolescents in kinship care that contributed to their inner self-assurance, in comparison with those in non-relative foster care. In their study, as in many other studies, those in kinship foster families had drifted less in the care system. They also felt their ties with the foster family would last. For example, the adolescent girls who were placed with kin reported greater closeness with the foster family, fewer tensions between the foster family and the biological family, and planned to keep in touch with the foster family in the future. Above all, they felt that the foster family was really an extension of their biological family. Those adolescents growing up in non-relative foster homes, on the other hand, felt that their care was a conditional arrangement, limited in time and contingent upon the foster-parents' decision (Mosek and Adler, 2001).

The literature reviewed in this and previous chapters provides overwhelming evidence that, in kinship care, family commitments are genuine, bound neither by time nor place. Such commitment, *inter alia*, enhances the child's sense of belonging, it makes the child feel loved and valued and, consequently, facilitates his/her adjustment to separation. In non-kinship foster care, in contrast, the commitment is conditional, the child or young person, the caregiver and the system are all fully aware that foster-care obligations and payments terminate on leaving care, on attaining the age of the age of 18. As Mosek and Adler (2001) rightly point out, underlying this scenario is the child welfare system's limited commitment to the young person. In other words, care terminates at a crucial phase of development, especially with respect to personal identity, and also when the young person needs family support most, as s/he takes his/her first step towards independence. Children growing up in kinship foster families do not usually face such a daunting prospect.

Stigma

Researchers and practitioners invariably list stigma as one of the negative attributes of child placement. Nonetheless, they generally agree that kinship care minimizes the shame attached to placement. For example, the social workers who participated in Peters' (2005) research (summarized above) identified reduced stigma as the dominant social factor in favour of kinship placement. Almost all of them acknowledged that there was little or no stigma attached to living with a relative for an extended period. Several of them reported having personal experience of informal or formal kinship care. Indeed, the supervisors and team leaders among the group noted that almost all their workers had an experience of kinship care, but often did not encode it as 'kinship care' because it was such a normal, accepted part of their experience (Peters, 2005). Anecdotal evidence supports Peters' findings; however, empirical evidence, besides anthropological reports, is scant.

Messing's (2006) study goes some way towards rectifying this situation. She reports that in her study, the children involved did not seem to feel ostracized from their peers on the grounds of their foster status, nor did they have qualms about talking about it with their friends or teachers. In fact, most children reported that they felt 'okay', 'good' or 'happy' with their living situation. The commonest reason they cited for these feelings was that their caregiver 'takes care' of them. An 11-year old boy is reported to have pointed out: '*I mean* [a lot] *of people now live with their grannie, aunties and stuff and not most people have a perfect family where they live with their mom and dad*' (in Messing, 2006, p. 1427). In other words, in this youngster's community, as in traditional communities where kinship care is normal, being looked after by a relative carried no shame. Indeed, in Messing's study, most of the youngsters stated that living with a relative is 'just the same' as living with a parent.

> In one of the focus groups there was some confusion about what it means to live with a relative ... when the facilitator told them that she did not know what it was like to live with a relative, one child raised her hand and asked if the facilitator had ever lived with her parents. There was a moment of confusion until the facilitator realised that this child was saying that the facilitator had also lived with relatives while growing up – her parents! This child did not sparse out 'living with a relative' and 'living with parents'.
>
> (in Messing, 2006, p. 1428)

Why should she have done so? It is doubtful if, while growing up, Nelson Mandela, or Bill Clinton or Barack Obama saw himself as a foster-child. Likewise, it is doubtful if many people would describe Obama's young daughters as fostered because their 'grandma' takes (full-time) care of them, while their parents are continually away from home sorting out the world's ills.

Identity and self-worth

One of the most frequently cited undesirable aspects of foster-care placement, in fact the public care system as a whole, is its negative impact on the child's self-esteem and identity. There is consensus among writers that kinship care can counteract this effect. This is because not only is the child encouraged to participate in the activities and rituals of the extended family and the community, or likely to have regular contact with at least one of his parents, but also, perhaps more importantly, she is loved and valued by committed caregivers. The voices of the children in the studies summarized in this section attest to this claim. One of Altshuler's respondents, a 15-year-old girl, removed from her mother at the age of nine, described her experience of living with her maternal grandparents:

> [t]hey just out there for us, tell us they love us. Like, they go shopping, they take us out to eat, they buy us stuff, do stuff like that, you know, we sit and we talk, and we argue. They're just so cool ... I love my grandparents. *It's like, a million and one times I can tell you that I can remember, 'cause I'm sure, I know, that they made me feel good about me.* They compliment us all the time, you know, 'you're so good, we love you', they want to go places with you and all that. They're cool.
>
> (in Altshuler, 1999, p. 225)

Altshuler notes the difficulty this girl had in pulling out one exemplar of her experiences living in kinship foster care. Altshuler's surmise is that it was the many acts of kindness that her grandparents performed that affirmed this girl's importance as a human being and, consequently, enhanced her wellbeing and self-worth.

Messing reports similar narratives from her participants. The youngsters described their caregivers variously as thoughtful: *'My grandma, she's thoughtful. She thinks about me, before she even thinks about herself'*; kind: *'Yea, nicer too,'cause they know what you've been through ... When you're crying they be, like, oh, poor baby'*; and available to fulfil their needs: *'[Be]cause her whole life is me, doctors appointments, and my sister'* (in Messing, 2006, p. 1427). Messing found that other children talked about their caregivers (especially grandparents) as strict; however, they appreciated that this was a necessary component of care-giving and, therefore, acceptable. As one girl stated: *'She yells a lot, but I still care for her because she, she takes care of me all the time, and she handles my problems'* (in Messing, 2006, p. 1427).

Summary

In all, Altshuler (1999) recognizes that it is the many acts of kindness that children in kinship care experience which offer them the opportunity to create their own futures, *'futures full of possibilities'* (p. 225). Besides the above, other research which has directly explored children's knowledge and perceptions of their family relationships and transition into kinship foster care reinforces Altshuler's claim (e.g., Aldgate and McIntosh, 2006; Chapman *et al.*, 2004; Mosek and Adler, 2001). In these studies, the children emphasized the importance of care-giving by loving and committed kin. They stressed also the significance of feeling safe and secure as a result of being in a permanent living arrangement. In these arrangements, as the studies summarized above indicate, children do not experience transition into care as distressing or traumatic or unduly so. They may be angry with or miss their parents, but they are content to be in the care of relatives. In the studies described above, the children spoke with affection about not only their primary caregivers (mostly grandparents), but also about their siblings, cousins, aunties and uncles. Namely, children in kinship care, relative to those in other types of placement, experience a broader sense of familial relationships, including relationships with their parents. These relationships are of great importance to them, they constitute the building block of a sense of socio-genealogical connectedness and, hence, identity and psychological wellbeing.

Theoretical perspectives of kinship placement

Readers might be tempted to deduce from the preceding discussion that children growing up in kinship foster care experience no difficulties at all. This would be hasty. On the contrary, it is fully acknowledged that kinship placement, like other placements, entails difficulties. Like other family forms, kinship or extended families are heterogeneous and, so, provide different experiences to their children. To reiterate, a question this chapter seeks to address is why children in kinship foster families, as a whole, fare better than those in non-relative foster care. The rest of this chapter now deals with this question, with reference to attachment theory and socio-genealogical connectedness theory.

Attachment theory

As previously pointed out, for several years now, many have tried to explain the emotional and behavioural vulnerability of separated children from the perspective of attachment theory. That is, [insecure] attachment has, for a long time, been regarded as the key underlying factor in the vulnerability of children in care. For example, we saw above Rutter and O'Connor's (1999) claim that attachment theory provides a *complete explanation* for the experiences of separation and relocation and their disruptive consequences for personality development. Likewise, Connor (2006) recommends attachment theory as a useful guide for understanding and helping children being cared for by their grandparents. Also, following Bowlby's (1969) recommendation, researchers and professionals alike predominantly regard attachment disorders as characterizing foster care. For example, Zeanah and Boris (2000) list attachment disorders among the most common underlying causes of the emotional and behavioural problems reported in children in foster care.

Attachment refers to the relationship between an infant and a primary caregiver. The nature, quality and continuity of this relationship are claimed to mould the infant's emotional life, that they are constitutive of the child's internal working models. To recapitulate, attachment theorists and research- ers list the following ingredients as essential for secure or healthy attachment and, therefore, personality development:

1. loving, unbroken relationship, characterized by continuous availability of the attachment-figure who responds with sensitivity to the child's physical as well as emotional needs;
2. the child's confidence in the availability of the attachment-figure must be established within a critical period (infancy to late childhood);
3. the varied expectations or experiences of the availability and responsive- ness of the attachment-figure.

In traditional societies, as anthropological evidence shows, things are often different. That is, the infant/child-caregiver relationship hardly follows this pattern (e.g., LeVine *et al.*, 1998; Whiting, 1963; Whiting and Edwards 1988). In these communities, children are frequently sent away from their parents to be raised by relatives and friends. Although Bowlby (1973, 1988) claimed that loss of the attachment-figure, the child's secure base, is an event which generates overwhelming anxiety, anger, grief and despair, and results in emotional and behavioural difficulties, anthropological evidence concern- ing fostering does not seem to support this claim. One reason for this, as Verhoef and Morelli (2007, p. 33) argue, might be that foster *'children's experiences are shaped more by the circumstances in which they are fostered than by being merely raised away from their parents'*. Rutter (1991) and Owusu-Bempah (1995, 2006, 2007) concur with this argument. The evidence examined so far suggests that the crucial difference in the circumstances in which children are fostered relate to the fact that some are raised in kinship foster families, while others are raised by strangers. This is clearly in line with the notion of socio-genealogical connectedness. That is, attachment theory does not explain the disparity in psychosocial developmental outcomes observed between children placed with kin and those placed with strangers. We must not lose sight of the fact that both groups of children come from similar, adverse family backgrounds.

Socio-genealogical connectedness

The literature is awash with assertions that, relative to other forms of child placement, kinship placement promotes the child's cultural, ethnic and personal identity and mental health. These claims are often presented as self-evident; explanations for why this is the case are rare and, where they are offered, tend to be lean and couched predominantly in attachment concepts. While attachment theory attributes the vulnerability of children in care and adopted children to separation, socio-genealogical connectedness regards doubts about their sense of belonging and identity or lack of feeling of connectedness, who and what one is, as a major underlying factor in the children's emotional and psychological susceptibility.

Wilson (2004) argues that although identity is referred to in various ways, in essence, it describes elements of self-definition and a subjective sense of integrated personality that refers to continuity and connectedness between one's past, present and future. William James (1890) described a sense of continuity as one of the essential elements of personal identity. He strongly believed it to be *sine qua non* for mental health. He saw the experience of continuity as precious to psychological wellbeing, so that disruptions to it are inimical to mental health. *'The worst alterations of the self are associated with disruption in identity fostered by a loss of continuity and distinctiveness'* (William James, 1890, p. 207). Most of us take these experiences for granted. *'Each of us when he awakens says, Here's the same old self again, just as he says, Here's the same old bed, the same old room, the same old world'* (William James, 1890, p. 334). This experience, a sense of continuity, is what most children in the public care system lack. Their feeling of sameness, of continuity, is constantly challenged by their constantly changing world through, typically, multiple placements. Thus, for a substantial number of them, when s/he awakens, s/he says: 'Here's another self, here's another bed, another room. Here's another self, the son/daughter of ... yesterday, but the son/daughter of ... today. Here is a strange new world.'

Knight and colleagues (2006) describe the experiences of a 16-year-old female interviewee who had experienced 12 placements in two years. Her experience reinforces James' concern. She narrated vividly how hard it was to adapt and settle, especially with little preparation:

> They put me in placements but they didn't sit down and say this is what the person's name is ... you don't get to meet the person before you go ... so there isn't any rapport there or anything so you are just ending up with people you don't know. It's quite distressing actually ... sometimes you get immune to it after a while, but how do they [social services] expect children *to be normal and behave well* ... they just live in a fantasy world of children who adapt to certain things ... we're not chameleons ... we don't adapt.
>
> (in Knight *et al.*, 2006, p. 60, emphasis added)

Socio-genealogical connectedness and kinship care

Whereas attachment theorists and practitioners attribute the psychosocial developmental problems facing children in care to insecure attachment, socio-genealogical connectedness theory emphasizes a sense of connectedness, a sense of continuity, a sense of personal as well as family identity, as a crucial factor in their general wellbeing, as it is in other children's wellbeing. It proposes that a feeling of socio-genealogical connectedness facilitates children's adjustment to separation; that it is an important determinant of their adjustment to separation and, hence, their mental health. The extent to which a child feels connected is, in turn, determined by the amount and nature of information the child possesses about his/her biological parents' backgrounds and, by extension, the child's hereditary backgrounds. It must be stressed that socio-genealogical information may be provided not only by the parents, but also by members of the extended family, especially grandparents who are the richest source of such information and often disseminate it liberally among their progeny. Why should they not? After all, as Schwartz (2007) points out, a primary role of grandparenting is the sharing of culture and family history. In order to be helpful, however, socio-genealogical information must be, on balance, favourable or undamaging.

In studies involving children of lone-parent families, Owusu-Bempah and Howitt (1997, 2000a) have tested the assumptions of socio-genealogical connectedness. Without direct comparisons between children raised by relatives and those raised by non-relatives, it could be argued that the evidence gleaned in this book indirectly supports socio-genealogical connectedness' assumptions as applied to children in care. That is, children cared for by relatives fare better than children looked after by non-relatives and those in residential settings because they experience a deeper sense of connectedness or continuity. Namely, while the constituents of a sense of continuity and connectedness and, therefore, mental health (William James, 1890) are very often absent in other placement settings, kinship placement, by its very nature, provides the child with ample opportunities to develop a coherent sense of personal identity or self-concept that incorporates the past, the present and the future. Since these constituents are embodied in socio-genealogical information, extended family members, among whom the child lives, and especially grandparents, constitute the foremost source of these ingredients.

Socio-genealogical information is transmitted trough family interactions, through language and rituals. Peters' (2005) participants did not miss this element in kinship placement.

> Kinship care 'helps the child stay familiar with the family, its rituals, habits, ways of operating;' it 'preserves long-term ties;' it 'maintains a child's sense of belonging'. Through this contact with family, the child develops a web of 'shared memories and experiences' which 'helps weave a fabric of integrated experience' such that the child 'knows their own story' with a full richness of detail which can never be achieved through a 'lifebook'.

> (Peters, 2005, p. 600)

From their study, Brown and colleagues (2002) provide further examples of socio-genealogical connectedness at work in kinship placements. They highlight kinship caregivers' belief in the importance of a sense of socio-genealogical connectedness to the child's wellbeing, and their efforts to provide it to the child. Apart from the children's comments, the caregivers in Brown's study reflected on their involvement with and attention to their foster child's experience of the extended family. Most of the caregivers used family visits as a useful vehicle for connecting the children to the extended family. For example, one caregiver was asked how she thought the child felt after visiting relatives. Her response is worth quoting at length:

> Oh, great, great. That's why I stay around them so often ... They [her relatives] have a nice place set out in the back for the kids. So usually when I go around the family, he gets a chance to be with the family. And ... they're all teenagers, his age now, and they really enjoy themselves ... once I go I know they'll want to spend the night. They don't want to come home ... We had family outings, picnics, and just sometimes being here at the house, family coming over, just enjoying sitting, talking. *And we have a lot of family videos and we sit down and look at these things, and look at them when they were just little kids. We go through the photo albums, the books, albums.* You'd be surprised how joyful it is ... It's very touching and to see them, how they've grown.
>
> (Brown *et al.*, 2002, p. 68, emphasis added)

This is a crystalline example of *socio-genealogization* (Owusu-Bempah, 2007), the process whereby a child acquires as sense of connectedness, of belonging to his/her kin.

Such experiences indicate that, relative to their peers in other placement settings, children in kinship care are at lower risk, if any, of what Shants (1964) described as 'genealogical bewilderment', or what Erikson dubbed 'identity confusion'. Most children in non-relative foster care lack such experiences. In the case of children who entered care as babies or infants, many of them are unlikely to even know who their biological parents are, especially those who are later adopted. Others, such as those who entered the care system in childhood, may have knowledge of their parents, but such knowledge is often fuzzy, or tainted by their negative experiences of the parents, often further reinforced by their in-care experiences. This is not to imply that children in kinship care may not have tainted memories of the parents. However, the care, love and emotional and other support they receive from their caregivers and other family members help to assuage those negative memories. Besides, as Rocco-Briggs (2008) and others have pointed out, not all children in care recognize that their parenting has very often been inconsistent, ineffective or abusive. It has long been recognized that most of those who do still do not want to be in foster care and continue to wish to be returned to the care of their parents (e.g., Palmer, 1990).

Following Freud and Burlingham (1944), many child welfare professionals, social workers and family therapists, for example, see the child's yearning for his/her parents and attempts to return to them as the child's efforts to keep an idealized image of his/her parents. From a socio-genealogical connectedness perspective, another way of describing these children's behaviour is that, since unfavourable information about one's parents is damaging or a threat to one's identity or feeling of connectedness, the children try hard to cognitively separate the parent as a person and a parent from his/her abusive behaviour. In other words, they detest the parent's abusive behaviour, they love him/her as a parent nonetheless (Owusu-Bempah, 2006, 2007; Owusu-Bempah and Howitt, 1997, 2000a). In plain language, they seem to believe in the old adage: 'condemn the sin but not the sinner'. Through information regarding the favourable aspects of the parents provided by the caregivers, children raised by relatives are better helped or motivated to achieve this and adjust better to placement than those in non-relative foster care.

Socio-genealogical connectedness offers a plausible explanation for the reported disparity in functioning between children in kinship care and those in non-relative foster care. It explains also the apparent differential psychosocial developmental outcomes between foster-children in traditional societies and those in foster care in Western societies. Erikson (1968) stressed the developing child's need for recognition and figures with whom to identify. He argued also that the self-identity, and therefore mental health, of all of us is largely founded upon our history, on what our parents and ancestors have been, spanning many generations. He argued furthermore that true personal identity depends on the support which the child or young person receives from the collective sense of identity which characterizes the social groups significant to him/her: his/her family, class and culture. Kinship care provides the child with not only positive role models and social and cultural capital, but also his/her history as well as support. Peters' respondents acknowledged this aspect of kinship families: *'kin are likely to accept the child as s/he is, and not be trying to fix the kid. The child therefore grows up in a normal, strengths-based environment feeling normal'* (in Peters, 2005, p. 600). In contrast, the respondents pointed out that children in non-relative foster care, especially those who are cared for by families from different cultural or socio-economic backgrounds, may be in 'limbo', belonging within neither the class/culture of their biological family nor that of the foster family. In other words, they are likely to experience identity confusion, with all its psychological ramifications which often manifest themselves in externalizing and internalizing behaviours.

Erikson argued that a child's efforts to establish identity intensify in adolescence. Frequently, the material, socio-genealogical information, that a child or adolescent requires to construct a personal identity is absent or lacking in the public care system. Studies have documented how children are frequently left with many unanswered questions about their individual histories when they enter care, which makes it hard for them to cultivate a sense of self and maintain self-esteem (Harrison, 1999; Triseliotis and Russell, 1984). Fahlberg (1991) agrees with Erikson and these investigators that the major psychosocial developmental task facing the adolescent is seeking satisfactory answers to the following questions about him/herself: Who am I? Where do I belong? What can I do or be? What do I believe in? Kinship care provides the child with answers to these fundamental questions.

Summary

The foregoing discussion describes what is special about kinship foster families. In kinship placement, children are socialized by and feel connected to their kin, their hereditary roots. As we saw in earlier chapters, and emphasized by Holtan (2008), kinship survives and flourishes on solidarity, love, confidence, reciprocity and resilience. All these are values and attributes that a child needs in order to function optimally. In spite of this, while kinship foster care is valued and accepted as normal in traditional communities, there is much ambivalence towards the practice in contemporary Western societies. Among childcare professionals, misgivings about kinship foster families are predominantly based on the idea of risk or generational abuse. Brown and colleagues (2002) point out that we tend to forget that these families are victims of the social structure, that they have suffered challenges associated with poverty, unemployment, drug/alcohol misuse, mental health, discrimination and other adversities. They argue that while kinship foster families may need additional social and economic support, especially when caregivers are poor and elderly, stigmatizing these families can create its own burdens and stresses. They therefore urge professional childcare workers not to associate them with pathology, as they routinely do.

On the question of risk to the child, based on the presumption that grandparents and other extended family members are responsible for their offspring's inadequacy, for their neglectful and abusive behaviour, Brown and colleagues argue eloquently:

> The problem with the 'risk' framework ... is that it creates associations between 'factors' and outcomes based solely on a probabilistic relationship. The reliance on probability may then create an association between a particular family form and an undesirable outcome without attention to causality. This statistical relationship then facilitates the slippage ... a slippage that allows ... families ... to be associated with risk to child well-being ... The risk model ends up blaming the victim by failing to understand whether particular 'risk factors' and 'negative outcomes' are themselves outcomes of other factors. We suggest here that the ... extended family [kinship foster family] be seen as a response to risk (the risk created by social and economic inequality) rather than a producer of risk.
>
> (Brown *et al.*, 2002, p. 72)

They conclude: '*Blaming the victim is a tired and futile way to avoid facing the real issues of institutionalized poverty, racism, and unequal opportunity ...*' (p. 72). Given the general profile of kinship placement providers, we must add to these issues, sexism, ageism and classism.

We saw in Chapter 1 that continuity of the clan was a major motive for adoption in ancient communities. Today, it continues to be a strong rationale for kinship foster care-giving and other acts of benevolence. The notion of inclusive fitness proposes that kin have a natural proclivity and commitment to helping and protecting their own; they have a vested interest in ensuring and safeguarding the continuity and identity of the family or clan. As such, a kinship caregiver can be expected to be committed to protecting the child from abusive parents. Evidence suggests that, in most situations, that is the reality. In short, it is a great disservice to a child to deny that child the opportunity to be cared for by relatives such as grandparents when the parents are unable to provide him/her with the standard of care required to promote his/ her growth and development.

Kidd and Storey (2006) point out that, in the UK for example, it is long established law that, to warrant the removal of a child from his/her genetic parent requires a positive decision on the part of the court that the natural parent is incapable of providing the child with the standard of care that it requires; that is, there is a presumption in favour of the natural parent. They quote Lord Templeman as best expressing this principle when he stated:

> The best person to bring up a child is the natural parent. It matters not whether the parent is wise or foolish, rich or poor, educated or illiterate, provided the child's moral and physical health are not endangered.
> (Lord Templeman, 1988, quoted in Kidd and Storey, 2006, p. 46)

Socio-genealogical connectedness fully endorses this principle. In the context of fostering, it goes further to argue that the second-best person to the biological parents to raise a child is kin and not a stranger, provided the child's 'moral and physical health' is not jeopardized or unduly compromised. Furthermore, it stresses that the decision as to whether or not to place a child with kin must be based upon facts, and not on stereotypes or conjectures.

8 Policy, practice and research implications

A child's identity is formed within a web of family relationships, in extended and augmented kinship networks which are part of a culture and embedded in a community.

(McFadden and Downs, 1995, p. 40)

Kinship care is a time-honoured childcare mechanism as well as a family support system. In many societies today, it is a taken-for-granted childcare practice. It is not regarded as care-giving separate from care provided by biological parents; indeed, a child is considered fostered only when fostering occurs outside the extended family. In these societies, fostering is an accepted means of meeting children's emotional, physical, cultural and spiritual needs as well as providing stability and promoting their identity. In some of these communities, looking after one's young relatives is a natural thing to do. Things are, however, transparently different in Western societies where many people feel uncomfortable about even the idea itself, where the mere thought of sending away one's offspring to be raised by another family makes many shudder. It is not surprising, therefore, that kinship care poses thorny questions for child welfare professionals, policy-makers and researchers. In terms of policy, these problems relate particularly to the kind and amount of support and services that should be committed to supporting kinship care as a viable service.

Regarding practice, many have documented practitioners' reluctance to operate not just with a view of family that transcends the nuclear definition of family, but also to consider the strengths of kinship arrangements (Brown *et al.*, 2002; Jackson, 1999; McFadden and Downs, 1995; Messing, 2006). In other words, they are unprepared to adopt an ecological perspective on human development, a perspective which recognizes the fact that the parent-child dyad is nested in a family system which is itself nested in a kinship system embedded in a cultural and historical context. Concerning research, studies needed to help policy-makers to commit appropriate and adequate resources to support and promote kinship care, and practitioners to adopt new approaches to childcare are scant. Extant studies tend to be narrow in their focus. This chapter considers the implications of the core arguments of the book for theory and research, policy and professional childcare practice.

Policy

> *Observers of child welfare systems assert repeatedly that the state makes a bad parent. This appears to be true when the state attempts to provide care for a group of children while dedicating inadequate public resources for this effort.*
>
> (Herring, 2005, p. 392)

International research reinforces Herring's concern; it raises fears about the ambivalence of the child welfare systems towards kinship care, towards kinship caregivers and the children in their charge. This ambivalence is nowhere more patently manifest than in the funding and services disparity between kinship and non-kinship caregivers. Observers (e.g., Hegar, 1999b; Schwartz, 2002) attribute this to the low value states attach to kinship caregivers and the children for whom they care. For example, Hegar (1999b) argues that, as an organized social service, as an adaptive mechanism, public recognition of kinship care is not patent, that state policies do little to recognize the funding issues involved in kinship care and often provide kin caregivers with less public financial support than non-relative caregivers. She argues further that the undervaluing of kinship caregivers and the children from the most vulnerable categories seriously questions societal commitment to child wellbeing in general.

Many share Hegar's concerns. For example, Schwartz (2002, p. 413) argues that the lack of public support for kinship care reflects society's reluctance to effectively deal with the many questions surrounding the subject, such as:

- How much financial support should the state provide to kin caregivers?
- What factors should determine whether a particular kin caregiver receives support?
- Should kin caregivers have to meet the same licensing standards as non-relative caregivers in order to receive the same level of financial support?
- How should informal kinship caregivers be funded in comparison with their formal counterparts?
- How should the responsibility individuals have towards children to whom they are related influence the funding kin caregivers receive?
- How does funding kinship care fit in with the mission of the child welfare system?

Rutter (2000, p. 694) raises similar concerns about the low value states attach to children and their carers: *'The basic question here ... is why does*

society value childcare so little and what should be done to change this?'
Rutter accepts that many people are likely to impugn the assumption that
childcare is valued lowly. Still, he reinforces his concern by stressing the fact
that financial rewards for providing childcare of all kinds are set at a low
level. Perhaps, he should have added that the financial reward for providing
care for a young relative is set at an even lower level.

The solution to the question of what should be done to rectify the situation
seems straightforward – treat all child caregivers even-handedly – provide all
foster families with adequate, appropriate and equitable support and services.
However, such an answer would be naïve, in that it ignores the ideological
context in which public childcare is organized, provided and supported.
Besides those outlined above, unresolved ideological questions surrounding the funding of kinship care, as outlined by Schwartz (2002) include the
following: 1) whether kinship care is good for the child; 2) the presumption
that the poor health of some kinship caregivers is disadvantageous to the
child; and 3) the presumption of a cycle of generational abuse, that children
living with relatives are not adequately protected.

Previous chapters addressed many of these issues. Regarding policy,
however, the question of funding remains unanswered and operates as a significant barrier not only to financial assistance, but also to services. Schwartz
argues that this is mainly because kinship foster families are powerless, they
are perceived as belonging to the underclass. As we saw in the preceding
chapters, in Western societies, the typical kinship caregiver is a member
of several underprivileged, undervalued social categories – female, older,
African-American (in the USA), low income. Both caregivers and children are
often vulnerable because of their low status in society. Kinship care policies
do little to ameliorate their vulnerability; rather, they render these families
more vulnerable by failing to provide them with adequate assistance. Like
Rutter (2000), Schwartz claims that not only do these policies undervalue the
care of vulnerable children, they also demonstrate a lack of societal commitment to child wellbeing in general by failing to recognize the public good
that kinship caregivers provide.

Detractors of adequate funding for kinship caregivers argue that, despite
the public good kinship care provides, it is inappropriate for relatives to be
monetarily recompensed for what they regard as a family or natural duty –
caring for a blood-related child. To this, Schwartz's reply is that we should
examine the matter from a service perspective. Her case is that if caregivers
were compensated not because of their relationship to a child, but because
of the service they provide to society, then the special benefits which children
experience in kinship care would command greater compensation of kinship
caregivers over non-relative caregivers. Thus argued, it becomes clear how
badly kinship caregivers are short-changed by society. Instead of seeing child-
rearing as a public good, society treats providing care for a related child as
a family affair or duty and, so, decides not to intervene, however grave the
foster family's financial circumstances may be. Even if, as individuals, we

accept that a child's welfare is his/her family's business, Schwartz still argues that if individuals cannot adequately care for their own children, it is the state's role to step in and assist them. After all, she stresses, a primary goal of the child welfare system is to safeguard and promote the general wellbeing of the child. That is to say, the system is founded on the principle of the 'interest of the child', and not that of the caregiver. Therefore, with respect to children growing up in kinship foster care, the system is badly remiss in its duty of care.

Financial support and services

Kinship foster care is indisputably a valuable service to society. The crucial question for policy-makers is what support, particularly in terms of financial assistance, should be given to kinship caregivers. Schwartz (2002) proposes a public good approach to rectifying the funding and services differential between kinship foster care and non-relative foster care. She argues that appropriate or increased compensation to kin caregivers should not be denied simply because of higher costs. In terms of cost-effectiveness, she argues that properly funded and greater use of kinship care would cut the costs of paying for more restrictive child placements, and that the cost of case management is also likely be lower because kinship caregivers require less supervision and the children require fewer placements. It should be added that the social and emotional costs to the children, their caregivers, biological parents and society at large are lower than that of other placement arrangements. Thus viewed, one could argue in support of Schwartz's contention that kinship care should demand higher compensation than non-kinship care since the children receive greater emotional, social, cultural and other benefits in kinship care relative to other placement arrangements.

Equitable services are also needed to ensure adequate support for kinship families – whether they care for children on a formal or an informal basis, and whether the arrangement is temporary or permanent. Among the many benefits of kinship care is its ability to maintain children within their own families and communities, thus averting the need for foster care entry. It provides children with stable, loving and permanent care when they cannot return to their parents (Freundlich *et al.*, 2003). These strengths of kinship care, if appropriately recognized and supported by policy and practice, can play a significant role in avoiding or, at the least, addressing many of the psychosocial developmental difficulties that children growing up in care face and which they continue to face after leaving the care system.

In short, the minimum policy-makers can do to support kinship care is to place it on a par with non-relative foster care. As many have argued, public policy genuinely intent on promoting and safeguarding the wellbeing of *all* children must provide assistance in order to improve the circumstances of kinship foster families, to lift them out of poverty and give them the necessary support and resources to fulfil their care-giving duties. Indeed, many are emphatic that society as a whole must grapple with its conscious regarding the unfair treatment of kinship foster families in spite of the public good they provide (e.g., Hegar, 1999a; Iglehart, 1994; McFadden and Downs, 1995; Scannapieco and Hegar, 2002; Schwartz, 2002). Society must muster the political will to resolve the funding disparity between kinship foster-carers and their non-relative peers. It will be a clear demonstration that we value children, regardless of their family backgrounds, class, race/ethnicity or religion. We can only do this by equally valuing those who provide care and guidance for vulnerable children, for children in need.

Approval

A significant hurdle facing kinship foster families with regard to access to funding and services concerns state and agency approval or licensing requirements. In order to receive support, in terms of financial assistance and services, a foster-parent must be approved or licensed by the state. In the UK, for example, local authorities are the bodies responsible for assessing and approving prospective foster-parents. As several researchers and professionals have noted, the complex system of approval and payments precludes many potential kinship foster-parents from meeting the required standards (Berrick, *et al.*, 1994; Broad, 2001a, b; Farmer and Moyers, 2008; Flynn, 2002; Sykes *et al.*, 2002). Because of age, restricted accommodation or lack of suitable housing and other poverty-related problems, many kinship caregivers are unable to meet the formal criteria for providing foster care.

Another factor which precludes kinship foster-carers from meeting approval standards is to do with the circumstances under which they undertake caregiving. As Farmer and Moyers (2008) point out, non-relative carers make a conscious decision to provide foster care. They then approach a child welfare agency (social services) for approval as prospective carers. Next, they are then given training regarding the role, expectations and relationships with the agency. If approved, a child is placed with them and they enter into a contract with the agency. Thus, the assessment of foster-carers is completed before a child is placed. Kin, on the other hand, as we saw in previous chapters, generally respond in emergency; they respond to adverse circumstances surrounding their young and vulnerable relatives with no or little preparation. As such, they frequently fall outside the childcare system and, so, are untitled to state funding and services, however dire their circumstances are. For example, in a recent UK study, Farmer and Moyers (2008) found that the carers who were at the greatest financial disadvantage were those who took in the child of a relative or friend without social services' involvement. In these cases, social services took the view that the children were not their responsibility and, so, refused payment when the caregiver later requested help. One such case involved a grandmother who was caring for her three granddaughters because of their mother's drug dependency and resultant incarceration. Social services refused her financial support, although she could clearly not cope financially.

To be considered for financial assistance and services, those who take their young relatives in and later come to the attention of child welfare agencies (social services) have to be assessed for their care-giving responsibilities. Nonetheless, research suggests that, aside from the barriers they face in accessing assistance and services, such as approval requirements, kinship caregivers tend to be less positive towards assessment which might enable them to access state funding and services because of their relationship with the child. Indeed, many find it unnecessary and intrusive (Altshuler, 1999; Berrick, *et al.*, 1994; Broad, 2001b; Brown *et al.*, 2002; Farmer and Moyers, 2008; Flynn, 2002; McFadden, 1998; Pitcher, 2002; Scannapieco, 1999; Sykes *et al.*, 2002). Those who subject themselves to assessment and are approved to care for their young relatives still often end up worse off, compared to their non-relative counterparts. For example, Farmer and Moyers found that social workers often put pressure on them to apply for a residence order which entails lower allowances than fostering allowances. Many carers agreed to do so, sometimes on the incorrect understanding that there would be no financial disadvantages. In other words, they felt tricked when they discovered the true situation. They were justified to feel duped; in some cases, their allowance dropped by £34 a week as well as losing entitlements, such as birthday and Christmas payments.

In a previous study involving seven local authorities in England, Sykes and colleagues (2002) reported similar disparities in allowances paid to kinship foster-parents and non-relative foster-parents. In short, kinship caregivers who meet the requirements for approval and become formal kinship foster-parents and the children in their care are still at a disadvantage, *vis-à-vis* their non-relative counterparts, in that they receive less funding and services. Also, for various reasons, some eligible kinship caregivers are reluctant to request financial assistance or services. For instance, Pitcher (2002) found a high level of anxiety among kinship foster-parents about requesting help. They did not request practical help when they badly needed help for fear that social services would construe their request as evidence of their inability to cope and, so, would take the children away and place them elsewhere.

In summary, formal or informal, approved/licensed or not, we must remember that kinship care is kinship care; kinship caregivers provide the full-time care, protection and nurturing that the child requires. Yet, through various manoeuvres, most of them are denied the financial assistance and resources or services they need to enable them to better carry out these duties. Approval or licensing requirements represent the biggest barrier to their access to funding and services. Very frequently, policies compound the disadvantaged position they are already in and which makes it hard for them satisfy those criteria. To many researchers and practitioners, the remedy to kinship caregivers' difficulty in meeting approval standards, especially with regard to financial and housing circumstances, is to lower the threshold for accepting kinship placements (e.g., Broad, 2004; Calder and Talbot, 2006; Farmer and Moyers, 2008; Flynn, 2002). This is well-meaning, but apologetic, if not ill-thought-out. In the interest of the child, an effective and equitable solution would be to raise their living standard in order to enable them to meet those requirements.

McFadden and Downs (1995) and Scannapieco and Hegar (2002), like many others, stress the crucial role of kinship caregivers in the public child-care system; that they constitute one of the most valuable resources available to the system in caring for children. Scannapieco and Hegar highlight the empirical evidence about the characteristics of kinship caregivers and argue that, in the light of such evidence, their needs for services and financial assistance should be assessed based on the unique circumstances of the family. In other words, assessment should take into account their socio-economically disadvantaged position, relative to non-relative foster families. The international evidence reviewed in the preceding chapters suggests that this fact is frequently ignored in the assessment of the financial, services and support needs of kinship foster families, leading to what amounts to discrimination against these families. Schwartz (2002), among many others, also emphasizes the inequity of this by stressing the obvious fact that, although individuals and families who provide non-relative foster care and kinship foster care are essentially contributing the same services to child welfare agencies, child welfare agencies seldom provide the same resources to kinship foster families.

Advocacy

Very few will disagree with Berry's (1998, pp. 6–7) assertion that '*preserving families is not dangerous, on balance. Impermanence and discontinuity of family and place is the enemy, and both adoption and family preservation are two means by which to vanquish that enemy*'. Berry (p. 7) rightly recognizes that '*to achieve that outcome, all parties – birth parents, adoptive parents and children deserve a fair shake*'. Kinship care provides permanence and preserves families. As such, it may be described as the 'enemy of the enemy', the enemy of family disintegration and impermanence. Yet, as research shows, through various means, some devious, society denies kinship care providers the fairness they need to overcome that enemy; we refuse to afford them and the children due value. Scannapieco and Hegar's (1999) analysis reinforces this claim. They argue that if social values were different, many of the concerns surrounding kinship foster care would cease to be concerns. To achieve this, they recommend that birth parents, kinship caregivers and non-relative foster-parents be equally eligible for public benefits and services. They believe that this will avoid many of the awkward questions about kinship care, questions which frequently result in unnecessary public care or leaving children looked after by relatives in poverty.

While many call for more research on frontline practices and kinship families themselves to understand better why services are not being accessed, others believe that what is required now is advocacy to dismantle the barriers to financial support and services which kinship caregivers face. Besides those sketched above, these barriers include caregivers' lack of information (e.g., Farmer and Moyers, 2008; Pitcher, 2002; Sykes *et al.*, 2002). In other words, many of them are unaware of their eligibility or might wish to avoid contact with child welfare professionals. In such cases, what they require is reassurance and easy, reliable access to advice and practical support. For example, many of Pitcher's (2002) grandparent caregivers expressed their wish for relevant information; they stated that clear, written information about entitlements should be given at the beginning of a placement, together with a package of help with transport and financial support.

Equally, some professionals are either ignorant or have misconceptions about services to which kinship foster families are entitled. For example, in Farmer and Moyers' (2008) national study, a number of workers commented that, unlike non-relative foster-carers, not only were kin carers ignorant of their entitlements, but also many of the children's key social workers did not know. Those who did know expected kinship caregivers to manage with little or no support at all. Such nonchalant attitudes among social workers towards kinship families were described openly by another social worker who explained that her team manager had instructed her, and presumably the rest of the team, that her role with kinship foster-carers was a strictly limited one: '*I remember the team manager saying that as far as families go, we don't really have an awful lot to do with them – except if there is a crisis or something goes wrong and then we sort of go down*' (in Farmer and Moyers, 2008, p. 192). In other words, the team's role was one of child protection, rather than family support. Some providers of kinship care may be unaware of their entitlements, but they still feel cheated by the childcare system and they are aware that the system discriminates against them (Farmer and Moyers, 2008; Flynn, 2002; Pitcher; 2002; Sykes *et al.*, 2002).

Relatives who assume the role of kinship caregiver may need assistance with housing, financial, legal, childcare and respite services (Calder and Talbot (2006). However, their access to these services and support is either restricted or denied, largely owing to their disadvantaged and powerless position. Many researchers and childcare professionals suggest the remedy to this unfair situation is advocacy; they suggest an alliance between professionals and kinship caregivers to advocate for increased support (McMillen, *et al.*, 2003; Sands and Goldberg-Glen, 2000; Schwartz, 2002). On top of this, Schwartz (2002) suggests establishing groups of 'professional' advocates or pressure groups to help relatives caring for children outside of the public care system to obtain financial benefits and other services and deal with any legal proceedings. For the children, McMillen and colleagues (2003) argue for a system of education advocates who work to develop and maintain suitable education placements for youth in foster care in general and help them receive the academic resources they need to succeed.

Intervention and support

One of the major roles that differentiate kinship care from non-relative care is that kinship care provides direct links to the child's socio-genealogical roots; it connects the child not just to his/her biological roots, but equally importantly, to his/her social, cultural and spiritual heritage. As Nisivoccia (1996) argues, organized kinship care rests on the philosophy of family preservation that acknowledges the strengths inherent in families, the positive influence of family ties on the child's growth and development. Kinship foster care provides internal commitment by way of maintaining family ties and ensuring the child's sense of continuity or connectedness. As such, many propose that intervention in kinship foster care should provide direct care and support to all involved: the child, the biological parent(s) and the relatives (Holtan, 2008; Mosek and Adler, 2001; Nisivoccia, 1996). McFadden and Downs (1995) reinforce this in arguing for appropriately assessed, planned for, and supported kinship care service that reflects the principles of child-centred, family-focused casework practice, the model of practice that child welfare practitioners should advocate as the unifying theme for child welfare services generally. Such childcare practice, according to proponents, strengthens a child's kinship network and so requires professionals to adopt and operate with a view of family that transcends the nuclear definition of family. This section examines some of the ways in which childcare practitioners may meet this challenge.

Scannapieco and Hegar (2002), concerned more about the children's wellbeing, argue that the needs of kinship caregivers may be different from those of non-relative foster-parents, but the needs of children in both types of placement are similar, and so urge child welfare agencies (social workers) to provide services that are more equitable across placements. This is a difficult argument to refute. A programme likely to ensure equity in service provision between kinship foster families and non-relative foster families requires a shift from the traditional 'child rescue' approach to one of family support. In the former approach, there is often a cognitive mismatch between social workers and kinship foster-parents. In other words, as Chipman and colleagues (2002) have observed, child welfare workers tend to focus on child safety and permanency issues in placement decisions; kinship caregivers, on the other hand, focus on their ability to provide the children with love and moral and spiritual guidance.

Various researchers and professionals have proposed a variety of programmes to achieve parity in financial assistance and services between kinship foster families and non-kinship foster families. These programmes are generally based not only upon the principle of morality, but also on the notion of empowerment in its true sense, a political activity. One such approach is what is commonly termed 'family conference' or 'family meetings'. Proponents of this approach, while recognizing the many challenges of working with kinship foster families, argue that kinship foster-parents and their families should be empowered to make decisions and identify their support and intervention needs along with the social worker. Many (e.g., Nisivoccia, 1996; Scannapieco and Hegar, 2002) argue that it is within the family conference or family meetings that the needs of kinship foster families should be assessed and reviewed. Scannapieco and Hegar (2002), for instance, suggest that in this endeavour, in assessing and meeting the needs of kinship foster families, four categories of needs should be considered:

- financial – among many other things, kinship care providers need financial assistance to cover such costs as clothing, transportation and so forth;
- services – the worker must examine the case management, legal, mental health, medical and dental services that are needed by the child in kinship care;
- social support – the worker is charged with helping families assess challenges in their social network and to make the appropriate connections to formal and informal resources in their communities to address them; and
- educational – the worker must seek and ensure appropriate education that meets the needs of children with special educational needs. (See Scannapieco and Hegar, 2002, for detailed discussion.)

While some researchers emphasize kinship foster-parents' financial and services needs, often, as outlined by the Child Welfare League of America (1994), others stress their family preservation role and the need for childcare practitioners to support them in this role. Nisivoccia (1996) provides one of the most comprehensive approaches to working with kinship foster families in this respect. It incorporates the family conference model and the notions of family strengths, empowerment and cultural competence. Nisivoccia recommends that effective practice with kinship foster families be guided by the following (summarized) overlapping precepts and strategies. The notion of socio-genealogical connectedness supports these guiding principles.

Kinship foster families are biological families: Socio-genealogical connectedness theory fully endorses this principle. Nisivoccia rightly makes no distinction between kinship foster family and biological family; in either family, the parents and the child are usually related by blood. She stresses the importance and strength of kinship ties and the common heritage, values, norms and world view that kinship foster-parents and the children share, and which have been passed down over generations. In brief, from a socio-genealogical connectedness perspective, kinship foster-parents have a vested interest in not only preserving family history and maintaining continuity and stability of their families, but also in fostering the child's sense of belonging and identity. Thus, in working with kinship foster families, Nisivoccia asks practitioners to be mindful of the obvious fact that kinship families have unique family stories, customs, beliefs, alliances and secrets which they share in common with the child and his/her birth parents. In terms of strategy, she suggests that the worker should explore life stories for a better understanding of family structure, roles and dynamics, as well as the kinship parent's interpretation of the current placement situation. She advises that the worker's intervention be appropriately timed, within context, and explained as not a matter of curiosity, but to understand the facts that might help the worker to assist the family.

Ethclass and culturally sensitive practice is needed: Nisivoccia suggests that it is essential for workers involved with kinship families to value and accept ethnic, class and cultural differences, especially as they relate to preserving and promoting the extended family and its structure. She emphasizes also that it is critical that the worker is aware of his/her own ethnic, class and cultural heritage, and acknowledges his/her bias and changes his/her attitudes which would otherwise create obstacles in building a relationship based upon trust with the kinship foster-parents. This approach, which Nisivoccia uses the phrase 'ethclass' to describe, takes into account the limitations of life chances and options imposed on families who are disadvantaged on the grounds of 'race', gender, ethnicity and class. These are social categories to which most kinship families belong in Western societies, especially the USA.

Work from a holistic perspective: Nisivoccia agrees with McFadden and Downs (1995) that family continuity practice, work with kinship foster families, must be based on an ecological perspective, on an approach which leads to a holistic assessment and intervention in the complex transactions of the kinship-foster family, and which enables the worker to provide an array of services which incorporate the needs of the whole family. They acknowledge that this approach requires the worker to assume a multi-role. They accept also that to be successful in the various roles, the worker must identify formal and informal systems in the kinship foster-parent's life which will provide extra support and resources, for instance, services within the community, neighbours and friends, church, schools, extended family, formal kinship support groups, home aid, day care and respite care. In other words, the worker must seek to exploit the social and cultural capital available within the family's community. This is consistent with Scannapieco and Hegar's third suggestion (above).

Start where the kinship parent is: Efficacious intervention necessitates empathy on the part of the worker. Nisivoccia suggests that the worker be able to anticipate the difficulties and struggles facing the family, so as to make appropriately timed, empathic interventions. The worker should assume that the agency's presence in the family's life is seen as an intrusion into a natural support system and, so, should attempt to develop parity in communication, to establish a cognitive match, in order to find solutions to or mitigate those difficulties and struggles.

Birth parents are important: This is one of the core assumptions of the theory of socio-genealogical connectedness (see especially Owusu-Bempah, 2007). It must be added that other relatives, siblings included, are important too. Whether biological parents are deceased or alive, present in or absent from the child's life, their presence is felt in the family's life, especially in the child's life. Most kinship foster-parents, particularly grandparents, appreciate the importance of the biological parents and siblings to the child's emotional wellbeing and adjustment to placement and, so, try to maintain contact between them, via whatever means safe and possible. For instance, several studies (e.g., Aldgate and McIntosh, 2006; Brown *et al.*, 2002; Chapman *et al.*, 2004; Cleaver, 2000; Hindle, 2000; Holtan, 2008; LeProhn, 1994; Owusu-Bempah 2007; Pitcher, 2002; Sanchirico and Jablonka, 2000; Triseliotis and Russell, 1984) indicate that kinship foster-parents see themselves as having responsibility for facilitating and maintaining the child's contact with his/her birth parents, siblings and other relatives. Such research shows also that it is something that most children in care, like other separated children, desire.

Most kinship caregivers rightly believe that the biological parents should not be excluded from the child's life. *'They need to see their mum; their mum is everything to them'* (in Aldgate and McIntosh, 2006, p. 66). Thus, it is important that workers do not allow themselves to be unduly swayed by the family pathology or dysfunctional family argument with respect to the child's contact, direct or indirect, with his/her biological parents and other relatives. That is, assessment regarding safety issues must be based on evidence, as opposed to stereotypes, preconceptions and misconceptions. Most importantly, as Nisivoccia suggests, such assessment issues must be conducted with the worker respecting and supporting the kinship foster-parent on this matter.

Assess and work from a 'strengths perspective': The preceding chapters highlight the strengths of the extended family network to care for and be a resource to one another in times of extreme need. It is important to assess and understand the strengths and limitations kinship foster-parents bring to the task of caring for a child. Focusing solely on deficits or weaknesses while making an assessment can lead to a self-fulfilling prophecy. Preoccupation with negatives underestimates and devalues kinship foster-parents and their role as active and valuable participants in the public childcare system. Instead, Nisivoccia recommends that the worker's helping role be one of avoiding blame and affirming problem-solving, self-determination and the preservation and autonomy of the family. This means enabling, supporting, fostering, coaching and providing optimism and insight to activate strengths and latent assets. She believes that the use of a strengths perspective enhances the kinship foster-parent's sense of power and equality in the helping relationship. Her advice is that interventions be directed at restoring responsibility to the birth parent and extended family to enable them to regain control over their collective life.

Work together toward empowerment: Empowerment, as propounded by Freire (1972), is a political activity requiring solidarity and personal commitment. It means working with the underdog, the undervalued and oppressed to identify their oppressors or the true causes of their socially disadvantaged position and, more importantly, to find ways of neutralizing their oppressors or finding solutions to the problems associated with their low social status. As evidence clearly shows, most kinship families in Western societies have suffered from the oppressive realities of discrimination based on class, age, colour and gender. Many kinship families already have a raised consciousness about dealing with oppression, for instance the injustice within the system. Thus, as Nisivoccia points out, they appreciate it if the worker also recognizes the social injustice they experience and wants to be in alliance with them to challenge oppressive forces. That is, Nisivoccia suggests that when blocks are located (including internalized oppression) the worker and kinship foster-parent together decide how to change the situation and take action. For example, the worker may validate concerns about powerlessness and promote and join in the reflection and action process. A worker who truly understands the notion of empowerment and genuinely believes in it will agree with Nisivoccia, (1996, p. 13) that '*We* cannot empower *kinship families, but we can* join with *them in efforts to empower themselves*' (emphasis added).

In a similar vein, Leonardsen (2007) has warned that social workers who possess only a limited or an individualistic grasp of the concept of empowerment are at risk of operating as moralizing agents rather than as agents of change. He argues that it is through the intricate interaction between a given socio-material situation and the individual capacity to understand and, more importantly, act that one finds the key to an empowerment worthy of its name. This, he claims, presupposes two things: 1) that social workers have, as a part of their education, theoretical knowledge about organizational structures, and 2) that they themselves have been empowered in ways that give them practical skills to act in relation to situations. They need the aptitude to appreciate the minutiae of interests and power present in any situation in society. According to Leonardsen, the implication of such recognition for social work education is clear: *the ideology of empowerment has to be contexualised* (Leonardsen, 2007, p. 3). Leonardsen's description of empowerment and its implications for professional practice reinforces an earlier argument by Spring (1994). Spring argues that to enable workers in the helping professions, such as social workers, teachers and psychologists, to be effective agents of change, their education and training, including the literature to which they are exposed, should be empowering. Their education and training must equip them with:

> The means to critically appropriate the knowledge existing outside their immediate experience in order to broaden their understanding of themselves, the world, and the possibilities for transforming the taken-for-granted assumptions about the way we live.
>
> (Spring, 1994, p. 27)

The above authors' suggestions together provide a useful tool for working with kinship families and other service users.

Permanency is the primary objective: Regarding kinship care, permanency planning applies only to formal arrangements. In such cases, the goals are different from a non-relative placement; they are different also from one kinship situation to another, since those goals are often inconsistent with the non-relative foster care or permanency planning options. Nisivoccia, therefore suggests that the worker study all of the child's existing relationships with kin, blood or fictive, to assess the validity of changing the child's legal status, if necessary, required or desirable, such as adoption or guardianship, to affirm an existing emotional relationship. In such a situation, she argues that permanency must be defined and operationalized in a way that preserves and supports the family, in addition to creating a supportive community, regardless of legal status. This may include birth parents, extended family network, or the new families added through foster care or adoption.

In applying these principles, we must bear in mind the child's need for socio-genealogical information. The present author, therefore, recommends incorporating the idea of socio-genealogical connectedness in these principles and strategies or in any practice with children in care and adopted children. In other words, without disregarding the child's other needs, consideration must be given to the person(s) amongst the child's kinship network who are suited to providing the child with the richest possible socio-genealogical information, those best equipped and prepared to connect the child to his/her hereditary roots. In fact, this applies to permanency planning for all children in the care system, regardless of the type of placement they are in.

Professional training

For social workers and other childcare agencies to appreciate kinship care as a valuable resource and so work effectively with kinship families, their training must equip them with the necessary knowledge and skills. Lamentably, such knowledge and skills are largely missing from training curricula. This is mainly because, in spite of being an ancient and customary mechanism of childcare, kinship care as an aspect of the public childcare system is an emerging phenomenon in contemporary Western societies. Thus, standard foster-care training concentrates mainly on topics such as facilitating the child's adjustment to their relocation (to a new environment), assessing foster-parents' capacity to parent, encouraging foster-parent role modelling, and helping workers to make permanency planning decisions (Jackson, 1999). Hence, when faced with kinship foster families, many practitioners feel inadequate and insecure.

They often project their feeling of inadequacy onto the family. For instance, Peters (2005) points out that many social workers do not feel confident in their skills and abilities to assess the likely level of dysfunction in kinship families or to deal with family conflicts related to past abuse. He interprets the 'apple does not fall far from the tree' metaphor, which some of the workers in his study used to rationalize their ambivalence towards kinship care, as '*not just a description of family members' ability to appropriately care for the child, but … also a description of the dynamic issues which are likely to confront the worker*' (Peters, 2005, p. 608). In short, Peters argues that kinship placement raises serious concerns for workers who feel that their training and skills are inadequate to face the complexity and power of dealing with the family dynamics which they encounter in kinship placements.

To better prepare workers for the task, Jackson (1999) recommends specialized training designed to increase the competence, knowledge and skill of family and child welfare professionals and to familiarize them with a system of social work practice that is unique to the kinship triad – child, parent and caregiver. Nonetheless, such training would still be incomplete without due consideration of the wider context in which this triad operates as a family. From socio-genealogical connectedness perspective, the ecology of kinship family transcends this triad; it includes the community at large. Training designed to equip practitioners to work effectively with kinship foster families, therefore, needs to take this into account, it must incorporate this perspective. In our pursuit of 'the best interest of the child', we must not overlook the child's right to continuity with respect to his/her family, kin and ancestors. As Yngvesson (2004) points out with regard to adoption, it is essential that we do not conflate an ideology of family permanence with the need of a child for continuity; in other words, a need for socio-genealogical connectedness.

Research

> *Nothing that is less than top-quality research should be regarded as good enough for policy and practice questions that are concerned with the future of a new generation of children.*
>
> (Rutter, 2000, p. 698)

Rutter considers the need for focused research in the area of public childcare generally to be acutely urgent. Like several others, he clearly acknowledges the pressing need for studies that provide better documentation on what is taking place in the field of provision of alternative parental care. Schwartz (2007) agrees with Rutter and notes that extant studies concerning the effects of kinship care, for example, tend to evaluate more tangible outcomes like physical health and scholastic achievement, rather than less concrete outcomes, such as identity. To deal with these and related concerns, Rutter (2000; p. 697) beseeches us to '*move beyond descriptive studies to research that can tackle questions on causal mechanisms (but recognising that multiple factors and indirect chain effects are likely to be the rule rather than the exception)*'.

One way of going beyond descriptive studies, with regard to the negative consequences of the public care system for psychosocial developmental outcomes, as Rutter suggests, may be to follow Little and colleagues' (2005) advice. Namely, in their examination of the impact of residential placement on child development, Little and colleagues (2005, p. 207) recommend *'less ideology and more science, alongside building expertise to apply research to policy and practice'*. These suggestions are noteworthy. Nevertheless, in order to provide top-quality research that will better inform policy and practice in the area of child welfare, we must go beyond not just descriptive studies; we must also expand our theoretical horizon. For example, in order to address adequately the question as to why different child placement settings result in different psychosocial developmental outcomes, why children placed with kin fare better than do those placed with non-relatives, who, in turn, fare better than those growing up in residential settings, we need to go beyond traditional and taken-for-granted attachment theory. For almost 70 years now, attachment theory has been used as a monocle, as the sole 'theoretical device' for examining the intricacies of child development. That is to say, it has been employed in a way that provides us with a monocular view of the world of the growing child and beyond, as a basis for research, policy and practice (Owusu-Bempah, 2007; Owusu-Bempah and Howitt, 1997; Rutter, 1991; Rutter and O'Connor, 1999). Consequently, we struggle for a satisfactory explanation for the disparate developmental outcomes between children raised by relatives and those looked after by strangers. This is by no means to suggest that we ignore attachment theory in our efforts to gain a better understanding of children's developmental needs. However, it is clear that we need something additional in order to gain a fuller insight into the world of the developing child.

The notion of socio-genealogical connectedness provides a promising approach. Atwool (2006, p. 231) suggests that if we rescue attachment theory from its shackles, *'from the perils of monotropism and monoculturalism, its focus on the significance of relationships provides a conceptual framework that encourages an integrated approach to understanding children's behaviour and the dynamics of resilience'*. Socio-genealogical connectedness obviously has a place in such an approach. It compliments attachment theory and vice versa. Thus, both theories may easily be amalgamated to formulate a unified framework which will help us not only to explain why children placed with kin or within their local community tend to fare better than those placed with non-kin or outside their community, but also to provide a better understanding of children's social and psychological functioning. It will also help us formulate and design appropriate policies, programmes and services that will serve the child's best interest, policies and interventions that will foster the child's growth and development.

Talbot (2006a, p. 9) argues: *'If kinship placements meet children's emotional, physical, cultural and religious needs, provide stability and promote identity, then they must be coherently and consistently promoted as the preferred placement option for all children and young people.'* Socio-genealogical connectedness postulates that kinship placement, indeed, achieves these objectives. However, to convince sceptics, research is needed to remove the 'if' from Talbot's suggestion. Research is urgently needed to establish the extent to which a sense of socio-genealogical connectedness makes an independent contribution to the adjustment and global wellbeing of children and young people growing up in care. Using, for example, such indicators as emotional wellbeing, academic achievement and conduct in a general population sample of children in care, such research can compare children and young people in care, children in informal or private childcare arrangements included, on these and other relevant measures. Such studies must not ignore the children's voices. In other words, their design must place equal weight on the children's placement experiences. Equally importantly, such studies must contain an action-research element designed to enhance its contribution to policy and practice or interventions with not only children in foster care, kinship or non-relative care, but also those in residential care and their families.

Bibliography

Achenbach, T. M. (1991). *Manual for the Child Behavior Check List/4–18 and 1991 Profile*. Burlington, VT: Department of Psychiatry, University of Vermont.

Ainsworth, M. (1967). *Infancy in Uganda: Infant Care and the Growth of Love*. Baltimore: Johns Hopkins University Press.

Ainsworth, M. (1989). Attachments beyond infancy. *The American Psychologist*, 44, 709–16.

Alber, E. (2003). Denying biological parenthood: fosterage in Northern Benin. *Ethnos*, 68, 487–506.

Alber, E. (2004). The real parents are the foster parents: Social parenthood among the Baatombu in Northern Benin. In F. Bowie (ed.), *Cross-Cultural Approaches to Adoption*. London: Routledge. pp. 33–47.

Aldgate, J. (1977). *Factors Influencing Children's Length of Stay in Care*. Ph.D. thesis, University of Edinburgh.

Aldgate, J. and McIntosh, M. (2006). *Looking After the Family: A Study of Children Looked After in Kinship Care in Scotland*. Edinburgh: Social Work Inspection Agency.

Aldgate, J. Colton, M., Ghate, D. and Heath, A. (1992). Educational attainment and stability in long-term foster care. *Children and Society*, 6(2), 91–103.

Aldgate, J., Heath, A., Colton, M. and Simm, M. (1993). Social work and the education of children in foster care. *Adoption & Fostering*, 17(3), 25–34.

Alexander, R. D. (1979). *Darwinism and Human Affairs*. Seattle: University of Washington Press.

Allott, A. N. (1966). The Ashanti law of property. *Zeitschrift für vergleichende Rechtswissenschaft*, 68, 129–215.

Altshuler, S. J. (1998). Child well-being in kinship foster care: similar to, or different from, non-related foster care? *Children and Youth Services Review*, 20(5), 369–88.

Altshuler, S. J. (1999). Children in kinship foster care speak out: 'We think we're doing fine'. *Child and Adolescent Social Work*, 16(6), 215–35.

American Psychiatric Association (1994). *Diagnostic and Statistical Manual of Mental Disorders* (DMS-IV). Washington, DC: American Psychiatric Association.

Anderson, G. (1999). Children in residential care and foster care – a Swedish example. *International Journal of Social Welfare*, 8, 253–66.

Anderson, G. (2001). The motives of foster parents, their family and work circumstances. *British Journal of Social Work*, 31, 235–48.

Anderson, K. (2004). *Urth noe e tat*: the question of fosterage in High Medieval Wales. *North American Journal of Welsh Studies*, 4(1), 1–11.

Arredondo, D. E. and Edwards, L. P. (2000). Attachment, bonding and reciprocal connectedness: limitations of attachment theory in the juvenile and family court. *Journal of the Centre for Families, Children and the Courts*, 2, 109–27.

Atwool, N. (2006). Attachment and resilience: implications for children in care. *Child Care Practice*, 12(4), 315–30.

Baran, A and Pannor, R. (1993). *Lethal Secrets: The Psychology of Donor Insemination – Problems and Solutions*. New York: Amistad.

Barth, R. P. (1990). On their own: the experiences of youth after foster care. *Child and Adolescent Social Work*, 7(5), 419–40.

Barth, R. P. (1997). Effects of age and race on the odds of adoption versus remaining in long-term out-of-home care. *Child Welfare*, 76(2), 285–308.

Barth, R., Crea, T. M., John, K., Thoburn, J. and Quinton, D. (2005). Beyond attachment theory and therapy: towards sensitive and evidence-based interventions with foster and adoptive families in distress. *Child and Family Social Work*, 10, 257–68.

Bartholet, E. (1999). *Nobody's Children: Abuse and Neglect, Foster Drift, and the Adoption Alternative*. Boston: Beacon Press.

Batty, D. (2003). *Catalogue of Cruelty*. Available online at http://www.guardian.co.uk/society/2003/jan/27/childrensservices.childprotection.

Bebbington, A. and Miles J. (1989). The background of children who enter local authority care. *British Journal of Social Work*, 19, 349–68.

Beck, A. (2006). Users' view of looked after children's mental health services. *Adoption & Fostering*, 30(2), 53–63.

Beeman, S. and Boisen, L. (1999). Child welfare professionals' attitudes towards kinship foster care. *Child Welfare*, 78(3), 315–37.

Beeman, S. K., Kim, H. and Bullerdick. (2000). Factors affecting placement of children in kinship and nonkinship foster care. *Children and Youth Services Review*, 22(1), 37–54.

Belsky, J. (2006). Attachment theory and research in ecological perspective. In K. E. Grossman, K. Grossman and E. Waters (eds), *Attachment from Infancy to Adulthood: The Major Longitudinal Studies*. London: Guildford Press. pp. 71–97.

Benedict, M., Zuravin, S., Brandt, D. and Abbey, H. (1994). Types and frequency of child maltreatment by family foster care providers in an urban population. *Child Abuse & Neglect*, 18(7), 577–85.

Benedict, M. I., Zuraman, S. and Stallings, R. Y. (1996). Adult functioning of children who lived in kin versus nonrelative family foster homes. *Child Welfare*, 75, 529–49.

Bengtson, V. (2001). Beyond the nuclear family: the increasing importance of multi-generational bonds. *Journal of Marriage and Family*, 63(1), 1–16.

Berrick, J. D. (1997). Assessing quality of kinship and foster family care. *Family Relations*, 46(3), 273–80.

Berrick, J. D. and Barth, R. P. (1994). Research on kinship foster care: What do we know? Where do we go from here? *Children and Youth Services*, 16(1/2), 1–5.

Berrick J. D., Barth, R. P. and Needell, B. (1994). A comparison of kinship foster homes and foster family homes: implications for kinship foster care as family preservation. *Children and Youth Services Review*, 16 (1/2), 33–63.

Berrick, J. D., Needle, B. and Barth, R. P. (1999). Kin as a family and child welfare resource: the child welfare worker's perspective. In R. L. Hegar, and M. Scannapieco (eds), *Kinship Foster Care: Policy, Practice, and Research*. Oxford: Oxford University Press. pp. 180–92.

Berridge, D. (1994). Foster and residential care reassessed: a research perspective. *Children & Society*, 8(2), 132–50.

Berridge, D. (1997). *Foster Care: A Research Review.* London: The Stationery Office.

Berridge, D. and Brodie, I. (1998). *Children's Homes Revisited.* London: Jessica Kingsley.

Berridge, D. and Cleaver, H. (1987). *Foster Home Breakdown.* Oxford: Blackwell.

Berry, M. (1998). Adoption in an era of family preservation. *Children and Youth Services Review*, 20(1/2), 1–12.

Bilgé, B. and Kaufman, G. (1983). Children of divorce and one-parent families: cross-cultural perspectives. *Family Relations*, 32, 59–71.

Bloch, M. and Sperber, D. (2004). Kinship and evolved psychological dispositions: the mother's brother controversy reconsidered. In L. Parkin and L. Stone (eds), *Kinship and Family: An Anthropological Reader.* Oxford: Blackwell. pp. 438–55.

Boada, C. M. (2007). Kinship foster care: a study from the perspective of the carers, the children and the child welfare workers. *Psychology in Spain*, 11(1), 42–52.

Bohr, Y. and Tse, C. (2009). Satellite babies in transnational families: a study of parents' decision to separate from their children. *Infant Mental Health Journal*, 30(3), 1–22.

Bowie, F. (2004). Adoption and the circulation of children: a comparative perspective. In F. Bowie (ed.), *Cross-Cultural Approaches to Adoption.* London: Routledge. pp. 3–20.

Bowlby, J. (1944). Forty-four juvenile thieves: their characteristics and home-life. *The International Journal of Psychoanalysis*, 25, 19–53.

Bowlby, J. (1969). *Attachment.* London: Penguin.

Bowlby, J. (1973). *Attachment and Loss: II. Separation Anxiety and Anger.* London: Hogarth Press.

Bowlby, J. (1980). *Attachment and Loss: III. Loss, Sadness and Depression.* New York: Basic Books.

Bowlby, J. (1988). *A Secure Base: Clinical Application of Attachment Theory.* London: Routledge.

Brady, I. (ed.) (1976). *Transactions in Kinship: Adoption and Fosterage in Oceania.* Honolulu: University of Hawaii Press.

Brand, A. E. and Brinich, P. M. (1999). Behavior problems and mental health contact in adopted, foster, and nonadopted children. *Journal of Child Psychology and Psychiatry*, 40(8), 1221–9.

Bretherton, I. (1985). Attachment theory: retrospect and prospect. In I. Bretherton and E. Waters (eds), *Growing Points of Attachment Theory and Research.* Chicago: Chicago University Press. pp. 3–35.

Bretherton, I. (1991). The roots and growing points of attachment theory. In C. M. Parkes, J. Stevenson-Hinde and P. Marris (eds), *Attachment Across the Life Cycle.* London: Routledge. pp. 9–32.

Bretherton, I. and Munholland, K. A. (1999). Internal working models in attachment relationships: a construct revisited. In J. Cassidy and P. R. Shaver (eds), *Handbook of Attachment: Theory, Research, and Clinical Application.* London: The Guildford Press. pp. 89–111.

Brian, J. and Martin, M. D. (1983). *Child Care and Health for Nursery Nurses.* Amersham: Hulton.

Broad, B. (1998). Kinship care: children placed with extended families or friends. *Childright*, 155 (April), 16–17.

Broad, B. (2001a). Kinship care: Supporting children in placements with extended family and friends. *Adoption & Fostering*, 25(4), 38–41.

Broad, B. (ed.) (2001b). *Kinship Care: The Placement Choice for Children and Young People*. Lyme Regis: Russell House.

Broad, B. (2004). Kinship care for children in the UK: messages from research, lessons for policy and practice. *European Journal of Social Work*, 7(2), 211–27.

Broad, B. (2006). Some advantages and disadvantages of kinship care: a view from research. In C. Talbot and C. Calder (eds), *Assessment in Kinship Care*. Lyme Regis: Russell House. pp. 13–24.

Bronfenbrenner, U. (1979). Contexts of child-rearing: problems and prospects. *American Psychologist*, 34(10), 844–50.

Bronfenbrenner, U. (1986). Ecology of the family as a context for human development: research perspective. *Developmental Psychology*, 22(6), 723–42.

Bronfenbrenner, U. (1992). Ecological systems theory. In R. Vasta (ed.), *Child Development: Revised Formulations and Current Issues*. London: Jessica Kingsley.

Brook, D. and Barth, R. P. (1998). Characteristics and outcomes of drug-exposed and non-drug-exposed children in kinship and non-relative foster care. *Children and Youth Services Review*, 20(6), 475–501.

Brown, S., Cohon, D. and Wheeler, R. (2002). African-American extended families and kinship care: how relevant is the foster care model for kinship care? *Children and Youth Services Review*, 24(1), 53–77.

Buehler, C., Cox, M. E. and Cuddeback, G. (2003). Foster parents; perceptions of factors that promote or inhibit successful fostering. *Qualitative Social Work: Research and Practice*, 2(1), 61–83.

Burnstein, E., Crandall, C. and Kitaya, S. (1994). Some neo-Darwinian decision rules for altruism: weighing cues for inclusive fitness as a function of the biological importance of the decision. *Journal of Personality and Social Psychology*, 67(3), 773–89.

Cairns, K. (2002). *Attachment, Trauma and Resilience: Therapeutic Caring for Children*. London: BAAF.

Calder, M. C. and Talbot, C. (2006). Assessment in kinship placements: towards a sensitive, evidence-based framework. In C. Talbot and C. Calder (eds), *Assessment in Kinship Care*. Lyme Regis: Russell House. pp 132–51.

Cantos, A. L., Gries, L. T. and Slis, V. (1997). Behavioral correlates of parental visiting during family foster care. *Child Welfare*, 76(2), 309–29.

Carlson, V. J. and Harwood, R. L. (2003). Attachment, culture, and the caregiving system: the cultural patterning of everyday experiences among Anglo and Puerto Rican mother-infant pairs. *Infant Mental Health Journal*, 24(1), 53–72.

Carpenter, S. C. and Clyman, R. B. (2004). The long-term emotional wellbeing of women who have lived in kinship care. *Children and Youth Services Review*, 26(7), 673–86.

Carsten J. (2000). 'Knowing where you've come from': ruptures and continuities of time and kinship in narratives of adoption reunions. *Journal of the Royal Anthropological Institute*, 6(4), 687–703.

Carsten J. (2007). Constitutive knowledge: tracing trajectories of information in new contexts of relatedness. *Anthropological Quarterly*, 80(2), 403–26.

Cashmore, J. and Paxman, M. (1996). *Longitudinal Study of Wards Leaving Care*. Sydney: University of New South Wales.

Castle, S. (1995). Child fostering and children's nutritional outcomes in rural Mali: the role of female status in directing child transfers. *Social Science and Medicine*, 40(5), 679–94.

Chapman, M. V., Wall, A. and Barth, R. P. (2004). Children's voices: the perceptions of children in foster care. *American Journal of Orthopsychiatry*, 74(3), 293–304.

Child Welfare Information Gateway (2006). *Sibling Issues in Foster Care and Adoption*. Available online at http://www.childwelfare.gov/pubs/siblingissues/index.cfm.

Child Welfare League of America. (1994). *Kinship Care: A Natural Bridge*. Washington, DC: CWLA Press.

Chipman, R. Wells., S. J. and Johnson, M. A. (2002). The meaning of quality in kinship foster care: caregiver, child and worker perspectives. *Families in Society: The Journal of Contemporary Social Services*, 83(5), 508–20.

Clausen, J. M., Landsverk, J., Granger, W., Chadwick, M. D. and Litrownik, A. (1998). Mental health problems of children in foster care. *Journal of Child and Family Studies*, 7(3), 283–96.

Cleaver, H. (2000). *Fostering and Family Contact*. London: The Stationery Office.

Coakley, T. M., Cuddeback, C. B. and Cox, M. E. (2007). Kinship parents' perceptions of factors that promote or inhibit successful fostering. *Children and Youth Services Review*, 29, 92–109.

Cole, S. A. (2005). Foster caregiver motivation and infant attachment: how do reasons for fostering affect relationships? *Child and Adolescent Social Work*, 22(5/6), 441–57.

Colton, M. and Hellinckx, W. (1996). Residential and foster care in the European community. *British Journal of Social Work*, 24, 559–76.

Colton, M., Roberts, S. and Williams, M. (2008). The recruitment and retention of family foster-carers: an international and cross-cultural analysis. *British Journal of Social Work*, 38(5), 865–84.

Connolly, M. (2003). *Kinship Care: A Selected Literature Review*. Wellington, NZ: Department of Child, Youth and Family. Available online at http://www.cyf.govt.nz/documents/about-us/publications/social-work-now/kinship-care.pdf.

Connor, S. (2006). Grandparents raising grandchildren: formation, disruption and intergenerational transmission of attachment. *Australian Social Work*, 59(2), 172–84.

Corlyon, J. and McGuire, C. (1999). *Pregnancy and Parenthood: The Views and Experiences of Young People in Public Care*. London: National Children's Bureau.

Courtney, M. E. (1994). Factors associated with the reunification of foster children with their families. *Social Services Review*, 68(1), 81–108.

Courtney, M. (1995). Reentry to foster care of children returned to their families. *Social Service Review*, 69(2), 226–41.

Courtney, M., Piliavin, I, Grogan-Kaylor, A. and Nesmith, A. (2001). Foster youth transitions to adulthood: a longitudinal view of youth leaving care. *Child Welfare*, 80(6), 685–717.

Courtney, M., Roderick, M., Smithgall, C., Gladden R. and Nagaoka, N. (2004). The educational status of foster children (*issue brief no. 102*). Chicago: Chapin Hall Center for Children, University of Chicago.

Courtney, M., Skyles, A., Mirinda, G., Zinn, A., Howard, E. and Goerge, R. (2005). *Youth who run away from substitute care*. Chicago: Chapin Hall Center for Children, University of Chicago.

Cowger, C. C. (1994). Assessing client strengths: clinical assessment for client empowerment. *Social Work*, 39(3), 262–8.

Coy M. (2008). Young women, local authority care and selling sex: findings from research. *British Journal of Social Work*, 38(7), 1408–24.

Crawford, S. (1999). *Childhood in Anglo-Saxon England*. Stroud: Sutton.

Cuddeback, G. S. (2004). Kinship family care: a methodological and substantive synthesis of research. *Children and Youth Services Review*, 26(7), 623–39.

Cuddeback G. S. and Orme, J. G. (2001). Training and services for kinship non-kinship foster families, *Child Welfare*, 81(6), 879–909.

Cusick, L. (2002). Youth prostitution: a literature review. *Child Abuse Review*, 11, 230–51.

Dando, I. and Minty, B. (1987). What makes a good foster parent? *British Journal of Social Work*, 17, 383–99.

Davis, I., Landsverk, J., Newton, P. and Ganger, W. (1996). Parental visiting and foster care reunification. *Children and Youth Services Review*, 18(4/5), 363–82.

Department for Education and Skills (2006). *Statistics of Education: Children Looked After by Local Authorities, Year Ending 31 March 2005. Volume 1: National Tables*. London: HMSO.

Dezeo de Nicora, M. (2006). Argentina. In Colton, M. and Williams, M. (eds), *Global Perspectives on Foster Family Care*. Lyme Regis: Russell House. pp. 1–9.

Donner, W. W. (1987). Compassion, kinship and fosterage: contexts for the care of the elderly in a Polynesian Community. *Journal of Cross-Cultural Gerontology*, 2 (April), 43–59.

Donner, W. W. (1999). Sharing and compassion: fostering in a Polynesian society. *Journal of Comparative Family Studies*, 30(4), 703–22.

Dozier, M. (2003). Attachment-based treatment for vulnerable children. *Attachment and Human Development*, 5(3), 253–7.

Dubowitz, H. and Sawyer, R. J. (1994). School behavior of children in kinship care. *Child Abuse & Neglect*, 18(11), 899–911.

Dubowitz, H., Feigelman, S., Harrington, D., Starr, R., Zuravin, S. and Sawyer, R. (1994). Children in kinship care: how do they fare? *Children and Youth Services Review*, 16(1/2), 85–106.

Dubowitz, H., Zuravin, S, Starr, R. H. Feigelman, S. and Harrington, D. (1993). Behavior problems in children in kinship care. *Developmental and Behavioral Pediatrics*, 14(6), 386–93.

Dumaret, A., Coppel-Batsch, M. and Couraud, S. (1997). Adult outcome of children reared for long-term periods in foster families. *Child Abuse & Neglect*, 21(10), 911–27.

Dwivedi, K. N. and Varma, V. P. (eds). (1996). *Meeting the Needs of Ethnic Minority Children: A Handbook for Professionals*. London: Jessica Kingsley.

Eagle, R. S. (1994). The separation experience of children in long-term care: theory, research, and implications for practice. *American Journal of Orthopsychiatry*, 64(3), 421–34.

Ehrle, J. and Geen, R. (2002). Kin and non-kin foster care: findings from a national survey. *Children and Youth Services Review*, 24(1/2), 15–35.

Elliot, A. (2002). The educational expectation of looked after children. *Adoption & Fostering*, 26(3), 58–68.

Emick, M. and Hayslip, B. (1999). Custodial grandparents: stresses, coping skills, and relationships with grandchildren. *International Journal of Aging and Human Development*, 48(1), 35–61.

Erikson, E. H. (1950). *Childhood and Society*. New York: Norton.

Erikson, E. (1968/1980). *Identity: Youth and Crisis*. New York: Norton.

Essen, J., Lambert, L. and Head, J. (1976). School attainment of children who have been in care. *Child Care, Health and Development*, 2, 339–51.

Euler, H. A. and Weitzel, B. (1996). Discriminative Grandparental Solicitude as Reproductive Strategy. *Human Nature*, 7, 39–59.

Euler, H. A., Hoier, S. and Rhode, P. A. (2001). Relationship-specific closeness of international family ties: findings from evolutionary psychology and implications for models of cultural transmission. *Journal of Cross-Cultural Psychology*, 32(2), 147–58.

Everett, J. E. (1995). Relative foster care: An emerging trend in foster care policy and practice. *Smith College Studies in Social Work*, 65(3), 239–53.

Fahlberg, V. (1991). *A Child's Journey Through Placement*. London: BAAF.

Farmer, E. and Moyers, S. (2008). *Kinship Care: Friends and Family Placements*. London: Jessica Kingsley.

Fauve-Chamoux, A. (1996). Beyond adoption: orphans and family strategies in pre-industrial France. *The History of the Family*, 1(1), 1–13.

Fletcher, J. A. and Zwick, M. (2006). Unifying the theories of inclusive fitness and reciprocal altruism. *The American Naturalist*, 168(2), 252–62.

Flynn, R. (2002). Kinship foster care. *Clinical and Family Social Work*, 7, 311–21.

Flynn, R. and Biro, C. (1998). Comparing developmental outcomes for children in care with those for other children in Canada. *Children & Society*, 12(3), 228–33.

Fonseca, C. (2002). Politics of adoption: child rights in the Brazilian setting. *Law and Policy*, 24(3), 199–227.

Fonseca, C. (2003). Patterns of shared parenthood among the Brazilian poor. *Social Text*, 21(1), 111–27.

Ford, T., Vostanis, P., Meltzer, H. and Goodman, R. (2007). Psychiatric disorders among British children looked after by local authorities: comparison with children living in private households. *British Journal of Psychiatry*, 190(4), 319–25.

Freire, P. (1972). *Pedagogy of the Oppressed*. London: Penguin.

Freud, A. and Burlingham, D. T. (1944). *Infants Without Families: the Case For and Against Residential Nurseries*. New York: International University Press.

Freundlich, M, Morris, L. and Hernandez, C. (2003). *Kinship Care: Meeting the Needs of Children and Families of Color. A Position Paper of the Race Matters Consortium*. New York: Children's Rights.

Fuller-Thomson, E. and Minkler, M. (2000). African American grandparents raising grandchildren: a national profile of demographic and health characteristics. *Health and Social Work*, 25(2), 109–18.

Gallagher, B. (1999). The abuse of children in public care. *Child Abuse Review*, 8(3), 357–65.

Gallagher, B., Brannan, C., Jones, R. and Westwood, S. (2004). Good practice in education of children in residential care. *British Journal of Social Work*, 34(8), 1133–60.

Garland, A. F., Landsverk, J. A. and Lau, A. S. (2003). Racial/ethnic disparities in mental health service use among children in foster care. *Childhood and Youth services Review*, 25(5/6), 491–507.

Geary, D. C. (2006). Coevolution of paternal investment and cuckoldry in humans. In J. A. Fletcher and M. Zwick (eds), *Female Infidelity and Paternal Uncertainty: Evolutionary Perspectives on Male Anti-Cuckoldry Tactics*. Cambridge: Cambridge University Press. pp. 14–34.

Gebel, T. (1996). Kinship care and non-relative foster care: a comparison of caregiver attributes and attitudes. *Child Welfare*, 75(1), 5–18.

Geen, R. (2000). In the interest of the children: rethinking federal and state policies affecting kinship care. *Policy and Practice of Public Human Services*, 58(1), 19–26.

Geen, R. and Berrick, J. D. (2002). Kinship care: an evolving service delivery option. *Children and Youth Services Review*, 24(1), 1–14.

George, C. and Solomon, J. (1999). Attachment and caregiving: the caregiving behavioural system. In J. Cassidy and P. R. Shaver (eds), *Handbook of Attachment: Theory, Research, and Clinical Implications*. New York: Guildford. pp. 469–96.

Gibbs, P. and Müller, U. (2000). Kinship foster care moving to mainstream: controversy, policy, and outcomes. *Adoption Quarterly*, 4(2), 57–87.

Giddens, A. (1991). *Modernity and Self-Identity: Self and Society in Late Modern Age*. Cambridge: Polity Press.

Gillen, S. (2002). Was race an issue? *Community Care*, 21–27 February, 30–32.

Gilligan, R. (2007). Adversity, resilience and educational progress of young people in public care. *Educational and Behavioural Difficulties*, 12(2), 135–45.

Gillis-Arnold, R., Crase, S. J., Stockdale, D. F. and Shelley, M. C. (1998). Parenting attitudes, foster parenting attitudes, and motivations of adoptive and nonadoptive foster parent trainees. *Children and Youth Services Review*, 20(8), 715–32.

Goddard, J. (2000). The education of looked after children. *Children and Family Social Work*, 5(1), 79–86.

Goldfarb, W. (1943). The effects of early institutional care on adolescent personality. *Journal of Experimental Education*, 12, 106–29.

Goldstein, J. Freud, A. and Solnit, A. J. (1973). *Beyond the Best Interests of the Child*. New York: Free Press.

Goodman, C. C., Potts, M., Pasztor, E. M. and Scorzo, D. (2004). Grandmothers as kinship caregivers: private arrangements compared to public child welfare oversight. *Children and Youth Services Review*, 26(3), 287–305.

Goodman, R. (1999). The extended version of the Strengths and Difficulties Questionnaire as a guide to child psychiatric caseness and consequent burden. *Journal of Child Psychology and Psychiatry*, 40, 791–9.

Goody, E. (1973). *Contexts of Kinship*. Cambridge: Cambridge University Press.

Goody, E. (1982). *Parenthood and Social Reproduction: Fostering and Occupational Roles in West Africa*. Cambridge: Cambridge University Press.

Goody, J. (1969). Adoption in cross-cultural perspective. *Comparative Studies in Society and History*, 11(1), 55–78.

Gordon, A. L., McKinley, S. E., Satterfield, M. L. and Curtis, P. A. (2003). A first look at enhanced support services for kinship caregivers. *Child Welfare*, 82(1), 77–96.

Goriawalla, N. and Telang, K. (2006). India. In M. Colton and M. Williams (eds), *Global perspectives on foster family care*. Lyme Regis: Russell House Publishing. pp. 29–38.

Greeff, R. (ed.). (1999). *Fostering Kinship: An International Perspective on Kinship Foster Care*. Aldershot: Ashgate.

Green, J. (2003). Attachment disorders best seen as social impairment syndrome? *Attachment and Human Development*, 5(3), 259–64.

Griffin, M. (2006). Covenants and adoption and land tenure in England and the Hawaiian Kingdom. *Adoption & Fostering*, 30(4), 39–51.

Grogan-Kaylor, A. (2000). What goes into kinship care? The relationship of child and family characteristics to placement into kinship foster care. *Social Work Research*, 24(3), 132–41.

Haley, J. (1996). *Learning and Teaching Therapy*. New York: Guildford Press.

Hamilton, W. D. (1964). The genetical evolution of social behaviour. *Journal of Theoretical Biology*, 7(1), 1–16.

Harrison, C. (1999). Young people, being in care and identity. In J. Masson, C.

Harris and A. Pavlovic (eds), *Lost and Found: Making and Remaking Working Partnerships With Parents of Children in the Care System*. London: BAAF.

Hayslip, B. and Kaminski, P. L. (2005). Grandparents raising their grandchildren: a review of the literature and suggestions for practice. *The Gerontologist*, 45(2), 262–9.

Hayslip, B. and Shore, R. J. (2000). Custodial grandparents and mental health services. *Journal of Mental Health and Aging*, 6, 367–84.

Heath, A., Colton, M. and Aldgate, J. (1994). Failure to escape: A longitudinal study of foster children's educational attainment. *British Journal of Social Work*, 24, 241–60.

Hegar, R. L. (1999a). Kinship foster care: the new child placement paradigm. In R. L. Hegar and M. Scannapieco (eds), *Kinship Foster Care: Policy, Practice, and Research*. Oxford: Oxford University Press. pp. 225–40.

Hegar, R. L. (1999b). The cultural roots of kinship care. In R. L. Hegar and M. Scannapieco (eds), *Kinship Foster Care: Policy, Practice, and Research*. Oxford: Oxford University Press. pp 1–13.

Hegar, R. L. and Scannapieco, M. (eds). (1999). *Kinship Foster Care: Policy, Practice, and Research*. Oxford: Oxford University Press.

Herrick, M. A. and Piccus, W. (2005). Sibling connections: the importance of nurturing sibling bonds in the foster care system. *Children and Youth Services Review*, 27(7), 845–61.

Herring, D. J. (2005). Foster care safety and the kinship cue of attitude similarity. *Minnesota Journal of Law, Science & Technology*, 7(2), 355–92.

Hill, C. and Thompson, M. (2003). Mental and Physical Health Co-morbidity. *Clinical Child Psychology and Psychiatry*, 8, 315–21.

Hindle, D. (2000). Assessing children's perspectives on sibling placements in foster and adoptive homes. *Clinical Child Psychology and Psychiatry*, 5(4), 613–25.

Hoigard, C. and Finstad, L. (1992). *Backstreets: Prostitution, Money and Love*. Cambridge: Polity Press.

Holman, W. D. (1998). The fatherbook: a document for therapeutic work with father-absent early adolescent boys. *Child and Adolescent Social Work*, 15(2), 101–15.

Holtan A. (2008). Family types and social integration in kinship foster care. *Children and Youth Services Review*, 30(9), 1022–36.

Holtan, A., Rønning, J. A., Handegå, B. H and Sourander, A. (2005). Comparison of mental health problems in kinship and nonkinship foster care. *European Journal of Child and Adolescent Psychiatry*, 14(4), 200–7.

Hornby, H., Zeller, D. and Karraker, D. (1995). Kinship care in America: what outcomes should policy seek? *Child Welfare*, 75(5), 397–418.

Horowitz, S., Simms, M. and Farrington, R. (1994). Impact of developmental problems on young children's exit from foster care. *Journal of Developmental and Behavioral Pediatrics*, 15(2), 105–10.

Howe, D. (1995). *Attachment Theory for Social Work Practice*. London: Macmillan.

Howe, D. and Fearnley, S. (1999). Disorders of attachment and attachment therapy. *Adoption & Fostering*, 23(2), 19–30.

Hukkanen, R., Sourander, A., Bergroth, L. and Piha, J. (1999). Psychosocial factors and adequacy of services for children in children's homes. *European Journal of Child & Adolescent Psychiatry*, 8(4), 268–75.

Hunt, J. (2003). *Family and Friends Carers: Report for the Department of Health*. Available online at http//www.doh.gov.uk/carers/familyand friends.htm.

Hussey, D. L. and Guo, S. (2002). Profile characteristics and behavioral change trajectories of young residential children. *Journal of Child and Family Studies*, 11(4), 401–10.

Hyun, I. (2008). Clinical cultural competence and the threat of ethical relativism. *Cambridge Quarterly of Healthcare Ethics*, 17(2), 154–63.

Iglehart, A. P. (1994). Kinship foster care: placement, service, and outcome issues. *Children and Youth Services Review*, 16(1/2), 107–22.

Iglehart, A. P. (1995). Readiness for independence: comparison of foster care, kinship care, and non-foster care adolescents. *Children and Youth Services Review*, 17(2), 417–32.

Isiugo-Abanihe, U. C. (1985). Child fosterage in West Africa. *Population and Development Review*, 11(1), 53–73.

Jackson, S. (1994). Educating children in residential and foster care. *Oxford Review of Education*, 20(3), 267–79.

Jackson, S. M. (1999). Paradigm shift: training staff to provide services to the kinship triad. In R. L. Hegar and M. Scannapieco (eds), *Kinship Foster Care: Policy, Practice, and Research*. Oxford: Oxford University Press. pp. 95–111.

James, W. (1890). *The Principles of Psychology*. New York: Holt.

James, S., Monn, A. R., Palinkas, L. A. and Laurel, K. L. (2008). Maintaining sibling relationships for children in foster and adoptive placements. *Children and Youth Services Review*, 30(1), 90–106.

Jendrek, M. (1993). Grandparents who parent their grandchildren: circumstances and decisions. *The Gerontologist*, 34(2), 206–16.

Johnson-Garner, M. Y. and Meyers, S. A. (2003). What factors contribute to the resilience of African-American children within kinship care. *Child and Youth Care Forum*, 32(6), 255–69.

Jolly, S. C. (1994). Cutting the ties: the termination of contact in care. *Journal of Social Welfare and Family Law*, 16(3), 299–311.

Kay, P. (1963). Tahitian fosterage and the form of ethnographic models. *American Anthropologist*, 65, 1027–44.

Keller, T. E., Wetherbee, K., Le Prohn, N., Payne, V., Sim, K. and Lamont, E. R. (2001). Competencies and problem behaviors of children in foster care: variation by kinship placement status and race. *Children and Youth Services Review*, 23(12), 915–40.

Kempton, T., Armistead, L., Wierson, M. and Forehand, R. (1991). Presence of a sibling as a potential buffer following parental divorce: an examination of young adolescents. *Journal of Child Psychology*, 20(4), 434–8.

Kidd, P. and Storey, P. (2006). Kinship care: the legal position. In C. Talbot and C. Calder (eds), *Assessment in Kinship Care*. Lyme Regis: Russell House. pp. 45–55.

Kirkpatrick, J. T. and Broder, C. R. (1976). Adoption and Parenthood on Yap. In I. Brady (ed.) *Transactions in Kinship: Adoption and Fosterage in Oceania*. Honolulu: University of Hawaii Press. pp. 200–27.

Klass, D. and Goss, R. (1999). Spiritual bonds to the dead in cross-cultural and historical perspective: comparative religion and modern grief. *Dead Studies*, 23(6), 547–67.

Klevius, P. (1996). Angels of Antichrist. *Issues of Child Abuse Association*, 8(2), 94–101.

Knight, A., Chase, E. C. and Aggleton P. (2006). Teenage pregnancy among young people in and leaving care: messages and implications for foster care. *Adoption & Fostering*, 30(1), 58–69.

Kosonen, M. (1999). Maintaining sibling relationships: neglected dimension in child care practice. *British Journal of Social Work*, 26(6), 809–22.

Kroll, B. (2007). A family affair? Kinship care and parental substance abuse: some dilemmas explored. *Child and Family Social Work*, 12(1), 84–93.

Landsverk, J., Davis, I., Granger, W. and Newton, R. (1996). Impact of child psychosocial functioning on reunification from out-of-home placement. *Children and Youth Services Review*, 18(4/5), 447–62.

Lataianu, C. M. (2003). Social protection of children in public care in Romania from the perspective of EU integration. *International Journal of Law, Policy and the Family*, 17(1), 99–120.

Leathers, S. J. (2002). Parental visiting and family reunification: could inclusive practice make a difference? *Child Welfare*, 81(4), 595–616.

Leiberman, A. F. and Zeanah, C. H. (1999). Contributions of attachment theory to infant-parent psychotherapy and other interventions with infants and young children. In J. Cassidy and P. Shaver (eds), *Handbook of Attachment*. New York: Guildford. pp. 555–74.

Leon, I. G. (2002). Adoption losses: naturally occurring or socially constructed? *Child Development*, 73(2), 652–63.

Leonardsen, M. (2007). Empowerment in social work: an individual vs. a relational perspective. *International Journal of Social Welfare*, 16(1), 3–11.

LeProhn, N. S. (1994). The role of kinship foster parent: a comparison of the role conceptions of relative and non-relative foster parents. *Children and Youth Services*, 16(1/2), 107–22.

Leslie, L. K., Gordon, J. N., Meneken, L., Premji, K, Michelmore, M. S. and Granger, W. (2005). Physical, developmental, and mental health needs of young children in child welfare by initial placement type. *Journal of Developmental Behavioral Pediatrics*, 26(3), 177–85.

LeVine, R. A., Dixon, S., Keefer, C. H. and Brazelton, T.B. (1998). *Child Care and Culture: Lessons from Africa*. Cambridge: Cambridge University Press.

Lewis, M., Feiring, C. and Rosenthal, S. (2000). Attachment over time. *Child Development*, 71(3), 707–20.

Lindheim, O. and Dozier, M. (2007). Caregiver commitment to foster children: the role of child behavior. *Child Abuse & Neglect*, 31(4), 361–74.

Little, M., Kohn, A. and Thompson, R. (2005). The impact of residential placement on child development: research and policy implications. *International Journal of Social Welfare*, 14(3), 200–9.

Littlefield, C. H. and Rushton, J. P. (1986). When a child dies: the socio-biology of bereavement. *Journal of Personality and Social Psychology*, 51(4), 797–802.

Lloyd, C. B. and Blanc, A. K. (1996). Children's Schooling in sub-Saharan Africa: The Role of Fathers, Mothers, and Others. *Population and Development Review*, 22(2), 265–98.

Lloyd, C. and Desai, S. (1992). Children's living arrangements in developing countries. *Population and Development Review*, 22(2), 265–98.

Lobo, J. (1978). *Children of Immigrants to Britain: Their Health and Social Problems*. London: Allen and Unwin.

McCann, J. B., James, A., Wilson, S. and Dunn, G. (1996). Prevalence of psychiatric disorders in young people in the care system. *British Medical Journal*, 313, 1529–30.

McCarthy, G. (2004). The developmental histories of children who experience high levels of placement instability in the care system. *Adoption & Fostering*, 28(4), 60–5.

McCarthy, G., Janeway, J. and Angus, G. (2003). The impact of emotional and behavioural problems on the lives of children growing up in the care system. *Adoption & Fostering*, 27(3), 14–19.

McFadden, E. J. (1998). Kinship in the United States. *Adoption & Fostering*, 22(3), 7–15.

McFadden, E. J. and Downs, S. W. (1995). Family continuity: the new paradigm in permanence planning. *Community Alternatives: International Journal of Family Care*, 7, 39–59.

McMillen, C., Auslander, W., Elze, D., White, T. and Thompson, R. (2003). Educational experiences and aspirations of older youth in foster care. *Child Welfare*, 82(4), 475–95.

McMillen, J. C., Zima, B. T., Scott, L. D., Auslander, W. F., Munson, M. R., Ollie, M. T. and Spitznagel, E. L. (2005). Prevalence of psychiatric disorders among older youths in the foster care system. *Journal of the American Academy of Child and Adolescent Psychiatry*, 44(1), 88–95.

Main, M. (1999). Attachment theory: eighteen points with suggestions for future studies. In J. Cassidy and P. R. Shavers (eds), *Handbook of Attachment: Theory, Research, and Clinical Applications*. London: The Guildford Press, pp. 845–87.

Maluccio, A. N., Abramczyk, L. W. and Tomlinson, B. (1996). Family reunification of children in out-of-home care: research perspectives. *Children and Youth Services Review*, 18(4/5), 287–305.

Marsh, P. (1987). Parental access to children in care – the research message. *Children & Society*, 1(1), 71–80.

Marsh, P. and Triseliotis, J. (1993). *Prevention and Reunification in Child Care*. London: Batsford.

Masson, J. (1997). Maintaining contact between parents and children in public care. *Children and Society*, 11(4), 222–30.

Meltzer, H., Corbin, T., Gatward, R., Goodman, R. and Ford, T. (2003). *The Mental Health of Young People Looked After by Local Authorities in England*. London: HMSO.

Meltzer, H., Corbin, T., Gatward, R., Goodman, R. and Ford, T. (2004a). *The Mental Health of Young People Looked After by Local Authorities in Wales*. London: HMSO.

Meltzer, H., Lader, D., Corbin, T., Goodman, R and Ford, T. (2004b). *The Mental Health of Young People Looked After by Local Authorities in Scotland*. London: HMSO.

Mendenhall, T. J., Berge, J. M., Wrobel, G. M., Grotevant, H. and McRoy, R. G. (2004). Adolescents' satisfaction with contact adoption. *Child and Adolescent Social Work*, 21(2), 175–90.

Mercer, J. (2001). Warning: Are you aware of 'holding therapy'? (letter to the Editor). *Pediatrics*, 107, 1498.

Messing, J. T. (2006). From the child's perspective: a qualitative analysis of kinship care placements. *Children and Youth Services Review*, 28(12), 1415–34.

Miller, P. H. (1999). *Theories of Developmental Psychology*. 3rd edn. New York: Freeman Worth.

Minkler, M. and Fuller-Thomson, E. (1999). The health of grandparents raising grandchildren: results of a national study. *American Journal of Public Health*, 89(9), 1384–9.

Minnis, H. (2004). How can foster carers help children with complex mental health attachment problems? *International Journal of Child and Family Welfare*, 7(4), 162–7.

Minty, B. (1999). Annotation: outcomes in long-term foster family care. *Journal of Child Psychology and Psychiatry*, 40(7), 991–9.

Moffatt, P. J and Thoburn, J. (2001). Outcomes of permanent family placement for children of minority ethnic origin. *Child and Family Social Work*, 6(1), 13–21.

Molloy, V. (2002). Identity, past and present, in an historical child-care setting. *Psychodynamic Practice*, 8(2), 163–78.

Montserrat, C. and Casas, F. (2006). Kinship care from the perspective of quality of life: research on satisfaction of the stakeholders. *Applied Research in Quality of Life*, 1(3/4), 227–37.

Mosek, A. (1993). Well-being and parental contact of foster children in Israel: a different situation from the USA? *International Social Work*, 36(3), 261–75.

Mosek A. and Adler, L. (2001). The self-concept of adolescent girls in non-relative versus kin foster care. *International Social work*, 44(2), 149–62.

Moynihan, D. (1965). *The Negro Family in the United States: The Case for Action*. Washington, DC: Government Printing Press.

Newton, R. R., Litrownik, A. J. and Landsverk, J. A. (2000). Children and youth in foster care: disentangling the relationship between problem behaviors and number of placements. *Child Abuse & Neglect*, 24(10), 1336–74.

Nicolas, B., Roberts, S. and Wurr, C. (2003). Looked after children in residential homes. *Child and adolescent Mental Health*, 8, 78–83.

Nisivoccia, D. (1996). Working with kinship foster families: principles for practice. *Community Alternatives*, 8(1), 1–21.

Nixon, K., Tutty, L., Downe, P., Gorkoff, K and Ursel, J. (2002). The everyday occurrence: violence in the lives of girls exploited through prostitution. *Violence Against Women*, 8(9), 1016–43.

Notermans, C. (2004). Fosterage and politics of marriage and kinship in East Cameroon. In F. Bowie (ed.), *Cross-Cultural Approaches to Adoption*. London: Routledge. pp. 49–63.

Nsameng, A. (1992). Perceptions of parenting among the Nso of Cameroon. In B. Hewlett (ed.), *Father-Child Relations: Cultural and Biosocial Contexts*. New York: Aldine de Gruyter. pp. 321–43.

O'Brien, V. (2000). Relative care: a different type of foster care – implications for practice. In G. Kelly and R. Gilligan (eds), *Issues in Foster Care: Policy, Practice and Research*. London: Jessica Kingsley.

O'Connor, G. C and Zeanah, C. H. (2003). Attachment disorders: assessment strategies and treatment approaches. *Attachment and Human Development*, 5(3), 223–44.

O'Sullivan, M. (1988). 'Salvation is a chameleon'. *The Idea of Salvation, Prudentia* supplement, pp. 43–8.

Oni, J. (1995). 'Fostered children's perception of their health care and illness treatment in Ekiti Yuroba households, Nigeria. *Heath Transition Review*, 5(1), 21–34.

Office for National Statistics (2006). Children looked after by local authorities: year ending 31 March 2005. London: ONS.

Oppong, C. (1973). *Growing up in Dagnon*. Accra: Ghana Publishing Corporation.

Orme, J. G. and Buehler, C. (2001). Foster family characteristics and behavioral problems of foster children: a narrative review. *Family Relations*, 50(1), 3–15.

Owusu-Bempah, J. (1995). Information about the absent parent as a factor in the well-being of children of single-parent families. *International Social Work*, 38(3), 253–75.

Owusu-Bempah. K. (2003). Political correctness: in the interest of the child? *Educational and Child Psychology*, 20(1), 53–63.

Owusu-Bempah, K. (2006). Socio-genealogical connectedness: knowledge and identity. In J. Aldgate, D. Jones, W. Rose and C. Jeffery (eds), *The Developing World of the Child*. London: Jessica Kingsley. pp. 112–21.

Owusu-Bempah, K. (2007). *Children and Separation: Socio-genealogical Connectedness Perspective*. London: Routledge.

Owusu-Bempah, K. and Howitt, D. (1997). Socio-genealogical connectedness, attachment theory, and childcare practice. *Child and Family Social Work*, 2(4), 199–207.

Owusu-Bempah, K. and Howitt, D. (2000a). Socio-genealogical connectedness: on the role of gender and same-gender parenting in mitigating the effects of parental divorce. *Child and Family Social Work*, 5(4), 107–16.

Owusu-Bempah, K. and Howitt, D. (2000b). *Psychology Beyond Western Perspectives*. Oxford: BPS/Blackwell.

Page, H. (1998). Childrearing versus childbearing: coresidence of mother and child in sub-saharan Africa. In R. J. Lesthaeghe (ed.), *Reproduction and Social Organisation in Sub-Saharan Africa*. Los Angeles: University of California Press. pp. 401–41.

Palmer, S. E. (1990). Group treatment of fostered children to reduce separation conflicts associated with placement breakdown. *Child Welfare*, 69(3), 227–38.

Pareto, V. (1963). *Treatise on General Sociology*. New York: Dover.

Parkes, P. (2001). Alternative social structures and foster relations in the Hindu Kush: milk kinship allegiance in former mountain kingdoms of Northern Pakistan. *Comparative Studies in Society and History*, 43(1), 4–36.

Parkes, P. (2006). Celtic fosterage: adoptive kinship and clientage in Northwest Europe. *Comparative Studies in Society and History*, 48(2), 359–95.

Pashos, A. (2000). Does paternal uncertainty explain discriminative grandparental solicitude: A cross-cultural study in Greece and Germany. *Evolution and Human Behavior*, 21(2), 97–109.

Payne-Price, A. C. (1981). Etic variations on fostering and adoption. *Anthropological Quarterly*, 54(3), 134–45.

Peers, L. and Brown, J. S. H. (2000). There is no end to relationships among the Indians: Ojibwa families and kinship in historical perspective. *The History of the Family*, 4(4), 529–55.

Peters, J. (2005). True ambivalence: child welfare workers' thoughts, feelings, and beliefs about kinship foster care. *Children and Youth Services Review*, 27(6), 595–614.

Platek, S. M. and Shackleford, T. K. (2006). Introduction to the theory and research on anti-cuckoldry tactics: Overview of current volume. In J. A. Fletcher and M. Zwick (eds), *Female Infidelity and Paternal Uncertainty: Evolutionary Perspectives on Male Anti-Cuckoldry Tactics*. Cambridge: Cambridge University Press. pp. 1–13.

Pitcher, D. (2002). Placement with grandparents: the issue for grandparents who care for their grandchildren. *Adoption & Fostering*, 26(1), 6–14.

Poehlmann, J. (2003). An attachment perspective on grandparent raising their very young grandchildren: implications for intervention and research. *Infant Mental Health Journal*, 24(2), 149–73.

Proch, K. (1982). Differences between foster care and adoption: perceptions of adopted foster children and adoptive parents. *Child Welfare*, 61(5), 259–68.

Quinton, D. and Rutter, M. (1984). Parents with children in care: intergenerational continuities. *Journal of Child Psychology and Psychiatry*, 25, 231–50.

Quinton, D., Rushton, A., Dance, C. and Mayes, D. (1997). Contact between children placed away from home and their birth parents: research issues and evidence. *Clinical Child Psychology and Psychiatry*, 2(3), 393–414.

Racusin, R., Maerlender, Jr., A. C., Sengupta, A., Isquith, P. K. and Straus, M. B. (2005). Psychosocial treatment of children in foster care: a review. *Community Mental Health Journal*, 41(2), 199–221.

Rak, C. F. and Patterson, L. E. (1996). Promoting resilience in at-risk children. *Journal of Counselling and Development*, 74(4), 368–73.

Richards, A. (2001). *Second Time Around: A Survey of Grandparents Raising Their Grandchildren*. London: Family Rights Group.

Richards, L., Wood, N. and Ruiz-Calzada, L. (2006). The mental health needs of looked children in a local authority permanent placement team and the value of the Goodman SDQ. *Adoption & Fostering*, 30(2), 43–52.

Richardson, J. and Goughin, C. (eds). (2002). *The Mental Health of Children Looked After*. London: Gaskell.

Roberson, K. C. (2006). Attachment and caregiving behavioral systems in intercountry adoption: a literature review. *Children and Youth Services Review*, 28(6), 727–40.

Robertson, J. and Robertson, J. (1971). Young children in brief separation: a fresh look. *Psychoanalytic Study of the Child*, 26, 264–315.

Rocco-Briggs, M. (2008). Who owns my pain? An aspect of the complexity of working with looked after children. *Journal of Child Psychotherapy*, 34(2), 190–206.

Roman, N. P. and Wolfe, P. (1995). *Web of Failure: The Relationship Between Foster Care and Homelessness*. Washington, DC: National Alliance to End Homelessness.

Rowe, J. (1984). *Long-Term Foster Care*. London: Batsford Academic and Educational.

Rubin, D. M., O'Reilly, A. L., Luan, X. and Localio, J. D. (2007). The impact of placement stability on behavioral well-being for children in foster care. *Pediatrics*, 119, 336–44.

Runyan, D. K., Hunter, W. M., Socolar, R. S., Amaya-Jackson, L., English, D., Landsverk, J., Dubowitz, H., Browne, D. H., Bangdiwala, S. I. and Mathew, R. M. (1998). Children who prosper in unfavourable environments: the relationship to social capital. *Pediatrics*, 101(1), 12–18.

Rushton, A. (2004). Scoping and scanning review of research on the adoption of children placed from public care. *Clinical Child Psychology and Psychiatry*, 9(1), 89–106.

Russell, M. and Taylor, B. (2005). Adult health and social outcome of children who have been in public care: population-based study. *Pediatrics*, 115(4), 894–9.

Russell, R. J. and Wells, P. A. (1987). Estimating paternity confidence. *Ethology and Sociobiology*, 8(3), 215–20.

Rutman, D., Hubberstey, C., Barlow, A. and Brown, E. (2005). *Promoting outcomes for youth from care: When Youth Age Out of Care Project: A report on baseline findings*. Http://soical-work.uvic.ca/research/projects.htm.

Rutter, M. (1972/1991). *Maternal Deprivation Reassessed*. (1991 2nd edn). Harmondsworth: Penguin.

Rutter, M. (1994). Family discord and conduct disorder: cause, consequences, or correlates? *Journal of Family Psychology*, 8(2), 170–86.

Rutter, M. (2000). Children in substitute care: some conceptual considerations and research implications. *Children and Youth Services Review*, 22(9), 685–703.

Rutter, M. and O'Connor, T. G. (1999). Implications of attachment theory for child care policies. In J. Cassidy and P. R. Shaver (eds), *Handbook of Attachment: Theory, Research and Clinical Applications*. New York: The Guildford Press. pp. 823–44.

Ryburn, M. (1999). Contact between children placed away from home and their birth parents: a reanalysis of the evidence in relation to permanent placements. *Clinical Child Psychology and Psychiatry*, 4(4), 501–18.

Sallnäs, M., Vinnerljung, B. and Westermark, P. K. (2004). Breakdown of teenage placements in Swedish foster and residential care. *Child & Family Social Work*, 9(2), 141–52.

Sanchirico, A. and Jablonka, K. (2000). Keeping foster children connected to their biological parents: the impact of foster parent training and support. *Child and Adolescent Social Work*, 17(3), 185–203.

Sands, R. G. and Goldberg-Glen, R. S. (2000). Factors associated with stress among grandparents raising their grandchildren. *Family Relations*, 49(1), 97–105.

Sargent, K. and O'Brien, K. (2004). The emotional and behavioural difficulties of looked after children: foster carers' perspectives and an indirect model of placement support. *Adoption & Fostering*, 28(2), 31–7.

Sawyer, R. J. and Dubowitz, H. (1994). School performance of children in kinship care. *Child Abuse & Neglect*, 18(7), 587–97.

Scannapieco, M. (1999). Formal kinship care practice models. In R. L. Hegar and M. Scannapieco (eds), *Kinship Foster Care: Policy, Practice, and Research*. Oxford: Oxford University Press. pp. 71–83.

Scannapieco, M. and Hegar, L. (1999). Kinship foster care in context. In Hegar, R. L. and Scannapieco, M. (1999). (eds), *Kinship Foster Care: Policy, Practice, and Research*. Oxford: Oxford University Press. pp 1–13.

Scannapieco, M. and Hegar, R. L. (2002). Kinship care providers: designing an array of supportive services. *Child and Adolescent Social Work*, 19(4), 315–27.

Scannapieco, M. and Jackson, S. (1996). Kinship care: the African American response to family preservation. *Social Work*, 41(2), 190–6.

Scannapieco, M., Hegar, R. L. and McAlpine, C. (1997). Kinship care and foster care: a comparison of characteristics and outcomes. *Families in Society*, 78(5), 480–8.

Schneider, R., Baumrind, N., Pavao, J., Stockdale, G., Castelli, P., Goodman, G. S. and Kimerling, R. (2009). What happens to youth removed from parental care?: Health and economic outcomes for women with a history of out-of-home placement. *Children and Youth Services Review*, 31, 440–4.

Schwartz, A. E. (2002). Societal values and the funding of kinship care. *Social Service Review*, 76(3), 430–59.

Schwartz, A. (2007). "Caught" versus "taught": ethnic identity and ethnic socialization in kinship and non-kinship foster placements. *Children and Youth Services Review*, 29, 1201–19.

Scott, S. (2004). Reviewing the research on the mental health of looked after children: some issues for the development of more evidence informed practice. *International journal of Child & Family Welfare*, 7(2–3), 86–97.

Sempik, J., Ward, H. and Darker, I. (2008). Emotional and behavioural difficulties and young people at entry into care. *Clinical Child Psychology and Psychiatry*, 13(2), 221–33.

Sengupta, S. (1999). Women keep garment jobs by sending babies to China. In Y. Bohr and C. Tse, Satellite babies in transnational families: a study of parents' decision to separate from their children. *Infant Mental Health Journal*, 30(3), 1–22.

Serra, R. (2009). Child fostering in Africa: when labor and schooling motives may coexist. *Journal of Development Economics*, 88(1), 157–170.

Shants, H. J. (1964). Genealogical bewilderment in children with substitute parents. *British Journal of Medical Psychology*, 37, 133–41.

Shlonsky, A., Bellamy, J, Elkins, J. and Ashare, C. J. (2005). The other kin: setting the course for research, policy, and practice with siblings. *Children and Youth Services Review*, 27(7), 697–716.

Shomaker, D. J. (1989). Transfer of children and the importance of grandmothers among the Navajo Indians. *Journal of Cross-cultural Gerontology*, 4(3), 1–18.

Shore, N., Sim, K. E., LeProhn, N. S. and Keller, T. E. (2002). Foster parent and teacher assessments of youth in kinship and non-kinship foster care placements: are behaviors perceived differently across settings? *Children and Youth Services Review*, 24(1/2), 109–34.

Shorkey, D. and Mitchell, B. (2003). Grandparents raising their children. In K. Kufeldt and B. McKenzie (eds), *Child Welfare: Connecting Research, Policy, and Practice*. Waterloo, ON: Wilfred Laurier University Press. pp. 147–56.

Silk, J. B. (1987). Adoption and fosterage in human societies: adaptations or enigmas? *Cultural Anthropology*, 2(1), 39–49.

Simon, A. and Owen, C. (2006). Outcomes for children in care: what do we know? In E. Chase, A. Simon and S. Jackson (eds), *In Care and After: A Positive Perspective*. London: Routledge. pp. 26–43.

Simms, M. D. (1991). Foster children and the foster care system, Part II: impact on the child. *Current Problems in Pediatrics*, 21(8), 345–69.

Simms, M. D., Dubowitz, H. and Szilagyi, M. A. (2000). Health care needs of children in the foster care system. *Pediatrics*, 106(4 Suppl.), 909–18.

Sinclair, I. and Gibbs, I. (1998). *Children' Homes: A Study in Diversity*. Chichester: John Wiley.

Sinclair, R., Garnett, L. and Berridge, D. (1995). *Social Work and Assessment with Adolescents*. London: National Children's Bureau.

Smith, M. C. (1998). Sibling placement in foster care: an exploration of associated concurrent preschool-aged child functioning. *Children and Youth Services Review*, 20(5), 389–412.

Solomon, J. C. and Marx, J. (1995). 'To grandmother's house we go': health and school adjustment of children raised solely by grandparents. *The Gerontologist*, 35(3), 386–94.

Sourander, A., Ellilä, H., Välimäki, M. and Piha, J. (2002). Use of holding, seclusion and time-out in child and adolescent psychiatric in-patient treatment. *European Child & Adolescent Psychiatry*, 11(4), 162–7.

Spence, N. (2004). Kinship care in Australia. *Child Abuse Review*, 13(4), 263–76.

Spitz, R. A. (1945). Hospitalism: An inquiry into the genesis of psychiatry conditions in early childhood. *Psychoanalytic Study of the Child*, 1, 53–74.

Spring, J. (1994). *Wheel in the Head: Educational Philosophies of Authority, Freedom, and Culture from Socrates to Paulo Freire*. New York: McGraw-Hill.

Sroufe L. A., Carlson, E. A., Levy, A. K. and Egeland, B. (1999). Implications of attachment theory for developmental psychopathology. *Development and Psychopathology*, 11(1), 1–13.

Sroufe, L. A., Egeland, B., Carlson, E. and Collins, W. A. (2006). Placing early attachment experiences in developmental context: the Minnesota longitudinal study. In K. E. Grossman, K. Grossman and E Waters (eds), *Attachment from*

Infancy to Adulthood: The Major Longitudinal Studies. London: Guildford Press. pp. 48–70.

Stack, C. (1974). *All Our Kin*. New York: Basic Books.

Stack, C. B. and Burton, L. M. (1993). Kinscripts: framework for studies on families. *Journal of Comparative Family Studies*, 24(2), 157–70.

Stanley, N., Riordan, D. and Alaszewski, H. (2005). The mental health of looked after children: matching response to need. *Health and Social Care in the Community*, 13(3), 239–48.

Starr, R. H., Dubowitz, H., Harrington, D. and Feigelman, S. (1999). Behavior problems in kinship care. In R. L. Hegar and M. Scannapieco (eds), *Kinship Foster Care: Policy, Practice, and Research*. Oxford: Oxford University Press. pp. 194–207.

Stein, E., Evans, B., Mazumdar, R. and Rae-Grant, N. (1996). The mental health of children in foster care: a comparison with community and clinical samples. *Canadian Journal of Psychiatry*, 41(6), 385–91.

Stelmaszuk, Z. W. (2006). Poland. In M. Colton and M. Williams (eds), *Global perspectives on foster family care*. Lyme Regis: Russell House Publishing. pp. 47–58.

Strijker, J., Zandberg, T. and van der Meulen, B. (2003). Kinship care and foster care in the Netherlands. *Children and Youth Services Review*, 25(11), 843–62.

Swain, D. (1995). Family Group Conference in Child Care and Protection in Aotearoa/ New Zealand. *International Journal of Law,Policy and the Family*, 9(2), 155–207.

Sykes, J., Sinclair, I., Gibbs, I. and Wilson, K. (2002). Kinship and stranger foster carers: how do they compare? *Adoption & Fostering*, 26(2), 38–48.

Talbot, C. (2006a). Kinship care: the research evidence. In C. Talbot and C. Calder (eds), *Assessment in Kinship Care*. Lyme Regis: Russell House. pp. 1–11.

Talbot, C. (2006b). Promoting contact between family and friends: research findings, cautionary notes and a structure for assessment. In C. Talbot and C. Calder (eds), *Assessment in Kinship Care*. Lyme Regis: Russell House. pp 124–9.

Talle, A. (2004). Adoption practices among the pastoral Maasai of East Africa: enacting fertility. In F. Bowie (ed.), *Cross-Cultural Approaches to Adoption*. London: Routledge. pp. 64–78.

Tapsfield, R. (2001). Kinship care: a Family Rights Group perspective. In B. Broad (ed.), *The Placement Choice for Children and Young People*. Lyme Regis: Russell House Publishing. pp. 85–91.

Tarren-Sweeney, M. and Hazell, P. (2006). Mental health of children in foster and kinship care in New South Wales, Australia. *Journal of Paediatrics and Child Health*, 42(3), 89–97.

Taylor, L. R. (2005). Patterns of child fosterage in rural northern Thailand. *Journal of Biosocial Science*, 37, 333–50.

Testa, M. F. and Slack, K. S. (2002). The gift of kinship foster care. *Children and Youth Services Review*, 24(1/2), 79–108.

Thoburn, J. (1994). *Child Placement: Principles and Practice*. Hampshire: Arena.

Titmus, R. M. (1970). *The Gift Relationship: From Human Blood to Social Policy*. London: Allen and Unwin.

Tizard, B. and Hodges, J. (1978). The effects of early institutional rearing on the development of eight-year-old children. *Journal of Child Psychology and Psychiatry*, 19(2), 99–118.

Tizard, B. and Rees, J. (1975). The effects of early institutional rearing on the behaviour problems and affectional relationships of four-old-children. *Journal of Child Psychology and Psychiatry*, 16(1), 61–73.

Tizard, B. and Phoenix, A. (1989). Black identity and transracial adoption. *New Community*, 15(3), 427–37.

Treide, D. (2004). Adoption in Micronesia: past and present. In F. Bowie (ed.), *Cross-Cultural Approaches to Adoption*. London: Routledge. pp 127–41.

Triseliotis, J. (1973). *In Search of Origins: the Experiences of Adopted People*. London: Routledge and Kegan Paul.

Triseliotis, J., Borland, M. and Hill, M. (1995). *Teenagers and the Social Work Services*. London: HMSO.

Triseliotis, J. and Hill, M. (1990). Contrasting adoption, foster care, and residential rearing. In D. Brodzinsky and M. Schechter (eds), *The Psychology of Adoption*. Oxford: Oxford University Press.

Triseliotis, J. and Russell, J. (1984). *Hard to Place: The Outcome of Adoption and Residential Care*. London: Heinemann Educational Publishers.

Trout, A. L., Hagaman, J., Casey, K., Reid, R. and Epstein, M. H. (2008). The academic status of children and youth in out-of-home care: a review of the literature. *Children and Youth Services Review*, 30(9), 979–94.

Turner, W., Macdonald, G. M. and Dennis, J. A. (2007). Behavioural and cognitive behavioural training interventions for assisting foster carers in the management of difficult behaviour. Available online at http://www.mrw.interscience.wiley.com/cochrane/clsysrev/articles/CD003760/frame.html.Tweedle, A. (2007). Youth leaving care: how do they fare? *New Directions for Youth Development*, 113, 15–31.

Tweedle, A. (2007). *New Directions for Youth Development*. No. 113, 15–31.

Umbima, J. K. (1991). Regulating foster care services: the Kenyan situation. *Child Welfare*, 70(2), 169–74.

Valsiner, J. (2000). *Culture and Human Development*. London: Sage.

van den Berghe, L. and Parash, D. P. (1977). Inclusive fitness and family structure. *American Anthropologist*, 79(4), 809–23.

van IJzendoorn, M. H. and Sagi, A. (1999). Cross-cultural patterns of attachment. In J. Cassidy and P. R. Shaver (eds), *Handbook of Attachment*. New York: Guildford Press. pp. 713–34.

van IJzendoorn, M. H., Juffer, F. and Duyvesteyn, M. G. C. (1995). Breaking the intergenerational cycle of insecure attachment: a review of the effects of attachment-based interventions on maternal sensitivity and infant security. *Journal of Child Psychology and Psychiatry*, 36(2), 225–48.

Vandermeersch, C. (2002). Child fostering under six in Senegal in 1992–1993. *Population*, 57(4/5), 659–86.

Verhoef, H. (2005). A child has many mothers: views of child fostering in Northwestern Cameroon. *Childhood*, 12(3), 367–90.

Verhoef, H. and Morelli, G. (2007). 'A child is a child': fostering experiences in Northern Cameroon. *Ethos*, 35(1), 33–64.

Vig, S., Chinitz, S. and Shulman, L. (2005). Young children in foster care: multiple vulnerabilities and complex service needs. *Infants & Young Children*, 18(2), 147–60.

Vinnerljung, B., Oman, M. and Gunnarson, T. (2005). Educational attainment of former child welfare clients – a Swedish national cohort Study. *International Journal of Social Welfare*, 14(4), 265–76.

Vorria, P., Rutter, M., Pickles, A., Wolkind, S. and Hobsbaum, A. (1998). A comparative study of Greek children in long-term residential group care and in two-parent families: social, emotional, and behavioural differences. *Journal of Child Psychology and Psychiatry*, 39(2), 225–36.

Vorria, P., Sarafidou, J. and Papaligoura, Z. (2004). The effects of state care on children's development: new findings, new approaches. *International Journal of Child and Family Welfare*, 7(4), 168–83.

Waterhouse, S. (2001). Keeping Children in Kinship Placement within Court Proceedings. In B. Broad (ed.), *The Placement Choice for Children and Young People*. Lyme Regis: Russell House Publishing. pp. 39–46.

Wehrmann, K., Unrau, Y. and Martin, J. (2006). United States. In M. Colton and M. Williams (eds.), *Global Perspectives on Foster Family Care*. Lyme Regis: Russell House. pp. 87–97.

Whiting, B. (ed.). (1963). *Six Cultures: Studies of Child Rearing*. Oxford: Wiley.

Whiting, B. B. and Edwards, C. P. (1988). *Children of Different Worlds: The Formation of Social Behaviour*. Cambridge, MA: Harvard University Press.

Williams, C. C. (2006). The epistemology of cultural competence. *Families in Society*, 87(2), 209–20.

Williams, S. C., Fanolis, V. and Schamess, G. (2002). Adapting the Pynoos school based group therapy model for use with foster children: theoretical and process considerations. *Journal of Child and Adolescent Group Therapy*, 11(2/3), 57–76.

Wilson, D. B. (1999). Kinship care in family-serving agencies. In R. L. Hegar and M. Scannapieco (eds), *Kinship Foster Care: Policy, Practice, and Research*. Oxford: Oxford University Press. pp 85–92.

Wilson, S. L. (2004). A current review of adoption research: exploring individual differences in adjustment. *Children Youth Services Review*, 26(8), 687–96.

Winokur, M., Rozen, D., Thompson, S., Green, S. and Valentine, D. (2005). *Kinship Care in the United States: A Systematic Review of Evidence-Based Research*. Fort Collins, Co: Social Work Research Centre, University of Colorado.

Witherspoon, G. (1975). *Navajo Kinship and Marriage*. Chicago: University of Chicago Press.

Wolkind, S. and Rutter, M. (1973). Children who have been 'in care': an epidemiological study. *Journal of Child Psychology & Psychiatry*, 14(2), 97–105.

World Health Organization (1992). *The International Statistical Classification of Diseases and Related Health Problems* (ICD-10). Geneva: WHO.

Yngvesson, B. (2004). National bodies and the body of the child: 'completing' families through international adoption. In Bowie, F. (ed.), *Cross-Cultural Approaches to Adoption*. London: Routledge. pp 212–26.

Zeanah, C. H. and Boris, N. W. (2000). Disturbances and disorders of attachment in early childhood. In C. H. Zeanah and N. W. Boris. (eds), *Handbook of Infant Mental Health*. 2nd edn. New York: Guildford Press. pp. 353–68.

Zeanah, C. H., Smyke, A. T. and Dumitrescu, A. (2002). Attachment disturbances in young children. II: Indiscriminate behaviour and institutional care. *Journal of the American Academy of Child and Adolescent Psychiatry*, 41(8), 983–9.

Zimmerman, P. (1999). Structure and functions of internal working models of attachment and their role in emotion regulation. *Attachment and Human Development*, 1(3), 291–306.

Zuravin, S. J., Benedict, M. and Stallings, R. (1999). Adult functioning of former kinship and nonrelative foster care children. In R. L. Hegar and M. Scannapieco (eds), *Kinship Foster Care: Policy, Practice, and Research*. Oxford: Oxford University Press. pp. 208–22.

Index